NIGHTMARE ON CHARLOTTE STREET

Tuesday, March 30, 1988. Chris Bryson revived about eight a.m., to find himself in pain, bound to a metal bed, and his mouth so tightly gagged he could hardly breathe. His head still hurt from the beating he'd received the night before from the man he knew only as "Bob."

He heard someone enter the room. It was him. Bob. Bryson's eyes popped wide open. Panic sped through his brain as the large man climbed on his chest and began to beat him repeatedly with an iron bar.

After what seemed like hours, Bob moved off him and onto the floor. Bryson began to feel sharp pain coming from his legs. His captor had attached metal clamps to him and was sending electrical charges through his body from a transformer near the bed. As Bryson snapped rigid with each jolt, he could see a flash and hear the whirring sound of Bob's Polaroid camera as he took photos of his agony.

The shocks, the torture, the photo flashes. Was this really happening to him? How much longer would this nightmare go on?

Chris Bryson had no way of knowing.

Bob had just begun.

RITES OF BURIAL

TOM JACKMAN
AND TROY COLE

PINNACLE BOOKS
WINDSOR PUBLISHING CORP.

PINNACLE BOOKS

are published by

Windsor Publishing Corp.
475 Park Avenue South
New York, NY 10016

Credits for cover photos:
  Top left: James Ferris (courtesy of Bonnie Ferris)
Top right: Jerry Howell (courtesy of Paul Howell, Sr.)
  Center: Robert Berdella (courtesy of Kansas City Police
          Department)
  Bottom: Robert Sheldon (courtesy of Kansas City Police
          Department)

Second printing: November, 1992

Printed in the United States of America

Chapter One

Though the desolate streets of downtown Kansas City assume an eerie calm after dusk, certain pockets of activity still seethe with life. For men seeking sex with other men, the area around 10th and McGee Streets has long been one of those sordid pockets. The tall buildings channel a cutting wind south from the Missouri River, causing the casually loitering young men to hunch their shoulders against the cold or duck into one of the shadowy doorways that line McGee Street. For years a Trailways bus station anchored the block, dropping newcomers and natives into the heart of the city. Across the street sat Joseph's Lounge, a quiet and uneasy gay bar. In many large American cities, bus stations have been perennial meeting places for male prostitutes. Homosexuals are thus drawn to certain grimy urban neighborhoods, where a quick, professional "date" can be found or, even better, a willing stranger, new to town, looking to make some fast dollars.

The bus station was gone, but the gaunt young men stayed. Cars circled the block frequently, at all hours, the drivers leaning down to check out the boys in their short jackets and tight jeans, trading glances, no subtlety. A lingering glance signaled a possible deal, a stroll over to the passenger window, then maybe an unlocked door, and a drive to another squalid part of town.

On a clear spring night, Chris Bryson stepped out of the shadows and into the dull glow of the street lights. As he strolled north toward 9th Street, he wore a black pullover short-sleeved shirt, blue jeans and tennis shoes, his light brown hair sprouting out of a part in the middle, his wide shoulders slightly tensed. Like many of the downtown hustlers, Bryson came from Kansas City's East Side, a large area of tightly packed, lower middle-class homes whose residents form a sort of gruff fraternity. There was no money to be made on the East Side, though. The johns were downtown. The male prostitutes, or "chicken hawks" as the cops called them, weren't necessarily gay; some were dropped off by their girlfriends or wives at the start of an evening. It was just a low-overhead, make-your-own-hours way to pull in some cash, mainly for food, booze or drugs.

One car that circled the block regularly was a copper-colored Toyota Tercel hatchback. Many of the chicken hawks were familiar with the driver, a heavyset man with wire-rimmed glasses and a mustache. Some even feared the man, and wouldn't go with him. Sometimes he stopped, sometimes he just circled and looked. Bryson hadn't seen him before. When the man asked if he wanted to party, Bryson opened the passenger side door and climbed in. It was about 1 A.M., Tuesday morning, March 29, 1988.

The slightly dangerous experience of getting into a stranger's car wasn't an entirely new one for Bryson. Though he was only twenty-two, he'd spent some time on the streets after dropping out of high school, at one point doing some burglary and a little prostitution to make a few extra bucks. The adrenaline rush of entering an unknown person's car added an edge to the scramble for spare change, change that often would go toward a few joints or a small packet of cocaine. It was a rush that Bryson hadn't pursued quite so often recently, after settling down, getting married, and fathering a child. But the charge of a quick hit of cocaine, smoked or snorted, was the familiar sensa-

6

tion Bryson sought again on this night, and hustling was a necessary means to that end.

The driver seemed harmless enough: maybe thirty-five or forty years old, average height, receding hairline, soft-spoken, a slight lisp. His rounded face featured a mustache which drooped past the sides of his mouth, and his sad eyes suggested the unthreatening look of a businessman acting on a hidden impulse.

"Want a beer?" the man asked. "They're in the back."

"Sure," Bryson said, reaching around to pull a can of beer from a cooler. "Want one?" Bryson asked the man.

"No," the man said.

Bryson popped his beer open.

"My name's Bob," the man told him.

"I'm Chris," Bryson said.

"What've you been doing?" the man asked.

"Oh, just partying a little, you know," Bryson replied.

"Oh yeah? What kind?"

"Oh, just, you know, a little coke."

"That's cool," Bob said. "I'm not that into uppers though, I'm more into downers." Bob listed a few of the depressants he preferred.

"Ever shoot any of those?" Bob asked.

"No."

"Well, I've got some Valiums at my place," Bob said.

We're going to his house, Bryson thought. Better than a sleazy hotel or a deserted lot. But Bob didn't seem gay, Bryson told himself, so maybe he didn't have to worry about turning a trick. Maybe just get stoned for an hour or two, then go home. Bryson knew that men who drive around late at night are often just lonely partiers, getting drunk or high or both. He glanced over at the paunchy man he'd just met, and decided he had nothing to fear from this guy. Bryson, streetwise and sturdily built, spoke in clipped, nasal tones with a natural swagger. He was confident he could take care of himself.

7

As they talked a little more, though, Bryson began to think that maybe Bob was looking for more than a party pal. As they drove south toward Bob's house, Bob asked him suggestively, "What are you into?" Bryson knew what Bob meant.

"Whatever," Bryson responded indifferently, resigning himself to having to earn his pay.

Bob parked his Toyota on Charlotte Street, and the two men climbed out. They walked up the concrete steps, then stepped on to the wooden front porch of a beige, three-story frame house with dark brown trim. Large wooden numbers nailed next to the doorway announced that this was 4315. Bob unlocked the door, opened it, and Bryson walked in first.

As Bryson stood in the front hallway, Bob moved to a set of closed French doors to the right. He opened them, and Bryson walked into a cluttered living room. Bryson sat down on the couch, pulled out his cigarettes and lit one. Bob walked out of the room and toward the kitchen.

"Want another beer?" Bob called out to Bryson.

"Sure."

Bob returned from the kitchen and handed Bryson another can of beer. Bryson could hear some dogs moving around in the back of the house. He glanced around at the mess—papers and magazines piled everywhere, antiques and other junk draped over chairs and tables. Bob had accumulated stacks of beads, pendants, paintings, books and assorted oddities ever since moving to Kansas City as a college art student in 1967. Even while growing up in Cuyahoga Falls, Ohio, Bob had shown a strong interest in art, and his interests had diversified as his curiosity grew. He never really specialized in any one area; he enjoyed dabbling, and over the years, parts of his house took on the look of a clogged museum. One of his upstairs bedrooms even had display cases filled with ceramics and small sculptures, while

8

masks and assorted artworks hung on the walls.

"Want to go upstairs?" Bob asked. "I've got some Chow dogs, and one of them just had puppies, so she's not too friendly right now, and she's running around down here. I've got a room upstairs with a couch and a TV and stuff."

"Sure," Bryson said. He picked up his beer and cigarettes off the table and headed toward the stairs. Bob followed him out of the room, and walked behind him up the stairs.

As Bryson reached the top of the stairs, Bob pulled out a two-foot-long iron pipe and smashed him once in the back of the skull. Bryson's vision blurred, and he was unable to cushion his fall as he landed face-first on the landing at the top of the stairs. He still had his beer in his right hand, pressed under his chest.

Bob moved above Bryson and leaned down on to his shoulders. He placed his left hand on Bryson's head, and with his right hand he took out a syringe and needle. He stuck the needle into the back of Bryson's neck and injected the contents into Bryson. Quickly, Bryson fell unconscious.

Bob climbed over Bryson and pulled his hands up over his head. He dragged Bryson into the bathroom and propped him up in the sitting position. Then he walked into his bedroom and got his Polaroid 600 camera. He returned to the bathroom and snapped a photo of the young man, his eyes slightly open, but his mind unaware of what was happening.

Next, Bob dragged Bryson back on to the floor. He stood above Bryson and clicked off another photo from the waist up, his arms bent over his head, his mouth open. Then Bob put the camera aside and started taking Bryson's clothes off. When he had finished, he stood back up over Bryson's waist and snapped two more photos from the waist up.

Bob put the camera back down and dragged him into

the bedroom by his legs. Bryson was five feet ten inches tall, weighing about 160 pounds, and lifting him onto the bed took some effort. Finally, Bob laid Bryson on his back. Using some bathrobe sashes, he tied Bryson's hands together and knotted the sashes around the bedposts. He moved down to the end of the bed and pulled Bryson's legs straight. Bryson roused briefly, looked down at Bob, then fell back into unconsciousness. Bob tied his legs to the bedposts with thin cord, then wrapped a washcloth around another length of cord, and tied the cord around Bryson's head, stuffing the washcloth into Bryson's mouth. He finished by attaching a dog collar and leash to his neck, then binding the leash to the bedposts as well.

Bob slept elsewhere in the house for several hours, then returned to the second-floor bedroom about 5:30 A.M. He brought in a spiral stenographer's notebook, and opened it past the dozens of pages filled with his systematic scrawl. He uncapped a pen and tested it at the top of a page. Bob hadn't used the notebook in almost nine months. He wrote in pen: Tues AM." He put the notebook inside a cabinet beyond the foot of the bed.

He then undressed himself, and moved over to the bed. Climbing between the legs of Bryson, he lifted the unconscious man up slightly, and had frictional sex with him, never actually penetrating Bryson. He next placed one of his fingers inside Bryson's anus.

When he was finished with this, Bob returned to the notebook. Beginning a new entry in the gruesome log, he wrote: "5:30-6. Tied on bar/Frt fu, finger."

At 7:30 A.M., Bob injected him with another syringe of clear liquid. This time, he put the shot into the man's shoulder: 3 cubic centimeters of acepromazine, an animal tranquilizer. After giving Bryson the shot, Bob recorded the dosage and where he had made the injection in his notebook. Then he returned to the bed and placed a pillowcase over Bryson's head.

At approximately 8 A.M. Tuesday morning, Bryson revived briefly. He realized he had a gag around his mouth, which scared him because he didn't normally breathe through his nose and began struggling against his restraints. Bob walked into the room, and lifted the pillowcase partially off Bryson's face. Bryson could barely see clearly. The bedroom was fuzzy and he saw only changing shapes. He fought harder to loosen his hands. Bob took his index finger and jabbed it directly into Bryson's eye repeatedly. Bryson could make no noise, because of the tightly tied gag.

Bob walked out of the room, but returned in moments. Bryson's eyes popped open wide, trying to imagine what terror could be next. Panic sped through his brain. But Bob had just begun.

Bob pulled out a cotton-tipped swab, wet with bleach or ammonia. He poked the swab into both of Bryson's eyes, as Bryson tried to writhe away from him. Bryson could feel his eyes stinging from whatever was on the swab. He thought Bob was trying to burn his eyes out. He struggled helplessly.

But Bob had another torture instrument handy. He returned with a two-foot iron bar and climbed on to Bryson's chest. As he straddled Bryson, he faced the bedposts, where Bryson's hands were tied over his head. He began battering Bryson's hands with the bar. Repeatedly. Bob was speaking to him, but Bryson could not understand him. The pain was agonizing.

Bob moved off of Bryson's chest, and down from the bed. Bryson began to feel sharp pain coming from his legs. He looked down and saw that Bob had attached two electrical clamps to him, with wires trailing away from the bed. One clamp was attached to Bryson's testicles, the other to his upper thigh. Bob was now standing at an electrical transformer, sending small jolts through the young man's body.

His body snapped rigid with each jolt. Bob had now turned his face into the bed, but he could still see the flash and hear the whirring sounds as Bob clicked off more photos with his Polaroid. Bryson dared not scream, for fear of the electricity intensifying. The shocks, the bondage, the photo flashes — was somebody really doing this to him?

After the shocks stopped, Bob administered two more injections. The first was 5 cubic centimeters of acepromazine, to reduce Bryson's resistance. The second shot was into the side of Bryson's neck: 2 cubic centimeters of drain cleaner, aimed near Bryson's vocal cords. This was to quiet Bryson's voice, in case he tried to scream while Bob was away.

"This is just for my security," Bob told Bryson. "But if I ever catch you yelling again, I'll put it straight into your vocal cords, and you won't have a voice anymore."

Bob pulled the pillowcase completely off Bryson. Bryson passed out.

About three hours later, Bob checked on Bryson. He made a notation in his diary: "11:45 Quiet." To be certain, he injected five more cubic centimeters of acepromazine into Bryson, this time into his leg. He wrote in his notebook that Bryson had "slight react" to this shot.

By 3:30 Tuesday afternoon, Bob's craving for action was gnawing at him once more. He returned to the bedroom. Bryson was still sleeping. His eyes were swollen. Bob filled up a syringe with penicillin and injected 3 cubic centimeters into Bryson's leg to fight any possible infections.

Bryson woke up. He moaned. Bob felt his forehead. It was hot.

"Be quiet," Bob commanded sternly. He moved to the foot of the bed and began untying Bryson's legs. As he

12

moved around Bryson, he told his young captive that he was now Bob's sex toy, and that he would not see the outside world again.

"The only thing you need to think about is you, me and this house." Bob said. "Don't try to fight me, or you'll just get more of what you had earlier." He reminded Bryson about the metal pipe, the electrical shocks and even mentioned a wooden glove, which Bryson hadn't seen.

"You see," Bob continued, "what you got is nothing compared to what you can have." Bob instructed Bryson that he was to ask permission to speak at all times, by placing his hand over his mouth. If Bob touched the hand, Bryson could talk. If Bryson spoke without requesting permission, he would be smacked with the iron bar.

Bob turned Bryson, still naked, on to his stomach. He moved between Bryson's legs, and had anal intercourse with him. Bryson closed his eyes tightly and prayed for it to end. When Bob was finished, he wiped Bryson's buttocks with a cold washrag, then turned him over again, on to his back. He began to speak to Bryson in soothing tones.

"You did not choose to be here, but you are," Bob lectured. "For you to survive being here and for you to, you know, make it, it could either be rough or it could be easy. If I grow to like you and trust you, then I could do special things for you, such as buy you cigarettes, pick up a movie on the way home from work and so forth."

Bryson listened, but didn't answer. He was still gagged.

Bob told him that if he did not cooperate, he would simply be left tied to the bed until he was ready for sex again. Or, he could move Bryson to the basement and tie him up there. He also said that he liked Bryson enough that he didn't want to share him right now. But if Bryson annoyed him, Bob knew people that would be glad to take advantage of a captive partner.

Bob began to spend more time with Bryson. That evening, after giving Bryson another shot of penicillin, Bob removed the gag from Bryson's mouth and the dog collar from his neck. He then pulled out his Polaroid camera and began snapping more photos of his naked captive. After having sex with Bryson again, Bob allowed him to go to the bathroom. Bob noted this in his log, along with the fact that Bryson's voice was hoarse. He washed Bryson's mouth out, brought him a can of soda, and talked with him some more.

Bryson told Bob he was only twenty-one years old, and Bob wrote down Bryson's address and date of birth, off by one year. He told Bob that he was married and had a son. Bob gave Bryson some cigarettes, and another soda. At 9 P.M. that Tuesday night, he gave Bryson another injection, dutifully noting the amounts of the various drugs he placed in the syringe. He warned Bryson against trying to escape, or trying to hurt him.

"The only ways you can harm me are with your arms or your teeth," Bob told Bryson that night. "I can make it so you'll never be able to use your arms again. And I can surely take care of your teeth. Try to escape and you'll be dead."

Bryson was already terrified. But the thought of trying to escape ran through his mind, parallel to the thought that Bob or his vicious dogs awaited him downstairs if he tried. Most of the time, over the next three days, Bryson didn't think too much; he either slept or was knocked out by the drugs Bob was administering to him.

By Wednesday morning, a routine had been established. Bob wanted sex when he awoke each day, and before he went to sleep each night. Bob told Bryson they could discuss the other types of treatment he was receiving, but there would be no negotiating on the sex. And no crying or bitching about it, Bob told him.

After sex each morning, Bob would place Bryson on his back, tie his hands and feet together, and tie him to the bedposts. Then he placed the washcloth gag over Bryson's mouth, and with a thin rope tied that to the bedposts, too. Finally, he attached the leash from the dog collar around Bryson's neck to the bed as well. Before leaving the room, Bob would switch on a television at the foot of Bryson's bed and turn the volume up so that Bryson couldn't hear him coming or going downstairs.

Besides the sex, the torture also continued. Bob continued to shock Bryson with electrodes attached to various parts of his body. He still beat Bryson with the iron bar, and injected drain cleaner into his throat. He also gave Bryson enemas occasionally before anal sex.

On Thursday, Bob chatted with Bryson about the increasing trust he had in Bryson, but made sure to add a warning: "I've gotten this far with other people before," Bob said, "and they're dead now, because of mistakes they made." The mistakes included not asking Bob for permission to speak, or resisting his advances. "Remember what happened, and what could happen," Bob told him daily.

Bryson began to feel feverish, so Bob gave him pills that he told Bryson were antibiotics. By Thursday night, Bryson was feeling slightly better, and Bob returned home with two rented video movies: *The Lost Boys* and *Robo Cop*. Bob also had cigarettes, and several packages of Polaroid film.

Bob loaded up the camera with film, and clicked off some shots of Bryson. Then he untied Bryson's hands and legs and led him by the dog collar into the bathroom. He tied the leash to a rail out of Bryson's reach, then returned to the bedroom and changed the sheets.

When Bryson finished bathing, Bob untied the leash and walked his captive back into the bedroom. He tied the leash to the bedpost, and told Bryson to start posing, flexing his muscles. Bob snapped off photos as if he were a

15

fashion photographer. Then, more sex before Bryson was tied down for the night.

Bryson still had hope of escaping. On Friday as he watched television while bound and gagged, he heard a basketball player talk about coming back from a debilitating injury. "I knew I was gonna have to go through a lot to get back out on the basketball court, but I knew one day I was gonna be there," the player said.

The thought stuck with Bryson. I've gotta get out of here. Whatever I have to do to see my wife and family again, Bryson thought. Whatever I have to do.

After asking for permission to speak, Bryson had convinced Bob on Thursday night that being tied to the bed with his hands over his head was extremely uncomfortable and cutting off circulation to his arms. So on Friday morning, after sex, Bob tied Bryson's hands in front of him, wrapping the rope around his legs. That day, Bryson found that he could loosen his hands if he worked at it, but he was still frightened of getting partially free and then having Bob discover him trying to escape.

By Saturday morning, Bryson had been in the house for four days. He now thought constantly of getting away. He prayed to God to give him a signal when the coast was clear.

Outside the house, Kansas City was enjoying a moment in the national spotlight. The college basketball "Final Four" championships were beginning that afternoon at Kemper Arena. As Bob retied Bryson after sex, Bryson asked Bob if he could videotape the basketball games that day so Bryson could watch them on Sunday. Bob told him the VCR was not set up to record programs. Bryson asked if he could have the television remote control placed between his legs, so he could change channels on the TV to watch the games. Bob agreed, and tied Bryson's hands in

16

front of him instead of over his head, as usual.

After Bob left the house, Bryson began squirming furiously to loosen the knots around his wrists. The ropes slowly gave way. About twenty minutes later, his right hand was free. Quickly, he worked to untie his left hand. When he was finished, he listened breathlessly to see if Bob was still in the house. He heard nothing.

Next, Bryson reached up and untied the gag that was knotted behind his head. He then pulled the leash off of the bedposts, but he couldn't manage to get the dog collar off his neck. No matter. His feet were still tied to the end posts.

Bryson's fear of being shocked was so great that he thought there might be an electrical charge running through the metal posts at the foot of the bed. He also was unsure how many knots had been tied around his ankles, since he could never see Bob tying those ropes.

However, he had kept his eyes on a book of matches lying on the left side of the bed. Bob had dropped the matches there after lighting a cigarette for Bryson that morning. Bryson leaned over and grabbed them. One by one, he carefully lit them and burned away at the ropes. When the rope would start to catch fire, Bryson would snuff it out with his fingers before the flames burned his legs. He had to burn through four ropes. Finally, they were all singed through. Bryson climbed off the bed, gingerly. His eyes turned toward the window.

It's probably nailed shut, Bryson thought. Or else it's a storm window, and can't be opened. Without even getting dressed, Bryson walked over to the window and tried to lift it up. It opened right away. Bryson couldn't believe it.

He looked down from the second floor. There was a sidewalk running along the side of the house, and a small patch of grass between the sidewalk and the fence separating Bob's house from his neighbor's. He climbed through the window, holding it open with one hand as he positioned himself on the windowsill.

Bryson grabbed the windowsill with his hands and hung down feet first. He decided to try to push out with his feet and land beyond the sidewalk on the grass. But the windowsill gave way before Bryson could push off, and he fell straight down.

He made it. A bone in his foot was broken, but he felt no pain. He ran down the slope leading up to Bob's house, and across Charlotte Street. He saw a meter man from the water department walking down the street. "Hey man," Bryson yelled, "call the police for me, that son of a bitch is crazy, he's trying to kill me."

The meter man and Bryson walked to the front porch of a house across the street from Bob's. They knocked on the door. Felix Duran Jr. looked out at them. He recognized the meter man, but not the naked man wearing a dog collar. He opened the door, and the meter man told him to call the police. Duran could see the naked man was scratched and limping, but he was afraid to let him into the house. He closed the door and dialed 911. After doing so, he returned to the front door and looked out the window. The naked man was sitting on his front steps.

It was 10:28 A.M., April 2, 1988. Neither Bryson, the neighbors nor the police had any notion of the years of horror that led up to that moment. In a quiet residential stretch of single family homes, Bryson's leap to freedom was the first real clue that inhuman atrocities had taken place in their midst, in an unremarkable house at 4315 Charlotte Street.

Chapter Two

The dispatcher's monotone sliced through the dull gray Saturday morning.

"213?"

"213, 41 and Gillham," answered Officer Lloyd Harvey.

"214?"

"214, Brush Creek and Troost," responded Officer Larry Lewis.

"213 with 214, check a nude, suspicious male sitting on the front porch of 4318 Charlotte."

Harvey and Lewis were both fairly close to Charlotte Street, and drove up in a matter of moments. Officer John Metzger and Sergeant Cynthia Cherry also heard the call, and with nothing better to do, headed over to see what was happening.

Lewis got out of his car first, and saw the meter man pointing to Bryson, who was facing the side of the house. Then he noticed the people inside the house, waving at him. He looked back at Bryson, and saw the naked man had something hanging down from his neck. Another damn bondage case, Lewis thought.

Lewis pulled out his notebook and walked up to Bryson.

"Did your lover do this to you?" Lewis asked bluntly.

Bryson looked up and started to speak, but his throat

hurt. The question flabbergasted him. He shook his head emphatically.

"How bad are you hurt?" Lewis asked, scanning Bryson and noticing the scars around his eyes, mouth, and wrists.

"I saw him jump out that window," the meter man piped in.

"Where were you?" Lewis asked Bryson. Bryson pointed across the street and up, to the southwest window on the second floor of 4315 Charlotte.

Lewis asked Bryson for his name and age, and what had happened. Harvey walked up and began listening to Bryson's tale. Not only had he been tortured and sodomized, but Bryson said this man named "Bob" had taken Polaroid photos of him, and shown him photos of other young men, who appeared to be dead. After a couple of minutes, Lewis decided to call for an ambulance, and to get a blanket from his car to cover Bryson.

Harvey asked Bryson what had happened, and Bryson told him he was near 9th and McGee when a man and a woman pulled up and asked him if he wanted to party. He rode with them to the house across the street, was walking up the stairs, and then the lights went out.

While Lewis stood at his car, Metzger drove up and walked over to Bryson and Harvey. Harvey turned to the young officer, put a hand on his shoulder and said, "This'll be a good learning experience for you."

Metzger backed away, thinking the naked man was some deranged person. "Yeah right, make me take the report on a crazy," Metzger said. He didn't want the paperwork.

Harvey resumed questioning Bryson, and Metzger became more interested. By the time the young officer's supervisor, Sergeant Cherry, arrived, Metzger volunteered to take the report.

Now Metzger asked Bryson to start again from the beginning. This time, Bryson said he was hitchhiking at 31st Street and Cleveland Avenue, on the East Side, when he was picked up by a man and a woman. Hours later, Bryson would admit there was no woman in the car with the man; he had said that because he didn't want the police to think he was "tricking." But he never again mentioned being downtown on McGee Street—instead, he stayed with his claim that he was merely accepting a ride home from 31st Street, and Bob convinced him to come to his house. Although Bryson didn't live far from where he claimed he was hitchhiking, and Bob would have been driving in an unfamiliar part of town where there are no male prostitutes, Bryson's revised story would go unchallenged.

While Metzger wrote down this version of how the men met, Harvey went across the street to see if Bob was home, and Lewis went inside Duran's house to use the telephone. First, he called a dispatcher and obtained the name that was listed for 4315 Charlotte: Robert A. Berdella. Then he had the dispatcher transfer him to the Crimes Against Persons division.

Working the day shift Saturday meant going home by 3:30, 4 P.M. at the latest. For Sergeant Troy Cole, a supervisor in the Kansas City Police Department's Homicide unit, that meant making it home in time to watch his beloved Oklahoma Sooners square off against the Arizona Wildcats. If he got home soon enough, Cole knew he could also see most of the first game, in which the University of Kansas would take on Duke University.

But Saturdays also meant that only one sergeant worked the entire Crimes Against Persons division, overseeing not just Homicide but the Robbery and Sex Crimes units as well. Weekends generally are slow for the detectives, but if a bank robbery or rape occurs, the Persons duty sergeant is the only supervisor available to make the calls when crucial decisions must be made about the early phases of an investigation.

21

Even after Cole got a phone call at 10:35 A.M. that Saturday morning, he didn't think his basketball watching would be disrupted. Lewis told him as many of the details of the crime as Bryson had related so far. The victim claimed he had been sexually assaulted, injected with Drano, electrically shocked and beaten. Wearing only a dog collar, the man also told the police that he had escaped from 4315 Charlotte by burning through ropes that bound him to the bed, then jumping from a second floor window.

Cole slowly shook his head, glancing out at the overcast, breezy morning. Homosexuals, he thought. Just another lovers' quarrel, maybe a little kinkier than most. Lewis told Cole that he had called an ambulance because the young man appeared to be injured.

"OK, give me that address again," Cole said, picking up his pen and leaning over the desk.

"4315 Charlotte," Lewis said.

"All right, we'll get somebody out there," Cole said.

Sounded like a sex crime, Cole thought, trying to decide which of his few detectives to send out. The victim claimed to have been sexually assaulted, but he might have been kidnapped or held hostage, crimes also investigated by the Sex Crimes unit. So Cole walked down the hall where Detective Ashley Hurn sat. He was the only member of the unit on duty.

"Hey Ashley," Cole said.

"What's up?"

"Need you to go out on something. We got some naked white guy out by Gillham Road," Cole said, referring to a nearby thoroughfare. Starting to smile, he asked, "Don't they have some kind of mental house out near there?"

"I think they still do, in the 4200 block of Locust," Hurn said.

"Well, I'm sure it's nothing more than a lovers' quarrel. Take Dupree with you, and find out if there's any substance to it," Cole said. The sergeant knew Hurn was hoping to leave early and added: "If it's nothing, you can come back here and then go home."

"OK, will do," Hurn said.

On his way back to homicide, Cole stepped in to the Robbery unit, and told Detective Darwin Dupree to accompany Hurn. Dupree and Hurn rode the elevator from the second floor to the ground floor at Police Headquarters, and took Hurn's unmarked police car south toward Charlotte Street.

Hurn had no plans to watch basketball that evening, but he thought the timing of this call was perfect. Maybe talk to the victim for a while, find out what really happened. By the time that was finished, it should be close to noon, Hurn figured. Since he started work at 7:30 and nearly five hours were in the can, he might be able to take the rest of Saturday off, then visit his parents living outside the city.

Hurn pulled his car onto Charlotte Street and parked. Metzger approached the detectives and related the basic story as Bryson had told it to him. Hurn looked over at Bryson who was facing away from the policemen, huddled under a blanket. His eyes were puffy and red, and he was having trouble adjusting to the light even though the morning sky was cloudy.

"I'm sure this is difficult for you," Hurn told Bryson. "I'm a detective. I'll probably be working this for the duration. Now I don't want you to think you're going to have to repeat this over and over again, but I need the highlights."

Bryson shot an odd glance at Hurn.

"No one is making light of this," Hurn quickly added, "but just give me the basics."

Bryson started from the beginning, saying he was hitchhiking at 31st and Cleveland, when he was picked up by a heavyset white man named "Bob" and a blond-haired white woman. He didn't know what happened to the woman. Though traumatized, Bryson still didn't want his family to know he'd been out hustling.

Hurn remained calm, almost nonchalant, as Bryson told his story. Nothing unusual or astounding about it at all. That was the impression Hurn tried to give all the sex crimes victims he encountered as they told him stories of sexual degradation. Though this story sounded as outlandish as anything Hurn had encountered in his ten years with the police department, he knew victims had a tendency to exaggerate, and that most cases weren't as bad as they initially seemed. But this victim did have a brown dog collar around his neck, with a long red leather leash attached to it. He also had red eyes, and scars on his face, arms, legs and back. And he was naked.

Hurn jotted down some notes in a small notebook, then asked Duran if he could use his telephone. He went inside and called Cole.

"There's much more to this than meets the eye," Hurn told Cole. "I don't know how much more, but this guy's telling a pretty harsh story about being captured and tortured. He's got deep rope marks on his wrists, mouth and ankles. It looks legit."

The two men then discussed whether to apply for a search warrant for Bob's house. Hurn figured that Berdella would probably come home, and then tell the police that Bryson liked to be tied up and treated roughly. He would allow a search of his house, nothing would be found, Bryson wouldn't want to prosecute, and Hurn could be at his parents' house in time for dinner.

Cole told Hurn to have the uniformed officers keep a discreet surveillance on the house until Berdella came home. In the meantime, Hurn could come back to the office and work on the paperwork for a search warrant, in case Bob turned out to be uncooperative. Hurn drove away as an ambulance arrived, and Bryson padded toward it for the short ride to the hospital.

Metzger followed the ambulance to Menorah Medical Center and explained Bryson's recent past to a supervisor while the patient was being admitted. Metzger then returned to Charlotte Street, parked several houses down from 4315 and began working on his report. Harvey and Cherry sat in the sergeant's car, chatting. Lewis informed everyone of the resident's name, which he had gotten from the dispatcher, then he walked around to the back of the house in case this "Bob" or Mr. Berdella arrived on that side.

At 11:30 A.M., Bob drove up in his Toyota Tercel. He parked the car in front of the house, then walked over to where Cherry and Harvey were sitting. Cherry rolled down her window.

"What's going on here?" the man asked innocently.

"Oh, not much," Cherry replied. "Who are you?"

"I'm Bob Berdella."

Cherry and Harvey exchanged electric glances: it's him. Harvey swiftly opened his door and darted around to Berdella.

"You're being arrested for investigation of sexual assault," Harvey told Berdella and read him his Miranda rights.

Berdella was stunned. He said nothing, but he began to shake involuntarily. Harvey moved behind him and handcuffed Berdella.

"Put him in your car, Lloyd," Cherry instructed. "Turn the radios off," she added, so Berdella wouldn't hear any internal communications about his case.

Harvey walked Berdella over to his empty squad car, opened the front passenger door, reached in and clicked off his police radios. Then he helped Berdella get in the front seat. Cherry walked over, followed by Lewis and Metzger, who both wanted a closer look at this suspect.

25

"What's happening here?" Berdella asked politely.

"Well," said Cherry, knowing she had to choose her words carefully, "we're investigating a report of an alleged sexual assault. Would you be willing to sign a Consent to Search to let us look in your house?"

"What for?"

"To check out the victim's report," Cherry said.

"What's his name?" Berdella said. Both Metzger and Lewis noticed that Berdella knew, or assumed, the victim was a man.

"Christopher," Cherry said.

"What's his last name?"

"I don't feel I'm at liberty to go into that right now," Cherry replied.

"Where is he?"

Lewis stepped in, irritated by Berdella's questions. "That's none of your business," Lewis told him pointedly. "We got him and he's talking."

"You don't have to sign the Consent," Cherry said, "but we can easily get a search warrant for your house."

"Well, if you won't give me any more information, I'll have to respectfully decline letting you into my house," Berdella said.

"OK, fine," Cherry said. She closed Berdella's door, and Harvey walked around to the driver's side.

Harvey started up the car, and Berdella watched him. Harvey could sense that Berdella wanted to talk.

"What is going on here?" Berdella wondered, his tone incredulous.

"Christopher says you've had him tied up for several days," Harvey said.

"This is not right," Berdella said. "This is not right."

"You don't have to talk, you know," Harvey said.

"This is not right," Berdella repeated. He murmured the same phrase several more times as Harvey drove him to police headquarters.

Berdella had been arrested before, and had had plenty of encounters with the police during his twenty years in Kansas City. As an art student in the late sixties he had been arrested twice, once for selling drugs, and once for possession, both minor violations. Several years after buying the Charlotte Street home in Kansas City's Hyde Park area, he had joined and then headed the neighborhood's crime watch association, getting to know the police department's community relations officers. And he'd been interviewed by detectives in recent years about a couple of missing young men who had last been seen with him. Berdella was not impressed by the investigative abilities of the Kansas City police. As he bumped along in Harvey's patrol car, he wondered what the police would be able to piece together about him this time.

Harvey and Berdella arrived at police headquarters about noon, and Harvey directed his prisoner into the jail elevator. Before riding up to the eighth floor, where the jail was located, they stopped at the second floor, longtime home of the Crimes Against Persons division. Harvey led Berdella to the Sex Crimes unit, where Hurn was sitting at a desk, working on an affidavit for a search warrant.

Harvey began telling Hurn that Berdella had driven up to his house, spoken to the officers, asked them for some information, and refused to let them search his house. Berdella stared hard at the floor. Hurn got up and walked over to him, but Berdella wouldn't look at him. Hurn bent over at the waist and leaned down, looking up at Berdella until finally the two made eye contact. Hurn slowly straightened up, with Berdella's eyes following him. When Hurn was upright, Berdella had a look of disgust on his face, as if Hurn had played a cheap trick on him.

"Do you understand what you're here for?" Hurn asked. Berdella said nothing.

"If you don't understand, someone has claimed that you held them against their will."

No response.

"Do you understand your rights?"

Still no answer.

Hurn began a second recitation of the Miranda rights.

"Officer," Berdella spoke up, "if you are an officer, maybe a detective—" he paused for several seconds, then said, "I have nothing to say at this time. As soon as I may, I'd like to make a telephone call." His tone was both polite and condescending. Hurn was chilled.

"You'll get your chance," Hurn said. He decided not to try to question Berdella, because police policy dictates that any prisoner who requests to speak to an attorney is not to be interrogated further.

Hurn watched as Harvey turned Berdella around and led him down the hallway out of the Sex Crimes unit. This is going to be a tough one, Hurn thought, very tough. Berdella's disgusted look, his condescending tone, his seeming lack of concern or fear; he'd be an extremely tough individual to break.

Harvey walked Berdella to the Homicide unit and told him to stand against a set of lockers just outside the unit. Cole looked up, expecting the visitor, then rose out of his chair to face the man who would become the dominant focus of his life for the next nine months.

"Are you Robert Berdella?" Cole asked.

"Yes," Berdella answered. The drawn-out "S" sound betrayed his slight lisp.

"You've been arrested for investigation of sodomy," Cole told him. "We're going to get a search warrant for your house unless you'll sign a Consent to Search form, and then we can avoid all that." Berdella eyed Cole anxiously. Again, his hands and shoulders started to shake, just barely, but enough for Cole to notice. He tried to appear calm.

"I'd better not sign anything until I talk with my attorney," Berdella said.

"Well," Cole said, "your attorney's going to advise you not to sign it, so we'll go ahead and get a search warrant."

"Can I call my attorney?" Berdella asked.

"You can call him when we get you upstairs," Cole replied.

Cole turned and walked back to his desk, opened up a drawer and pulled out a small pad of arrest authorization forms. He filled in Berdella's name, time and location of arrest, the reason for arrest, and signed his name. He handed the form to Harvey, who then led Berdella to the jail elevator. But before he got there, Hurn reappeared for one last second-floor formality: a snapshot for the case file. Hurn took two Polaroid pictures. The first one didn't develop. The second one captured Berdella staring straight at the camera, emotionless, his hair slightly awry, but seemingly unfazed.

Hurn returned to his desk to finish filling out the search warrant forms, in which police explain the circumstances of the alleged crime and what police hope to find if they get the search warrant. Meanwhile Cole called the police Crime Scene Investigation unit and told Detective Mel Beverlin that they would need assistance in photographing, diagramming and otherwise processing a house where an alleged sodomy had occurred. They would also need photos of the victim, who was already at the hospital. Beverlin, in an office about seven blocks from police headquarters, prepared to head out.

At the front of the Crimes Against Persons offices, Hurn sat down with a typist and began dictating a rough outline of Bryson's tale. Hurn's meticulous work habits would prove useful in this case. Known, even as a street officer, for writing lengthy, detailed reports of events most officers would summarize in a page or two, Hurn knew he had to demonstrate emphatically that this was no ordinary

29

search warrant. He mentioned Bryson's claims that he had been injected with Drano, sexually humiliated, drugged and tied to a bed for days. He quickly filled up the space allotted for explaining the offense, and added five more pages of information. This case feels like a big one, Hurn thought, don't miss anything.

When he was finished, Hurn took the application into Cole's office for a final check before taking it to a judge's house for his signature. Cole examined the paperwork and told Hurn to call him once the judge had approved the warrant, so he could meet the detectives at Berdella's house before they went in.

Hurn arrived at Associate Circuit Judge Vincent Baker's house shortly before 1:30 P.M. Hurn explained briefly what police knew so far, which was basically just Bryson's claims of being held against his will and sodomized. Baker read the police paperwork and shook his head several times. How could one human being do this to another, Baker wondered. This guy is in a moral vacuum.

He signed his name at the bottom of several pages and handed them back to Hurn. Hurn asked if he could use the phone, then called Cole to tell him the warrants were in hand. Then he returned to his car and drove back to Berdella's house.

After Cole hung up with Hurn, he called a young robbery detective, Chris Mahlstadt, to accompany him on a search warrant. The two men walked out to Cole's unmarked police car as Cole filled in Mahlstadt on what was happening. Again, Cole restated his belief that it was just a "lovers' quarrel." Often in police work, though it isn't immediately apparent, detectives find a relationship between the victim and the suspect that provides a motive and context for the crime.

Cole and Mahlstadt arrived at Berdella's house shortly

before 2 P.M., and Hurn pulled up minutes later. Beverlin, the Crime Scene investigator, had already photographed Bryson's injuries at the hospital and was outside the house with another Crime Scene specialist. The detectives noticed that a truck from the city's Animal Control department was parked near Berdella's house. Cherry told Cole that neighbors had informed her that Berdella kept large, vicious dogs in the house, so Cherry had requested Animal Control's help.

With two Animal Control employees trailing behind them, Cole, Cherry, the detectives, the Crime Scene investigators, a patrol duty captain, Metzger and Lewis walked up the front steps to 4315 Charlotte Street. Hurn knocked on the door and shouted, "Police officers, search warrant." He tried the doorknob. It was locked. The detectives all wore street shoes, but Metzger had black boots on, so he was nominated to kick the door in. With his third assault on the knob, the door blew backward. At 2:12 P.M., police had their first look inside Berdella's house.

The Animal Control handlers entered first, and headed toward the back of the house to corral the dogs. The uniformed officers followed, then the detectives. Everyone had the same initial thought: the clutter was unbelievable. As they scanned the first-floor hallways and rooms, there was very little empty floor space. Almost every inch was occupied by stacks of papers, brown paper bags filled with books and magazines, plastic garbage bags bulging with clothes, large and small artifacts, trash. The man was either a collector or an incredible pack rat, the detectives thought.

Next they noticed the odor. Piles of dog excrement were noticeable in several places around the house. Simply moving around on the first floor often required the detectives to maneuver carefully. When they reached the kitchen, another contributor to the household smells—a spoiled turkey carcass in a pot on the stove—was discovered. Dirty

31

dishes filled the sink. Everyone was careful not to touch anything. No one knew what was evidence and what was junk. As they glanced around, the Animal Control handlers dragged three Chow Chow dogs, one of them very large with a lionlike mane and one a small puppy, out to a cage in the back of their truck.

"Let's try to go upstairs," Cole instructed the rest of the group. He knew that was where Bryson claimed he had been held. The officers picked their way through the clutter and tromped up the staircase.

The group reached the second-floor landing. Officers leaned their heads into each room, and saw nothing like what Bryson had described. Must be on the next floor, they thought. So the group headed up to the third floor and again ducked into each room. Again, nothing.

"Did we miss it?" Hurn asked. He also wondered if someone had gotten in the house and cleaned up the crime scene.

The officers split up and started exploring the house. On the second floor, Metzger walked through a bedroom filled with clothes, bags and furniture. He noticed another door in the room, and heard a television. He walked toward the door, which was closed, raised his shotgun and tapped the door open.

"Sarge, here it is," he yelled.

The investigators clambered past Metzger into the room. Hurn approached the bed and found burnt ropes attached to the posts at the foot of the bed. Sashes, as if from bathrobes, were tied to the head posts. The window was slightly ajar, and the storm window outside was loose. On the floor was an electric transformer, its cord plugged in to a wall socket, with wires leading toward the bed. On a table next to the bed sat a metal tray with syringes, small bottles apparently filled with prescription drugs, some ointments and some eye drops.

Metzger left the room and started looking around in the

adjoining room he had just come through. Against one wall stood a wooden wardrobe cabinet with two doors, a shelf and five drawers inside. Sitting on the shelf was a shoebox. A sheaf of Polaroid photographs stuck above the side of the box. Metzger pulled them out of the box. The first few photographs were all of the same man. It was Bryson. He was pale, naked, obviously in pain.

"Look at this," Metzger called to no one in particular.

"Jesus Christ," one of the officers said.

Hurn came in and flipped through the rest of the photographs. There were dozens, all of Bryson. In some, he had a bag or pillowcase over his head. In others, he was facedown, his hands tied behind his back. In all of them, he appeared to be tortured.

Back in the bedroom, Cole thought: this is the Crime Scene all right. He scanned the room. Lying on the floor near the bed were several all-male pornographic magazines, some wide leather belts, and various lengths of rope. Another small table in the room had some more small bottles of liquid drugs. The bed had vertical steel posts at both the head and foot, and both ends had been painted white. The paint on two of the middle posts at the head of the bed had been completely worn away.

On the mattress at the foot of the bed, a twenty-nine-inch iron pipe was lying alongside a remote control television box and a book of matches. A small table at the end of the bed supported a portable television and two video recorders. So far, everything matched the once incredible story Bryson had been telling them.

Maybe this guy's telling us the truth, Cole thought to himself. But the sergeant also figured that this was no stranger-to-stranger relationship. If Berdella really did tie up and torture Bryson, somewhere along the line detectives would probably find that the two men actually knew each other.

The detectives fanned out through the rest of the house.

33

The two Crime Scene investigators went to brief their commander, Captain Ronald Canaday, who had just arrived along with the director of the Regional Crime Lab, Gary Howell. Beverlin had called Canaday after speaking with Bryson at the hospital and realizing how unusual the case was going to be. Canaday would eventually supervise the entire search and cataloguing of the house, and Howell's crime lab would become crucial in discovering physical evidence, such as blood stains, hair strands and fingerprints.

Cole thought the commanders in the Sex Crimes unit would want to know what was going on, since it appeared to be their case. He checked a list of phone numbers in his notebook, then called the captain in Sex Crimes, Captain Marylyn Brauninger, and gave her a summary of what he knew so far. Brauninger then phoned one of her sergeants, Roy Orth, and instructed him to head over to 4315 Charlotte.

When Orth arrived about 3 P.M., Cole turned the investigation over to him. The search of the house was still in its early stages, but the physical evidence to corroborate Bryson's story appeared to be all there in the second-floor bedroom, Cole told Orth. A Sex Crimes detective, Hurn, had been present from the start and could handle the investigation in later stages. Orth nodded in agreement, and Cole and Mahlstadt returned to Cole's car and drove back to police headquarters. Cole didn't want to be away from headquarters for long, since he was the only one there who could authorize bookings into the city jail.

That must be one strange individual, Cole thought of Berdella as he drove back downtown. In his mind, he pictured the man he had spoken with briefly outside the homicide unit three hours earlier: high forehead, his hair combed straight back, wire-rimmed glasses, thick mustache, rounded jaw, paunchy, slumped shoulders, slight lisp. Didn't seem like the kind of guy to take a sexual captive, but then not many criminals give obvious signs of a

34

twisted nature in their appearance.

When he returned to the Homicide unit, Cole finished some paperwork, briefed the night shift duty sergeant on Bryson's case, told him which detectives were still at the scene and headed for his car. No homicides or serious assaults on his shift. That meant no overtime. On the twenty-minute drive to his south Kansas City home, he turned on the radio and listened to the game between Kansas and Duke. Kansas leapt out to a huge early lead, and began pummeling Duke in front of an appreciative Kansas City crowd. As the game got boring, the announcers soon turned their patter to the second game, the *real* game for the national championship, between Oklahoma and Arizona. Cole smiled in anticipation.

Cole loved police work, but he was also a sports nut. It wasn't uncommon to find him leaning back in the Homicide unit, a detective or fellow sergeant standing nearby, heatedly discussing the previous night's ballgame. Sports had been his means of escape from tiny Keota, Oklahoma, where he was the youngest of nine children. Cole played baseball, football and basketball constantly while growing up in the tiny town, eventually being named all-conference in high school as a quarterback in football and a guard in basketball.

But it was baseball where Cole really starred. Though he wasn't a big teenager, he developed a tricky knuckleball that helped him become an ace starting pitcher, and to win a full scholarship to a junior college in Muskogee, Oklahoma. His coach there later went on to coach the University of Oklahoma baseball team, and Cole's loyalties to the Sooners were sewn up. Long after he'd moved away from Oklahoma, he kept close tabs not only on the Sooner baseball team, but on every powerhouse Oklahoma football team. And when the basketball team also reached national prominence, it became inevitable that Saturday afternoons in the winter would be spent

35

in front of the television whenever Oklahoma was on.

Back at Berdella's house, Orth summoned two more detectives from police headquarters to help scour the cluttered residence. The more they searched, the stranger their findings were, so Orth also decided to notify the Jackson County prosecutor's office. The prosecutor's office liked to be aware of big cases from the very start, since it would be their job to prosecute the suspects somewhere down the road. Orth called Rick Holtsclaw, a member of the prosecutor's Sex Crimes unit.

The house was buzzing with activity when Holtsclaw arrived. A second bedroom upstairs was jammed with artifacts and weird items. Another new arrival to the house, Detective Randall Morris, stepped carefully through the mess, stopping in the middle of the room to look at a human skull. It was sitting under a glass dome, on top of a small table. Could this be real? Morris wondered. There must be thousands of things in this one room alone, he thought. I hope we don't have to itemize every one of them for the search warrant.

Morris slowly made his way toward the back of the room, thinking unkind thoughts about a man who would live in such a mess, much less tie up and sexually torture someone. The detective bent down and picked up a couple of books. One was titled *Satanic Interpretation and Lifestyle*. Another was called *How to Create Poisons and the Antidotes to Them*.

He stepped over another pile of books to reach the bedroom's closet. Morris pulled the door open, and immediately stared at the closet's center shelf: another human skull stared back at him. This one looks real, Morris thought.

"Hey, we got a skull over here," Morris called out. Footsteps started to thump in his direction. Morris leaned in for a closer look, and noticed two lumpy envelopes lying on the lower shelves. He picked up one of the envelopes, which wasn't sealed, and opened the flap. Inside was a cluster of human teeth.

Morris went to tell Orth of his discovery, but Orth and Hurn were making discoveries of their own. In the bedroom that detectives would later call the "torture room," Hurn found a stenographer's pad on top of a chest of drawers. He flipped through the pages and found numerous notations, almost all with dates and times, apparently starting on "6/23/87." Hurn opened the chest of drawers. In addition to clothes, he found thirteen audio cassette tapes. He didn't touch them, but he made a note of them in his notebook.

Orth circled around the bed in this room, then lifted up the mattress and looked underneath. He spotted a large clear plastic bag. He reached in with one hand and pulled it out. More photos. He opened the bag and started looking at the Polaroid prints, which were mainly of naked men. Also in the bag were fourteen pages of handwritten notes, again including dates and times. The photos were organized into four separate sets, either with rubber bands or plastic baggies, each grouped with a few pages of notes.

Orth put the notes down and resumed examining the photos. In several of the shots, men were shown with a cucumber or a carrot protruding from their anus. Orth didn't know whether to be amused or disgusted, but after hearing Bryson's claims, he wasn't surprised. At least, not until he came to the photo of the naked man hanging upside down. The man was tied with rope at both ankles, and was hanging from a ceiling, apparently in the basement next to a water heater. Orth studied this photo for a long time. The man had discoloration down by his hands and arms, as if blood had settled there. His mouth was open, his eyes apparently closed. He didn't look to be in any pain. He didn't appear to be alive.

"Holy shit," Orth muttered softly. He set that photo apart from the others.

Morris entered the room with an excited look on his face.

"Have you been in that other room yet?"

"There's two human skulls in there."

Orth's eyes grew wide.

"Oh shit," he said.

Orth immediately turned to seek out higher authority. Captain Canaday, the crime scene commander, was walking through the first floor. Orth went downstairs to speak with him.

"Captain, I think we might have more than a sodomy on our hands here," Orth said.

"Why's that Roy?" Canaday asked.

"Morris says we've got two human skulls in one of the rooms upstairs."

"Well let's go have a look."

Morris led the tour back into the junk-strewn southwest room on the second floor. Canaday looked first at the skull under glass, then moved over to the closet to inspect the skull lying next to the envelope. Morris explained that there were teeth in both envelopes.

"Well, hell, I don't know if these are real or not," Canaday said. "Anybody that collects this much junk would probably know where to get a human skull." Canaday suspected the second one was real. Gary Howell, director of the crime lab, moved in for a look. He also couldn't tell if the skulls were genuine.

"Think we ought to call in somebody to find out if these are real?" Orth asked.

"Yes I do," Canaday said, and he went to call an anthropology professor at the University of Missouri. But it was Easter weekend, and none could be reached. So Howell called Dr. Michael Finnegan, a forensic anthropologist from Kansas State University in Manhattan, Kansas.

38

Finnegan had assisted various police departments as well as consulted on dozens of archeological and historical mysteries in which human or animal parts had been found. Finnegan said he'd be there as quickly as he could make the two-hour drive.

Meanwhile, Orth went back downstairs, then into the kitchen to use Berdella's phone. He called police headquarters to get the home phone number of the Homicide commander, Captain Sylvester Winston, then informed him about the skulls and the photograph.

"I'll get some people over there," Winston told Orth. After they hung up, Winston phoned Sergeant Cole.

By 6:15 P.M. that evening, Cole was barely started watching the Kansas-Duke game. It was a blowout. His wife, Jan, had fixed dinner, and Cole was sitting in an easy chair with a portable tray in front of him. Jan answered the phone when it rang, then called her husband over and handed him the receiver.

"Yeah, it's Winston."

"What's up, sir?" Cole asked.

"Yeah, seems like we got something going on over at 43rd and Charlotte. Were you out there earlier today?"

"Yes sir, on a sodomy."

"Apparently they've got a couple of human skulls," Winston said, "and some photos of some dead males, I don't know what else. You want to go on down there and check it out?"

"Sure, I'll get right to it."

Cole hung up.

"Shit. I've got to go back out on a possible homicide," Cole said. Jan knew that meant missing the Oklahoma game.

"At least you can tape it," she said.

Cole agreed, set the timer for the second game, then returned to the telephone to call one of his detectives, John Fraise, to meet him at Berdella's house.

Cole and Fraise arrived at the house about 7:15 P.M. As they went inside, Cole gave Fraise the background on Bryson's case, and what had been done by the time Cole went home at 4:00. Fraise nodded, looking around at the covered floors and furniture of Berdella's entryway, living room and dining room.

Canaday came downstairs and introduced Finnegan. He led Cole and Fraise up to the second floor, and told them that while the skull found under glass was an old artifact, the skull in the closet was definitely that of a more recent human being, probably a younger white male. He said the teeth in the envelopes appeared to go with the skull.

Orth entered the room, and told Cole, "I've already got Eikel working on a second search warrant—for murder." Both Orth and Cole knew that the first warrant was for sexual assault, and that any evidence of murder found while looking for sexual assault evidence might not be admissible in court. What they didn't know was that Detective Tom Eikel, putting together the application for a search warrant, had been to Berdella's house before, as an undercover detective. Eikel would fill them in on that later.

For now, Eikel had the task of visiting Judge Baker at home again and asking for a second set of signatures. He told Baker what detectives had found as a result of the first search warrant, and that his approval might be needed again the next morning on a criminal warrant charging Berdella with sodomy. Baker, alternately interested and amazed by how the case was unfolding, told Eikel that would be fine. He signed the second set of search warrants about 7:30 P.M.

Even as Eikel was waiting for the judge's signature, the detectives continued to comb through Berdella's house. Detective Jon Jacobson, digging around next to the second-floor closet where the skull was found, picked up a brown suitcase and unlatched it. Inside were two more clear, plastic Zip-Loc bags, with yet more Polaroid photos of men being tortured. Some of the men had plastic garbage bags over their heads. Also in one of the bags were three more sheets of paper, this time yellow, lined pages with times and dates.

Elsewhere in the suitcase, Jacobson found a brown cloth wallet. He opened it up and pulled out a driver's license. "Walter James Ferris," the identification said. Jacobson thought he had just seen that name. He glanced back at the yellow paper in the plastic bag. At the top of one of the notated sheets was the heading "Ferris."

Orth walked in, and Jacobson showed him the latest discovery. "Wouldn't it be wild if this guy turned up missing?" Orth said. He told Jacobson to call the dispatcher and run Ferris's name through the police computer. Jacobson called. Ferris was a missing person.

On the first floor, Cole and Fraise were rooting through the dining room. The dining room table was piled high with papers—invoices, bills, letters, junk mail, boxes, magazines. Fraise picked up a brown expandable folder. On the outside was written "House Guests." Inside were several manila folders with different headings, including one folder with several newspaper clippings from the *Kansas City Star* about a missing young man named Jerry Howell. Next to the clips were some handwritten notes with the heading "Howell."

Down in the basement, the Crime Scene investigators were looking around to see if the photo of the man hanging by his ankles had been taken there. It sure looked like it, they agreed. Near one wall, a sack of dog food had dried blood on it. Beverlin and Canaday looked up at the ceiling and speculated that the blood appeared to have dripped down from the first floor. Then they noticed what appeared to be some sort of smudged footprint, or sock print, on a beam in the ceiling. Either someone had been walking upside down, or someone had been hanging from this beam, they figured. A nearby styrofoam cooler also had blood drops on the lid. In addition, in one corner of the basement, a rectangular area in the floor about three feet long by four feet wide had been recently filled in with fresh concrete.

We're going to be spending a lot of time in this basement, Canaday thought.

Chapter Three

> *"The Dragon Nagari*
> *I rise from death, I kill death, and death kills me. I re-*
> *suscitate the bodies I have created and, alive in death, I*
> *destroy myself. Although I carry poison in my head*
> *the antidote can be found in my tail, which I bite with*
> *rage. Whoever bites me must first bite himself; other-*
> *wise, if I bite him, death will bite him first in the head.*
> *Biting is a remedy against bites."*
> *— Inscription on Bob Berdella's business cards*

"Jesus, what is that smell?"

"Fraise, did you track that shit up here?"

In the middle of serving the second search warrant on Bob Berdella's house, a group of detectives began the schoolyard game of Who Stepped In It? "It" was the dog feces that were dropped around Berdella's house. The detectives lifted their feet and inspected their soles, but throughout the night the pungent odor would trail them through the house. Nearly everyone who entered Berdella's house for the first time was struck by the putrid air, which included the stench of the decaying food in the kitchen and the pesticide chlordane which Berdella had sprayed heavily throughout the house.

Some of the investigators in the house were now wearing white paper overalls and plastic booties over their shoes, to protect their clothes from the dust, dirt and assorted debris that coated Berdella's belongings. In addition, the police had an unspoken paranoia about contracting the AIDS virus from touching something of Berdella's. They had no reason to think Berdella was infected, but if he was gay, they reasoned, AIDS was possible.

Sergeant Cole assigned detectives to sift through certain areas of the house. He knew that a complete, top-to-bottom scouring of the house would take days, if not weeks, so he just wanted a light run-through this first night. Conclusions about Berdella at this point were impossible; this was simply the time to start collecting the raw data.

It wasn't just the clutter, though, that concerned the police. It was the type of clutter. There were strange masks scattered about the house, including a frightening, hairy mask of dark fur, which was propped on a post in an upstairs bedroom. In the room next door, where Bryson had been held, a black, dashiki-style shirt with zippers and colorful designs was pinned on the wall over the bed. Elsewhere in the house, small plaster masks were found on shelves and in drawers, sometimes resembling shrunken heads. Most of these items, including the two skulls already found, were in a third bedroom on the second floor, which the detectives dubbed the "artifact room."

In a hallway between the bedrooms, Detective Bill Earhart opened a closet door to see what new treasures he could uncover. As he rooted through the papers, linens and assorted clutter, he found a clear plastic bag with bones inside. He picked the bag up and examined the contents, unsure what type of bones he was looking at. With all the weird stuff in this house, Earhart thought, this may as well be dinosaur bones. Orth walked by and took a look at Earhart's discovery.

"Those are human vertebrae," Orth said flatly. Earhart turned to look at Orth and fought the urge to drop the bag to the floor. Instead he noted where he'd found the bag and went to notify a Crime Scene investigator so the bones could be labeled and taken to the crime lab.

On the third floor of the house, where a small stereo sat above a pile of albums, the record on the turntable was entitled *Black Mass for Lucifer*. The detectives had already counted twenty books on Satanism or witchcraft in the house. Was Berdella some sort of devil worshiper? Neither Cole nor anyone else in the house had ever encountered a case with that twist to it. But earlier in the year, in a rural Missouri town about 120 miles southeast of Kansas City, two teen-aged boys had beaten a third boy to death with baseball bats as part of a Satanic ritual. The possibility that Berdella had some type of cult involvement promised to make investigating him that much more difficult.

The thought that police might suspect him of devil worshipping hadn't occurred to Berdella until it started to appear in news reports. His father, Robert Berdella Sr., was a Catholic of Italian descent. Berdella was baptized a Catholic, and attended Catholic Mass and religious education courses while growing up in Cuyahoga Falls. But when Berdella was a teenager in the 1960s, his father began to get more involved in the local church, and became disillusioned with its internal politics, passing those sentiments on to his oldest son. Berdella questioned the supposed infallibility of the priests, and disagreed with the concept of confession and forgiveness. Do these robed men actually speak to God? Only God could really forgive someone, Berdella once told a friend. The young Berdella also wrestled with the church's doctrines on divorce and birth control.

On Christmas Day 1965, the Berdella family drove down to Canton, Ohio, to visit relatives. That evening, the senior Berdella suffered a sudden heart attack and was hospitalized. Two days later, Robert Berdella Sr. died at the age of thirty-nine. His oldest son was shocked, and hoped the

45

church might provide solace, but it did not. The sixteen-year-old grew more impatient with Catholicism's inability to answer the spiritual questions he asked. He stopped attending services altogether, but a certain guilt would trail him the rest of his life.

Gradually, Berdella developed a cynical attitude toward all organized religions. He read extensively about many faiths and ideas, but never embraced any of them. The ceremony and ritual of these groups could be attractive, but their theologies weren't appealing to Berdella. Instead, he developed a flair for showmanship. After he enrolled in the Kansas City Art Institute, in the fall of 1967, Berdella grew long hair and a full, bushy beard and mustache. While a student, Berdella once constructed a small maze, and handed those entering the maze a baby chicken to hold. At the end of the maze, the participant watched a short film of another small chick pecking away at some food, then a sudden explosion as the chicken on the film was shot to death. This sometimes caused the participant to squeeze the live chicken involuntarily, while Berdella watched with enjoyment. Berdella's circle of friends also enjoyed attention-grabbing stunts, and at one time even planned to stage a mock "Black Mass" on the front yard of a nearby Christian youth home.

Drawing attention to himself was a new experience for Berdella, something he rarely did in Cuyahoga Falls, a city of about 49,000 on the northern border of Akron in northeastern Ohio. As a child, he was highly intelligent but quiet and aloof. Neighbors recalled that he appeared to have no friends in the newly built neighborhood on Curtis Avenue, where small, nearly identical houses were packed closely together. The Berdellas moved into their one-and-a-half-story home in 1954, when "Robbie" was five, after his father took a job as a die-setter in a Ford Motor Company plant north of Cuyahoga Falls. Mr. and Mrs. Berdella were well-liked by neighbors and co-workers, occasionally socializing with the neighbors, and Mr. Berdella would gladly help others with

46

chores or household handiwork. A second son, Daniel, was born in May 1956.

But little Robbie almost never played outside and rarely had friends come to visit him. Instead, he stayed inside and read books, or worked on his coin and stamp collections. As an adolescent in the early 1960s, he spent much of his time writing letters to pen pals in Vietnam, Burma, Jamaica, France, Japan and Canada. Berdella wrote long, serious letters, and his distant friends wrote back with an earnestness that hadn't yet been darkened by the cynicism of the late sixties. The young Ohioan related details of his life, including mention of a girlfriend, and his pen pals did the same, often enclosing new stamps for Berdella's collection. Berdella also began to develop an interest in painting, and sometimes sent some of his paintings to his friends. In turn, Berdella received photos of his correspondents and their families. Keeping dialogues going with as many as six people at a time meant coming home from school each day with the possibility of a new surprise in the mail. Ever the collector, Berdella kept every one of the letters he received, even after he moved away to Kansas City in 1967.

It may have been the lasting correspondences with his far-flung friends that piqued Berdella's later interest in multi-headed dragons and spark-spitting oriental toys. He began collecting such oddities in college and eventually opened a shop specializing in offbeat collectibles. Berdella once described his shop as filled with "ethnological curiosities from the world's far corners," which he later sold or traded to others with similar interests.

Cole glanced around at the artifacts in Berdella's house, some stored in wood and glass display cases, and returned to the torture room. As the detectives buzzed with each new, weird finding, they continued to talk about the Polaroid photos that kept turning up. The one photo that particularly held their interest was the shot of the naked man hanging upside down by his ankles. Cole picked it up off the bed.

He stared at the photo a long time. There definitely was some discoloration toward the ends of the man's arms. But that would happen even if the man were alive, he thought. The man's mouth was open. Maybe he was just amazed that someone was taking his picture, Cole thought. Or else asking to be cut down. Cole glanced down at some of the other photos on the bed. Clearly, there were men in these photos who were acting consensually. They were kissing and performing sex acts with each other in some of the shots.

"Whaddya think, Sarge? Dead or alive?" a detective asked.

"Hell, I don't know," Cole replied. He wasn't convinced. He wasn't sure this whole house wasn't just one big homosexual party palace. There was only one victim so far, and he wasn't dead.

One concern Cole had was the huge number of scraps of paper with people's names on them. Mostly men's names. On the mantel over the first-floor fireplace was a man's passport, not Berdella's. There were letters addressed to men other than Berdella. All manner of bills and shipping invoices contained dozens of different names. If there really were a homicide in this house, any one of those names could be a crucial clue. He told the detectives to jot down every name they encountered during their sifting, and the investigators could work on tracking them down later, if necessary.

Though Cole was unimpressed, many of the detectives scavenging through the house were gripped by a sense of uncertain anticipation. They felt this case had the makings of a big one, but they weren't sure exactly why. The photos, the skulls, Bryson's appalling tale; this Berdella had the early indicators of a true psychopath. But there were no bodies, and therefore no need to jump to wild conclusions.

As the night wore on, the house grew stifling. Shortly before midnight, Detective Fraise told Cole that he was about to pass out from the heat. Though it was only about sixty degrees outside, the paper suit Fraise wore over his own suit was suffocating him. Cole saw that Fraise looked pale, and told him to go home. Cole still didn't think this was a homicide case, and didn't see a need to keep a homicide detective at the scene any longer.

The remaining detectives stayed in the house until nearly 2 A.M. Finally, Cole sent them home, but told three of them they would have to be back at police headquarters at 9 A.M. that morning. The detectives nodded, half expecting such an order—even though it was Easter Sunday.

Sergeant Orth and Detective Hurn had another concern: they had to get some sort of charges filed against Berdella, and fast. Missouri law requires that police obtain charges against a suspect within twenty hours of his arrest, or he must be released. Berdella had been arrested at 11:30 A.M. Saturday. That meant the detectives would have to get an arrest warrant for him by 7:30 A.M. Sunday, or Berdella would go free.

As Saturday night flowed into Sunday morning, Hurn and Orth found Rick Holtsclaw, the assistant prosecutor, in an upstairs bedroom and began planning how they would get charges filed against Berdella. They would need to have Bryson pick Berdella out of a lineup, probably a lineup of photos if Bryson was still in the hospital. They would need to make sure Bryson wasn't acting consensually when he was in Berdella's bed for four days. "Try to check on his history too," Holtsclaw advised the policemen, which meant trying to determine if Bryson will make a credible witness in court.

Holtsclaw had already jotted down some notes about Bryson's claims, which he could use to determine how many counts could be filed against Berdella. He decided to drive down to the prosecutor's office, in the Jackson County courthouse, to start drawing up the charges. Hurn and Orth would return to police headquarters to compose a Statement of Probable Cause, which would explain for both judge and prosecutor the circumstances of the crime for which they were seeking a warrant. They would also put together a lineup of photos for Bryson to examine, and if Bryson picked Berdella as his assailant, take the whole package to Judge Baker to sign a warrant.

As a member of the county prosecutor's Sex Crimes unit, Holtsclaw was one of three assistant prosecutors with specific responsibility for rapes, sodomies and kidnappings. While he drove toward downtown, he thought back to the previous weekend, when he and nine other Jackson County prosecutors attended a seminar on serial murderers and rapists. At one point during the seminar, one of the prosecutors had cracked: "Thank God this kind of thing doesn't happen in Jackson County."

Holtsclaw entered the empty courthouse and took the elevator up to his office on the seventh floor mezzanine. When he reached his desk, he pulled out a charge book that helped prosecutors determine what statutory crimes had been committed, or at least what they could prove in a courtroom. He glanced at his notes, and estimated that Bryson had been sodomized at least seven times. He'd also been beaten and shocked — first-degree assault — and tied to the bed — felonious restraint. Nine felony counts in all. He phoned a secretary from the warrant desk, and asked her to come downtown and type up the paperwork, which was kept on a standard form in a computer at the warrant desk.

Diagonally across 12th Street, Hurn and Orth were working rapidly. At the entrance to the Crimes Against Persons division, Hurn hunched over his notes next to a typist and began dictating the Statement of Probable Cause. Back in the Sex Crimes unit, Orth phoned Holtsclaw several times to ask for guidance on the specific elements that needed to be included in the paperwork. When Hurn finished dictating, he picked up a police show-up folder, which has six numbered windows where detectives can place mug shot photographs. Instead of looking at an actual lineup with six men standing against a wall, a victim can look at six photographs and try to pick out the suspect. Hurn flipped through the mug shot files on the second floor, trying to come up with five white, mustachioed men who resembled Berdella. He taped Berdella's photo into the number two space. In a hurry, he could find only four other photos of men who looked like Berdella.

As Hurn was finishing the menial task of taping photos into the folder, Holtsclaw appeared, paperwork in hand. The formal complaint and the arrest warrant were ready to be signed by Judge Baker. As Holtsclaw read Hurn's Probable Cause statement, Hurn phoned the judge at home, waking him up. Customarily supportive of the police, the judge told Hurn he was expecting a call at some point, since he'd already signed two search warrants. Come on over, he said. Holtsclaw told Hurn the Probable Cause looked fine. As long as Bryson stood by his story, and could pick Berdella from the lineup, they had a case.

It was after 2 A.M. when Hurn and Orth got into Orth's unmarked police car and drove south toward Menorah Medical Center. They arrived at the hospital and explained their situation to the nursing supervisor. She instructed a nurse to awaken Bryson, then allowed Hurn and Orth to visit him.

"Hi Chris," Hurn said, entering the darkness of Room 3113. "Remember me? I'm Detective Hurn, and this is Sergeant Orth. I'm sorry to get you up, but we've got some things we've got to take care of right away, and we need to take another short statement from you."

"OK," Bryson said. His voice was raspy and low, as if it hurt him to speak. Clear red marks trailed away from the corners of his mouth, where a gag had once been tightly tied. His body trembled constantly, uncontrollably, and Orth had to urge Bryson several times to calm down when his emotions began to overwhelm him.

Hurn told Bryson, "I don't want you to have to go back through the whole thing, but you might very well be a sole survivor of these events, if they happened to someone else."

Bryson nodded, his blinking eyes still stinging.

"What you tell us has to be 100 percent of the truth," Hurn continued. "The well being of other people may hinge on your being truthful." Hurn then asked Bryson if there was anything about his original statement that he wanted to change now. Bryson told him there really hadn't been a blond woman in the car with Berdella, as he originally said, but everything else was the truth. He said that after Berdella picked him up on the East Side, Berdella asked him if he had been "tricking," and Bryson told him he had only wanted a ride home. Berdella's attitude seemed to change, and Berdella just invited him over for a beer. Hurn asked Bryson if he would take a lie-detector test, and Bryson said he would.

Bryson tried to recall specifics about the inside of the house and what Berdella had said to him, but his head was still hazy, and he had difficulty placing events in chronological order. He remembered that Berdella frequently made notes in a spiral notebook, and kept his syringes and drugs on serving trays. He also remembered that bright, buzzing Polaroid flash exploding in his eyes, and then he recalled that Berdella had shown him Polaroid photos of other young men, in similar positions. He couldn't tell if they were asleep or dead.

Then, some of Berdella's intimidation tactics started to come back to Bryson.

"He told me he was never going to let me go," Bryson told Hurn, "but if I cooperated, he'd take me to someplace in Wyoming where the nearest civilization was an hour away, and there was other people there who liked to do what he does. And he told me if I didn't do everything he told me to do, every time, he'd kill me."

Bryson paused, then added: "I think he was just trying to totally dominate me, mentally, so I'd do everything he wanted. He just wanted total control."

Hurn pulled out his show-up folder, with five mug shots taped inside. He asked Bryson if the man who assaulted him was shown in the folder. Bryson immediately pointed to Number Two. Hurn handed Bryson the folder and a black ballpoint pen, and told Bryson to initial the back of photograph Number Two. Orth and Hurn thanked Bryson, then got up and left his room.

As the two policemen drove toward Judge Baker's house, the vast possibilities of the case practically overwhelmed them.

"How many guys do you think he's done this to?" Orth asked.

"Geez, I don't know, but I don't think we know the whole score," Hurn said. "Did you see all those books on witchcraft, and all that satanic stuff?"

"Yeah, it makes me wonder what happened to all those guys in the photos," Orth responded. "If they're all dead, where are all the bodies?"

"Let's hope they're not all dead."

"Yeah, well you're taking Bryson's statement," Orth said, referring to the detailed recounting Bryson would have to give when he was able.

The two men pulled into Baker's driveway, got out and knocked on his door. It was after 3 A.M. Baker invited the policemen in and led them to his kitchen table.

"What have we got here, Ashley?" Baker asked.

"This could be another John Wayne Gacy," Hurn said, alluding to the serial killer from Chicago who killed thirty-three young men and buried most of them in the crawl space of his house.

"Good God," Baker rasped. "This is a sick world we've got here." He read the Probable Cause and was disgusted further. I've been through a war and seen a lot of things, Baker thought, and I've never seen anything this degrading done to a human being.

"Do we know anything about this guy Berdella?" Baker asked.

"Just that he runs a shop in Westport," Hurn answered.

"Westport huh?" Baker grunted. A yuppie? Westport had once been the Bohemian hangout for Kansas City's offbeat and hippie types in the late sixties and seventies, but a flurry of new bars had sprung up in the eighties, and a different crowd now flooded the area. Baker began signing the pages of the Probable Cause, and then the complaint and the warrant. He thought about the bond amount he should set for someone who might do something like this. With the police obtaining two search warrants already, and probably wanting more, he didn't want this suspect going back into the house and messing with the evidence. On the line marked, "Bond set at" Baker wrote "No bond."

Not long after Hurn and Orth returned the signed warrant to the jail at police headquarters, where Berdella was being kept, another group of detectives woke up and tried to explain to their families why they had to work on Easter Sunday.

By 9 A.M. Cole had assembled five detectives and his commander, Captain Winston, for a meeting to plan the next stages of the search. Cole told the men they would be working closely with the Crime Scene Investigations unit, which would be photographing nearly everything and documenting where it was found. When they got to the house, each detective would be assigned one room, and his task would be to leave no shrunken head or strange amulet unlisted, Cole said. He reminded them to make a note of every name or address or phone number; there was no way yet to tell what was valuable information and what was useless.

The detectives arrived at Berdella's house about 10 A.M.,

54

and found a welcoming party awaiting them. Captain Canaday and several of his Crime Scene investigators were there, as was Dr. Finnegan, the anthropologist, and even Orth. The Sex Crimes sergeant didn't need much sleep, and had headed back to Berdella's house after showering and changing his clothes.

Once Cole and Canaday had paired up the detectives and assigned them to various rooms inside the house, the two men walked around the outside. They stepped into the overgrown backyard, toward Berdella's rear property line.

"What have we got here?" Canaday said.

They stood over a rectangular area, not as grassy as the rest of the yard. It appeared to have been dug up in recent months. Planks of wood outlined the area, which was about four feet by six feet long. As Canaday and Cole looked around the small, grassy backyard, they saw other, smaller shapes outlined with rocks.

"Think we got a body under here?" Cole asked, nodding down at the plot.

"I don't know," Canaday said, "maybe we've got the bodies that used to be attached to those skulls inside."

"Maybe we've got some more skulls," Cole said.

"It's not really big enough to be a grave," Canaday noted.

"Nope. Could be anything," Cole said, still skeptical. He remembered that a neighbor had told one of his detectives that Berdella used to work in his backyard flower beds after dark. Cole didn't know if that was suspicious or just weird.

"Well, there's only one way to find out," Canaday said. "But I think we ought to get a backhoe out here rather than digging it up with shovels, it'll go faster. Let's call the city and see what they've got."

"Might have some trouble contacting anyone on Easter," Cole noted.

"Well, let's give it a shot," Canaday concluded. "We'll go down about two feet, and if we hit something, we'll dig by hand."

"What about his vehicle?" Cole asked.

"Probably ought to get a search warrant for that today too, go through it," Canaday said. "Where's this guy work, did somebody say he owned his own business?"

"Yeah, looks like it, some place over in Westport called Bob's Bazaar Bizarre," Cole said. Stationery and business cards inside the house provided the name of Berdella's shop.

"That sounds about right, I guess," Canaday said. "Well, we've got to search that too. Let's get a warrant for that while we're at it."

Detective Tom Eikel, who had prepared the second search warrant for the house, was awarded the task of filling out the paperwork for warrants on Berdella's Toyota Tercel and his shop in the Westport district, Bob's Bazaar Bizarre. The detectives all thought that name was too good to be true, but they also figured it might explain why Berdella had so many different artifacts in his house. The police had no idea if any of the items they examined were valuable — they just knew there were a lot of them.

Berdella's shop had begun simply as a side business out of his Charlotte Street home, after he dropped out of art school back in the late sixties. To help pay off the lawyer fees and fines from his drug arrests, Berdella had started working as a short-order cook in various restaurants around Kansas City, but he also made a little extra money by selling his collected folk art and artifacts, mainly antiques and items from the Middle East. He had business cards and stationery printed up with the words "Dragon Nagari" and a dragon logo next to his address and phone number. It derived from an ancient legend Berdella had picked up out of an old book, and he thought the dragon would stick in people's minds.

Both of Berdella's livelihoods flourished. He became more accomplished as a cook and worked as a chef at several renowned Kansas City restaurants and country clubs. He joined the local chefs association, and helped set up training classes for aspiring cooks at a suburban community college. At the same time, his antiques and artifacts business grew more and more profitable. He started to rent space at the Old Westport Flea Market, an indoor collection of clothing and collectibles merchants in Westport.

As he grew bored with the restaurant business, he devoted more time to his Flea Market booth, and to the intriguing deals he cut with importers and merchants in New York, Europe and South America. His contacts were improving steadily. By 1981, Bob's Bazaar Bizarre was his full-time job.

The money wasn't great at Berdella's shop — Berdella cleared about one thousand dollars per month — so he used other means to get by. He participated in several "barter systems," in which merchants can trade goods or services for credits, and then redeem the credits with some other merchant participating in the system. He took in some rent from his various boarders, who also performed household repairs or worked at his shop. Berdella also was known to scrounge for items that he could use in his house or sell at his booth. John Stith, who had known Berdella since the late sixties, recalled Berdella once climbing perilously to the roof of an old barn to snatch a weathervane for later sale.

Though Berdella wasn't often described as charitable by friends and neighbors, they had to admit he did his share of good deeds. Besides helping to set up a crime watch program for his part of the Hyde Park Neighborhood Association, he also served as the association's liaison to a couple of nearby homes for wayward youths. Once, Berdella even carted a vanload of kids to Stith's farm south of the city. It was the first time many of the youngsters had been outside the city, and was just as jarring a sight to the farm's rural neighbors. Stith and his wife, Mary Lou, didn't think Berdella particularly liked children, but they gave him credit for organizing the expedition. For some of his older boarders, Berdella would take time to drive them to temporary employment agencies such as Manpower, or to the barter group Intra-World, trying to help them find work. Berdella also assisted the local public television outlet with their annual fund-raising auction, pushing fellow Flea Market merchants to donate goods, then participating in the televised auction.

A less formal way of serving the community was to take in young men and try to give them guidance. At a block party on Charlotte Street one evening, neighbor Mike Calderon remembered, Berdella respectfully told a group of neighbors that he "hoped they didn't mind" when they saw young men running in and out of his house from time to time. He was going to be a "big brother" of sorts to these men, who were mostly runaway kids, he said. The neighbors looked at each other, slightly surprised, and told Berdella they had no problem with that. For several years after that, different cars would be parked in front of Berdella's house, and shaggy, skinny men would pass by on the street, smoking a cigarette, not hurting anyone. Another neighbor recalled lending his lawn mower to one of these young men a couple of times, a talkative guy from Kansas named Larry. He seemed all right, the neighbor thought at the time. His view began to change when he glimpsed a naked Chris Bryson limping around in the street nine months later.

Mostly, the neighbors liked Berdella. He was a bit eccentric — he once hung an eerie doll in a window to intimidate a neighbor — and his house wasn't exactly well-kept. Logs for his fireplace were strewn about the front yard, and miscellaneous junk piled up on his porch. But he usually offered a wave and a "hi" when he went by, and he'd been in the same house twenty years, keeping the block stable. So when he was arrested, the neighbors weren't only shocked. Some of them felt used. Some of the nearby families were close friends with Berdella, and they couldn't believe that they didn't notice anything wrong occurring inside his house. Were they just a front for Berdella's secret, dark life? Some grew bitter and moved away, so as not to be reminded of Berdella by having to look at his house daily.

But Berdella's friends who weren't his neighbors never noticed any change in Berdella either. He had a mild temper, but nothing explosive. He complained frequently, and carried a "me against the world" attitude into most situations: someone was always trying to screw him. He filed numerous small claims suits against various boarders and businessmen he felt had cheated him. But actual violence was almost unheard of. From a tall and lean physique when he first arrived in Kansas City, Berdella had filled out to a pudgy pear shape, soft and unthreatening. He gradually became self-conscious about his looks, and sometimes talked about having surgery to improve his jutting jaw. When he told friends he was "rehabilitating" the young men who accompanied him, most figured he was more interested in seducing them.

It appeared to his friends that Berdella had no long-term, intimate relationships with anyone. Several knew that Berdella's sexual preferences ran as far as bondage, but again, nothing violent.

Despite the Easter holiday, Canaday eventually located a Water Department supervisor, who rounded up a driver and a backhoe. At the same time, Eikel took two more search warrant applications to Judge Baker, who was having Easter dinner at a relative's house. By now, the judge was intrigued.

"What the hell you guys got out there?" he asked.

"Don't really know, sir," Eikel said. "You need any fresh vegetables for your Easter salad?"

Baker laughed. "Found any bodies yet?" the judge asked.

"No sir, not yet," Eikel said. "But we've got pictures you wouldn't believe."

"Got any of those with you?"

"No sir, but it's bigger than anything I've ever worked in Sex Crimes."

"Are they kids?"

"It looks mainly like younger males."

"Well let me know if you need any more help."

Eikel drove to the police tow lot, where abandoned and confiscated cars are taken. A crime scene investigator met him there, and the two of them dug through Berdella's compact car thoroughly. Berdella's wallet and checkbook were inside, along with another spiral notebook and two unmarked videotapes.

Shortly before 5:30 that afternoon, Hurn and Detective Lee Floyd drove to Bob's Bazaar Bizarre. The booths of the Flea Market, all with antiques and vintage clothing stacked to the ceiling, adjoined a bar and restaurant that was open on Sunday. In one window of the Flea Market, looking in on Berdella's booth, hung a neon sign announcing Bob's Bazaar Bizarre. But below the sign was a shelf. On the shelf were four human skulls. A piece of paper taped to the shelves had the handwriting: The Final Four.

Hurn and Floyd looked at each other in astonishment.

"Holy shit, look at that," Hurn said, tapping Floyd on the shoulder.

"Yeah," Floyd said, laughing and coughing at the same time.

"Must be a basketball fan, huh?" Hurn said. Floyd nodded. "I want to get a closer look at those things," Hurn said.

Floyd, a longtime detective who also made and collected jewelry in his spare time, had been in Berdella's shop before, though he never paid the proprietor much attention. He remembered that whenever he was there with his wife, Berdella would speak only to him, even if his wife had asked a question. Other patrons recalled similar quirks by Berdella, which they mainly wrote off to rudeness or condescension. Usually, Berdella liked repartee with customers. "There is nothing like wanting to smart-ass with people and having customers love to have you smart-ass with them to really kind of make your day," Berdella once said. But if the customers didn't know what they were talking about, or didn't have a genuine interest in the subject, Berdella could be impatient, even mean.

Floyd also knew one of the Flea Market's Managers, a former Kansas City policeman named Steve Grosko. He asked Grosko to let them into Berdella's booth, which normally was open on Sundays. The detectives walked over to "The Final Four," but it was clear to Grosko and Floyd that the skulls were artifacts. Floyd noted that he'd seen skulls in Berdella's booth before, so having them there this weekend was not particularly unusual. The detectives poked around the small booth for more than an hour, as Grosko watched with interest. Floyd and Hurn soon decided that it didn't appear Berdella had stashed any bodies in his store. They gathered up a few items, including one Polaroid photograph, and left.

The long flatbed tractor trailer rumbled slowly down Campbell Street, a New Holland backhoe as its only cargo. Berdella's house did not have a driveway on either side, so the only way to get the backhoe to the backyard was through the yard of the house behind Berdella's. Several officers pulled down part of a small wooden fence on Berdella's property to clear a path. The backhoe operator, Michael Oswald, rolled his powerful wheeled shovel off the flat bed and into Berdella's backyard, parallel to the rectangular plot.

"OK, let's do this real slowly," Canaday told Oswald. "You take it one scoop at a time, and then we'll sift through the basket and see if we've got anything."

Cole looked at his watch. It was almost 3:30 P.M. This has the makings of another long night, he thought.

By the time the backhoe had positioned itself, Cole and Canaday were back inside the house, examining the recently poured cement in the basement. Some officers had attacked the small area with pickaxes, but uncovered nothing.

Outside, Orth and Earhart stood by the backhoe's scoop,

joined by Detective Robert Dodds of the Crime Scene unit, and Detective Bill Wilson of the Homicide unit. The noisy backhoe cranked up its heavy arm, and plunged into the area marked off by the boards. As it pulled up a load of moist dirt, the investigators stepped closer, then started rooting through the soil with gloved hands. Nothing.

The operator dumped the load of dirt off to one side, then positioned his scoop over an untouched portion of the plot. He lowered it sixteen inches into the ground, then pulled it back up with another full load of soil.

Almost immediately, they spotted it. Before Oswald could even raise the scoop to eye level, two of the detectives yelled *"Stop!"* Visible through the top of the soil was something white and round. There was hair attached, and clumps of it nearby. This wasn't just a skull; it was a human head. The detectives, all veterans, knew immediately. Orth darted across the backyard to tell Canaday and Cole. Detective Steve Brauninger, another Crime Scene investigator, came out to help Dodds unearth this latest find.

The smell of decomposition, of death, swept out of the newly created hole, and the detectives looked down to see if there was a body in there. There wasn't, but the lower jaw to the head had been separated by the force of the scoop, along with some white matter and a dirty cloth or rag. Dodds and Brauninger began working quietly with tongue depressors to clear away the mud from the head. They could see that this one had hair, teeth, even some skin and tissue.

A silence of slow realization enveloped the group. No one was really surprised, because after seeing the photos and finding the skulls in the house, they all half expected that the backyard might be a burial ground. Dodds and Brauninger scraped away quietly at the head, then lifted it out of the backhoe's scoop. Unlike such a scene in the movies, there was no excitement, no chatter. Little was said. The detectives scanned the rest of the backyard.

At last, Cole was convinced. This whole yard is probably a

graveyard, he thought, looking around at the various areas that seemed to be marked off. We've got a major investigation on our hands. His mind flashed to the hundreds of photographs of men that the detectives had found. Most appeared to be in the middle of being tortured. Had Berdella killed all of them? he wondered.

"I better get on the phone," Canaday said. He started back toward the house to notify the top police commanders that he had something of interest out here. He called the head of the Investigations Bureau, Colonel Robert Jenkins, and told Jenkins: "My God, there's going to be dozens of bodies out here." Canaday had a tendency to exaggerate, but if they found a head on the second scoop, who knew what they would uncover after excavating the whole yard.

Holtsclaw was inside the house, and he called the Jackson County prosecutor, Albert Riederer. "I think this is more than a sex crimes case," Holtsclaw said with understatement. "We just dug up a head." Riederer told Holtsclaw to stay and monitor developments. Holtsclaw then called the top homicide prosecutor, Pat Hall. He told Hall what he knew about the case, and that Berdella's first court appearance would be tomorrow, Monday morning. Holtsclaw couldn't handle it because he was scheduled to prosecute another case, in another county, that morning. Hall had a trial scheduled for Monday morning, so he phoned another homicide prosecutor, Marietta Parker, and asked her to handle Berdella's morning arraignment. Hall explained that Holtsclaw had recommended trying to have Berdella held without bond, and he related what details he knew about the torture, the photos, and the skulls.

When Parker hung up, she shivered. She walked around her house closing all the window blinds. "You can't believe what people *do*," she told her husband.

Somehow, the word also had leaked to the news media. Even as early as Saturday night, an off-duty detective had seen a newspaper reporter at the Final Four at Kemper Arena

63

and mentioned to him that he might want to check with homicide about something at 43rd and Charlotte. The reporter nodded as if interested, but then ignored the tip and went back to his seat to watch the second game. By Sunday afternoon, however, television reporters from two different stations had gotten similar leads, and shortly after the backhoe unearthed the latest skull, their video photographers were jockeying for the best angle into Berdella's backyard.

With the heavy police presence in the neighborhood, drivers started to slow down in front of Berdella's house to gawk. Uniformed officers were called to the house to keep the traffic moving. Police commanders gathered around the small hole in Berdella's backyard, and discussed what to do next. They decided to stop digging. Every step now needed to be a cautious one. The consensus was that there was no longer a need to do anything hurriedly. Berdella was in jail with no bond. The evidence for the sodomy case had pretty much been discovered, but the evidence for a murder was modest at best. The house needed to be fully searched and catalogued, with an abundance of lab tests to follow. The entire backyard no doubt needed to be excavated. A logical plan needed to be hatched. Bringing in bright lights and a generator, to illuminate the backyard for more digging, was considered and then rejected. The commanders decided to resume the excavation Monday morning, and regroup with a special squad of detectives.

Cole headed back to police headquarters, where detectives were waiting to fill him in on what else had been happening on Sunday. Hurn told him what they had found at Berdella's shop, which was mainly some papers, three bottles of pills, a bag of tablets, and one Polaroid photo of a man lifting barbells. Floyd reported that he had interviewed a man and a woman who had known Berdella through the flea market for years. The woman told Floyd that Berdella was "snotty" toward her and didn't seem to like women. She thought Berdella was gay. No shit, Cole thought.

Detective Fraise had more interesting news. Shortly before 6 P.M., he had gotten a call from Harriet Sanders, the mother of Walter James Ferris. Also on the line was Ferris's wife, Bonnie Ferris. They had just seen the 5 P.M. television news, which carried a segment on Berdella being arrested and a skull being discovered. The women asked if any remains had been identified. Fraise said he didn't think so. He didn't know that other detectives had found Ferris's wallet in the artifact room the night before.

Bonnie Ferris told Fraise that the last time she had seen her husband, in September 1985, he told her he was going to see Bob Berdella. He hadn't been seen since. She also said that her husband had a friend named Gene who told her that Berdella "used to get his jollies" by injecting Ferris with Thorazine and other drugs, and then watching Ferris collapse. Berdella supposedly kept a variety of drugs hidden in a secret compartment, Gene had told her. She gave Fraise Gene's phone number.

Later Sunday night, while the detectives were writing out their reports to be typed, a twenty-five-year-old man named Foster Simmons approached a uniformed officer guarding Berdella's house and told him he used to live there. The officer had Simmons taken down to headquarters, and Floyd interviewed him shortly after 9 P.M.

Simmons told Floyd that in the early 1980s, a friend named Freddie had introduced him to Berdella, and that Berdella offered Simmons a place to stay. In return, Simmons performed odd chores around the house, cared for Berdella's dogs and also looked after Berdella's shop occasionally. One night, Simmons found a set of nude photographs of Freddie in explicit positions, and he deduced that Berdella and Freddie were lovers. He also told Floyd that he was present when parties would start with a group of young men, but when the action started to take on a homosexual tinge, he would leave. Simmons said he moved out after about nine months.

Floyd asked Simmons if he thought Berdella was involved in the occult. Simmons said he never saw anything like that, but he thought it was weird that the second floor room at the top of the stairs was always locked. He never saw inside that room, Simmons told Floyd. What about drugs? Floyd asked. Simmons said he had seen Berdella inject Freddie with Thorazine on more than one occasion, and that he had also used the drugs on his dogs to calm them down.

After Simmons finished, Floyd took out the photograph that he and Hurn had found that afternoon at Berdella's shop. Simmons said the man with the barbells was Freddie, and he apparently was standing in the room on the third floor, where a weight bench and barbells were kept. Floyd thanked him, and arranged for a ride for Simmons back to the midtown area.

Floyd went in and told Cole about the interview. Now police had three people — Bryson, Bonnie Ferris and Simmons — who told them that Berdella liked to inject people with drugs, and that he was gay. Did that make Berdella a murderer? Could that have been how he killed his victims? A thousand questions raced through his head. No answers came back.

Chapter Four

Berdella spent Saturday night, all of Sunday, and Monday morning in the city jail, on the eighth floor of police headquarters. He phoned two lawyers on Saturday afternoon, and one came to visit him on Sunday. By then, all the lawyer could do was tell Berdella to wait until his arraignment Monday morning, when another judge might set a bond amount for Berdella. Earlier Sunday, when the first judge wrote "No bond" on the initial warrant, Berdella knew that wasn't a good sign.

Berdella exchanged the black, button-down shirt he'd been wearing when he was arrested for a light blue paper prison top, then ripped the sleeves up the side to loosen it. He sat silently on the steel benches inside the city jail cell, staring at the floor. For the first time, he began to confront the actions he'd taken over the last several years. As a man whose emotions often affected him physically, Berdella became practically paralyzed.

For years, Berdella had refused to deal with what he was doing. It was like it didn't happen. Easily, in the past, he turned his attention to other things, such as his shop; it required a great deal of work to keep weird and intriguing items on the shelves. He had numerous friends in Kansas City from his days as a student at the Art Institute and also from his work in various restaurants as well as his decade as a shop merchant in Westport. His shop was respected not only for its esoterica but for its quality, and also for Berdella's knowledge of the background and value of all of its beads, jewelry, primitive trinkets and paintings. His sharp mind retained details.

When he wasn't focused on his shop, Berdella worked around his house, and he got to know some of the neighbors. He appreciated the history and charm of communities such as Kansas City's Hyde Park, filled with Victorian-style two- and three-story frame houses. In the late 1970s, he helped organize the South Hyde Park Crime Prevention and Neighborhood Association, and even became its chairman in the early 1980s, attending occasional meetings with the police, urging neighbors to install porch lights and get involved in "block watching." Part of Berdella's civic-mindedness stemmed from his desire to be liked by his neighbors, to be a positive presence in the community, friends said. Another part stemmed from his fear of having his house burglarized, and his valuable artifact collection stolen or damaged. He also took out homeowners' insurance, steadily increasing the coverage for his personal property. But by the middle of the eighties he relinquished his position with the neighborhood association and stopped attending meetings. His neighbors noticed that he became more sullen, less talkative. Where once he waved and smiled as they went by, now he rarely made eye contact.

In addition to lawyers, Berdella also called his mother in Ohio, and told her he'd been arrested. Without knowing the details, she was merely stunned. She and her second husband, whom she married shortly after her first husband's sudden death, decided to go to Kansas City to offer what support they could, and to help get Berdella's finances in order. Berdella was still close to his mother, calling or writing her from time to time, occasionally making the fourteen-hour drive to northern Ohio to visit. But he had resented the fact that she remarried, and so soon after his father's death. He told friends he felt betrayed by her, and that he didn't care for her new husband, a businessman of Middle Eastern descent. Through the years, the sense of betrayal dimmed, and Berdella's relationship with his mother and stepfather gradually improved.

He sat alone in the jail cell, his mood dark, a pair of gray days leaking scant sunlight through the barred windows. He wasn't sure what to feel. He wondered about his future, and whether he could really be sent to prison. On Monday, he would finally get to appear before a judge to have a bond set. He wondered about paying for a lawyer, and whether he would have to sell his shop or house. He found it easy not to think about his past—he was still emotionally insulated from that. Mainly, he felt relief. The nightmare was finally over, he thought. But only he knew what the nightmare really was. And he wasn't sure he was ready to tell anyone else yet.

Several floors below Berdella various police commanders and detectives discussed the case. On the fifth floor, where the chief and his colonels worked, the top brass traded what information they had, and made suggestions to Lieutenant Colonel Robert Jenkins, head of investigations, on how he should instruct his charges.

On the third floor, Sergeant Laura Mulloy's phone was ringing continuously before she ever stepped into the office. She expected that. As the department's media liaison, she had been called out to Berdella's house Sunday afternoon to brief the gathered reporters about the main aspects of the story. This helped keep the press off the backs of Cole and his detectives, but as the news organizations quickly realized the possibilities of the story, they demanded more access. On Sunday, Mulloy told the reporters only about the head found in the backyard, but not about either of the two skulls in the house. She told them that the head had been found after a man who was hitchhiking several days earlier had been picked up by Berdella and sexually tortured for days. No mention was made of anything found in the house—the notebooks, the photos, the torture items—because police wanted to be cautious about discussing possible evidence. But on Monday, as reporters obtained Detective Hurn's Statement of Probable Cause from the court records, and began talking to detectives and commanders familiar with the case, details poured out. After handling inquiries for about an hour, Mulloy decided to head to Berdella's house and handle the media there, at least to keep from being stuck at her desk all day.

On the second floor, the tension was immediately apparent. Cole arrived at 7:30 A.M., and met with Winston and the other homicide sergeants to brief them on what was happening in the case. The phones rang just as frequently as they did in Mulloy's office, as radio reporters with hourly deadlines trolled for the latest information, with television and newspaper reporters right behind them. The sergeants ignored the din and focused on the case. Berdella was charged with nine felony counts, so there was no apparent need to rush the investigation, they decided. There were no signs that anyone else was in any imminent danger because of Berdella. And though the trail that murder investigations follow is hottest immediately after the killing, if Berdella had murdered anyone, there were no hints that it had happened recently.

Lieutenant Colonel Jenkins came down from the fifth floor and met with Cole. He told Cole he had decided to form a special, twelve-man squad, composed of eleven detectives and one sergeant—Cole.

70

The case was definitely his now. For a moment, Cole sat and wondered how he'd ended up with what could be the biggest investigation in Kansas City's long, violent history. Though he'd grown up and attended college in Oklahoma, he had originally moved to the Washington, D.C. area. His first job, in 1968, was a desk position with the Central Intelligence Agency, where he received a bureaucratic assignment in the White House. But his tasks were unexciting, and by 1970, he had joined the D.C. Police Department, where he got a street-level taste of homicide investigations in the violent 10th Precinct. While living in northern Virginia, near CIA headquarters, he met his future wife, Janet Boyd. They married in 1969 and had a son, Stan, in 1970. Cole named the boy after his old baseball idol, the St. Louis Cardinal great Stan Musial.

In late 1971, wanting to move back to the Midwest, Cole applied to the Kansas City Police Department. He had friends in Kansas City, and was back in uniform by January 1972, attending his second police training academy. Besides spending several years in the police department's Intelligence unit, Cole also worked for three years as a Homicide detective. It was a busy, high pressure job. Kansas City has a higher homicide rate, per capita, than far larger, seemingly more violent cities such as New York, Los Angeles or Chicago. The overall crime rate in Kansas City is also higher than those cities, and annually reaches one of the highest rates in the country among large cities.

Cole left the Homicide unit in 1978, and later was assigned to the Intelligence unit, where he tracked organized crime members and assisted the FBI in its attempts to break up the Kansas City mob. After being promoted to sergeant, Cole returned to the world of everyday murder when he was reassigned to homicide in September 1987. He had attended several homicide investigation seminars, stood over countless dead bodies, and examined the photographs of hundreds more murders and suicides. But in every other homicide he'd handled, whether a mob slaying or a drive-by shooting, he had a body and no suspect. This time, he had a suspect and no body. Putting this together would be the puzzle of a lifetime.

Jenkins told Cole that he could pick six of the detectives on the squad, and that commanders from other units would select five more. The squad would be called the Berdella Task Force, and they would set up in a back room of the second floor used for meetings, larger investigations, and showing police lineups to victims and witnesses — the "show-up" room, detectives called it. There was no guidance offered on what to do with the swarm of phone calls, and Cole was almost looking forward to going back to Berdella's house, where the only sounds he heard were of digging in the backyard, and an occasional "Holy shit" from a detective rooting through the house.

Cole quickly selected six detectives, including Hurn and Eikel from Sex Crimes, and the Robbery and Special Investigations units soon made their assignments. As the detectives gathered in the show-up room, they began sifting through enlargements of some of Berdella's Polaroids. Gary Howell, the crime lab director, had taken the originals back to the lab Sunday evening and had his technicians work through the night making numerous blow-ups so the detectives could have several sets of copies to work with. Word shot out from the room and through the department that this case was something different.

The phones kept ringing, but as the morning wore on, many of the calls weren't from the media. People who had read the morning paper or seen the TV newscasts were beginning to call. People who knew Berdella from somewhere, or knew something strange about Berdella, or knew someone missing who might be linked to Berdella, or people who were just plain curious. Cole, trying to read the reports written the previous night, handled all the calls, and his patience rapidly grew thin.

At one point in the confusion, Cole walked upstairs to the third floor to the Fugitive Apprehension unit. The detectives there had been quietly shaking their heads since they first heard of Berdella's arrest. Several years earlier, they had followed Berdella, questioned him, watched him, harassed him. But they could never prove that Berdella had done anything illegal, and eventually they left him alone.

The Fugitive unit also investigates missing persons cases, and detectives had interviewed Berdella about two cases: The disappearance of a nineteen-year-old man in July 1984 named Jerry Howell, and the disappearance of twenty-five-year-old James Ferris in September 1985. When they'd asked Berdella about Howell, he told them he'd dropped Howell off at a 7-11 store on Main Street on the day Howell was last seen. A year later, when detectives went back to question him about Ferris, Berdella told them Ferris had stayed with him for three days before he kicked Ferris out, for stealing from him.

Detective Charles Neuner was assigned the Howell case in 1984, and he had worked it particularly hard for two reasons: he knew Howell's father, Paul Howell, and the elder Howell had convinced him that Jerry wasn't just a runaway. Also, another Fugitive detective, Tom Marquis, had once taken an undercover assignment at 10th and McGee Streets to deal with the male hustlers there, and his street sources told him this Berdella character was the type to prey on transient young men.

After Paul Howell filed the missing person report on his son, he told Neuner and Marquis that Berdella helped kids who were in trouble, but also liked to give them drugs and stick needles in them "for the hell of it." So the detectives interviewed Berdella, who showed up at police headquarters with a lawyer. Berdella perspired and appeared openly

73

nervous as he told Neuner and Marquis he had dropped Jerry Howell off shortly after he'd met him at Paul Howell's shop. The interview ended with little of substance revealed, other than that Berdella now feared Paul Howell.

The detectives began to look for friends of Berdella who might have known Howell, and two weeks later they found Todd Stoops, a street hustler who, along with his wife, had lived in Berdella's house on two separate occasions earlier in 1984. Stoops told Neuner that he thought Berdella had given Jerry Howell "a hot shot," or injection, and Howell could have died from it. Later, he said he had seen Howell at Berdella's house, passed out drunk on a couch, on the night he was last seen alive. It turned out Stoops was lying—he was in jail the night Howell was last seen—but this stuff about injecting kids kept coming up. Marquis had spoken to Freddie Kellogg, another former Berdella housemate, who said the same thing. Neuner later advised Stoops, "Man, don't go back out there."

Still, the Fugitive unit had no solid evidence that Berdella had done anything with Howell other than see him last. The unit didn't have the manpower to keep investigating Berdella, so they asked the undercover, Special Investigations division, to put Berdella under surveillance. The Career Criminal unit got the call, and Detectives Tom Eikel and Terry Rogers were assigned to Berdella. After speaking with Paul Howell, they went to the streets, to 10th and McGee. "Everybody knew Berdella," Eikel said. He was a guy you could call for a ride late at night, or maybe to buy a bag of pot or a quick shot of dope. One night, as Eikel and Rogers spoke to a hustler, they decided to try to get inside Berdella's house under the pretense that they wanted to buy some drugs.

"Can you get us in there?" Eikel had asked the hustler.

"No way, you look too old," the hustler replied. "Anyway, he'll want to party with you." Dope dealers know undercover cops don't stick around to use what they've just bought.

"One of us has got to get in there," Eikel told Rogers.

"Well, let's just go knock on the door and see if he'll sell," Rogers said.

"OK, we'll flip for it," Eikel said, taking out a quarter. He flipped the coin, and won. Rogers would try to make the buy. He had gray hair, but the next night Rogers slicked it back and stuffed it under a baseball cap. They visited their street friend again. He laughed.

"Bob'll never go for it," the hustler said.

Eikel and Rogers looked at each other. "We could have the kid make a controlled buy," in which an informant buys from the drug dealer.

"No way," the hustler said, alarm in his voice.

"Why not?"

"The word on the streets is he does bad things to kids."

"Well, we'll just try it ourselves, see what happens," Eikel said. "Maybe we'll see something."

The detectives drove to Berdella's house, both got out and walked up to the front door. They knocked. No answer.

Eikel and Rogers then decided to begin surveillance on Berdella. They drove to the Flea Market, saw his car there, and waited for two hours to see if Berdella would go anywhere. He didn't. Several days later, Eikel sat outside Berdella's house for four hours, but Berdella didn't leave. The next day, Eikel went to the Flea Market and went inside for two hours. Berdella ate lunch, and had no customers. The day after that, Eikel and Rogers sat outside the Flea Market for four hours, but again Berdella did nothing suspicious. Eikel and Rogers moved on to other cases, but Neuner and Marquis went to visit Berdella at home again later that month, to bring up Todd Stoops's claims about seeing Jerry Howell passed out. Berdella grew indignant, denied everything, and told the detectives to talk to his lawyer.

The following fall, in 1985, Bonnie Ferris reported her husband missing, with Berdella as the last person who had seen him. It was the first case any of the fugitive detectives had encountered in which the same man was linked to two missing persons. A close friend of Ferris's, Gene Shaw, said he and Ferris had injected drugs at Berdella's house. This time, Detectives Robert Rogge and Luther Buford went to visit Berdella. Berdella invited them in, and told them he hadn't seen Ferris in two weeks. He denied injecting drugs into other people, and said he didn't like "needle drugs." Rogge said he had heard Berdella liked to chain people to a wall in the basement and sexually torture them. Berdella denied that, and took Rogge down into the basement to show him it was clean. When that was finished, Rogge asked if he could see the upstairs rooms, too. Berdella flinched, then asked if it was necessary. Rogge said if it was necessary, he would have gotten a search warrant. "No, they're not clean right now," Berdella told him.

The Fugitive unit now had its antennae up. Informally, one detective said, "there was a standing order to fuck with Berdella whenever possible." A new, more aggressive sergeant, Tom Moss, could sense something suspicious about Berdella. Detectives stopped by the Flea Market to chat with him. Berdella would affect a pained look, asking Rogge one time, "Why would you guys come and do this to me at my place of business?" The investigators would drive past both the Flea Market and Berdella's house whenever possible, just to see what they could see. Rogge and his wife even argued about Rogge's penchant for always driving down Westport Road to glance at the Flea Market.

About a month later Rogge was leaving the office and

76

heading toward the midtown area. Neuner heard where Rogge was going; he had a job to perform in the same area and asked to ride along. Rogge said sure. When Rogge arrived at his destination, it was 4315 Charlotte Street.

"Hey, that's Berdella's house," Neuner said.

"That's right," Rogge said with a straight face.

They knocked on the door, and Berdella let them inside. Rogge had a theory: when he'd visited the basement before, maybe Berdella had cleaned up whatever illicit activity he had going on. But visit him later, and perhaps find something else. While Neuner kept Berdella occupied, Rogge sneaked down into the basement for a quick look. Nothing. He returned upstairs, joined the conversation about the missing young men, and then the two detectives left. They thought Rogge had made it into the basement unnoticed, but Berdella's lawyer later called Sergeant Moss. When he told Moss to "stay the fuck away" from his client, Moss figured that Berdella had noticed. Having been directly confronted by Berdella's attorney, Moss didn't want to risk accusations that he was harassing Berdella. So he tried to get the undercover Special Investigations division involved again, as they had the previous year. He sent them a copy of the case file, but never heard anything more.

Also keeping the detectives' interest up was Bonnie Ferris, who called the Fugitive unit several times a week. "Buford, have you found out anything?" she once asked, as Buford realized she was setting the record for most inquiries on a missing adult case. Ferris called Buford again on her husband's birthday. "If he were alive, he would call," Bonnie Ferris told the detective. "He might not say where he was, but he'd call." She wanted the police to just burst in on Berdella. Buford told her that wasn't possible. "But something is going to happen that's going to give us a reason to go into the house," Buford said.

Cole knew about James Ferris because his wife and mother had called last night, but he'd never heard of Jerry Howell. After Neuner filled him in on the two investigations, Cole went back downstairs to discuss the cases with Eikel, who by coincidence was now on his squad. When Eikel finished, Cole told him to write down everything he could remember about his investigation of nearly four years earlier, and also to track down the dental records of James Ferris and Jerry Howell, to see if either of them matched up with the two skulls.

Pacing the sidewalk in front of Berdella's house Monday morning, Paul Howell seethed. I knew it goddammit, I knew it, he kept thinking to himself. He had tried to tell the police for almost four years now that Berdella had killed his son. Even though there was no proof that Berdella had killed anyone, the mass of police cars, officers, reporters and television cameras surrounding the house convinced him that his suspicions were right on from the start.

Howell was a longtime street tough who was proud of his survival abilities and the fact that he'd raised a family of two daughters and three sons. He was a junk collector, not unlike Berdella in a way, and for a time he had a booth in the Flea Market, just a few feet away from Bob's Bazaar Bizarre. He had known Berdella for years, and had introduced Berdella to Jerry in the late 1970s. Jerry would hang around Berdella's booth while his father was working, seemingly intrigued by the fact that Berdella was openly gay. Jerry and another friend would sometimes tease Berdella about this, and on one occasion Jerry offered to sell his friend to Berdella for the night, for fifty dollars. Berdella told him that was "about thirty dollars over market." Jerry continued the joke until Berdella got irritated and told him that, unless he was serious, it was getting out of hand.

Jerry was a short, wiry, adventurous kid, about fourteen or fifteen years old when he first met Berdella. He had had a few minor scrapes with the law, nothing major. He liked to help his dad find valuable scrap that could be resold for a profit. But in the early eighties he turned to another means of making pocket change: prostitution, in the downtown area of 10th and McGee Streets. One afternoon, Jerry confided in Berdella that he'd started hustling. Berdella was surprised. He thought Jerry was too young, too lacking in street smarts, to survive that part of the city. He tried to tell Jerry how tough that area was, how dangerous the neighborhood, the johns, the competition, could all be. Jerry wasn't interested in being lectured, especially by Berdella.

Berdella thought he should do something, but he didn't know Paul Howell very well. So he mentioned the conversation to Grosko at the Flea Market, who in turn relayed it to Howell. Howell was furious at his son, and told him so very forcefully. But that still didn't deter Jerry. Several weeks later, Berdella actually saw Jerry at 10th and McGee. Again, he relayed the message, and again Paul Howell became enraged. Berdella subsequently heard that Howell had beaten Jerry, and told Howell he didn't think that was a very productive way to handle the situation. Howell told Berdella, "Well, at least Jerry isn't doing robbery or burglary like his friends."

Jerry was upset at Berdella for having told his father about his activities, and he stopped visiting the Flea Market. For some months in 1983, Jerry moved out to Los Angeles and held a part-time job. Then he moved back to Kansas City, and Paul Howell rented a small space in the Flea Market for Jerry to operate on his own. At first, Jerry refused to even acknowledge Berdella. But by early 1984,

Jerry had been arrested several times for fighting, stealing some lawn mowers and failure to pay traffic tickets. He needed some help paying the fines and maneuvering through the legal system, but he didn't want to go to his father, who had already set him up with his own shop. Jerry knew Berdella had had some contact with the police through the neighborhood crime prevention group, and that he had helped some other young men. Berdella told Jerry he would help him hire and pay for a lawyer, if Jerry would help him by doing repair and yard work around his house. Jerry agreed.

Eventually, Jerry and Berdella became friends again, and by March of 1984, they were meeting outside the Flea Market to see movies, eat dinner, get high and hang out at Berdella's house. Besides providing Jerry with a joint or a couple of pills of Valium when they were together, Berdella occasionally did favors for Jerry, such as helping him buy a car, or helping him to get some dental work done. Sometimes, Jerry and Berdella had sex, but Jerry would always try to get home before his father awoke in the morning. By this time, Paul Howell had moved out of the Flea Market into his own store at 39th and Main Streets, and his family lived above the shop in the same building. Howell didn't particularly like Berdella and he didn't like his son spending a lot of time with Berdella. But Jerry was now nineteen, and there wasn't much Howell could do to control his son's behavior.

Late on the afternoon of July 5, 1984, Berdella drove over to Howell's shop to pick up Jerry. They left the shop shortly before 6 P.M. Jerry told some friends he was going to meet them at a club in Merriam, Kansas, a suburb of Kansas City, and he hoped Berdella would give him a ride, maybe get him high first. Jerry was never seen again.

Paul Howell became concerned when his son didn't come home that weekend to pick up the tickets he had for the widely promoted concert kicking off the national tour of Michael Jackson and his brothers at Arrowhead Stadium. He asked Berdella when he'd seen Jerry last, and Berdella told him the story about dropping Jerry off at the 7-11, just four blocks from where he'd picked him up. This explanation hardly satisfied Howell. He always thought Berdella was weird. Howell hounded the fugitive detectives, but he also conducted his own search. He had fliers printed with his son's photo and description on them. He drove through the sleazier parts of the city, including 10th and McGee, stopping to question people about the last time they saw Jerry. He went to the media and explained his story, and the *Kansas City Star* printed a Sunday article about Jerry, and his father's search, accompanied by a photo of Howell and his wife forlornly standing next to one of the fliers.

Howell also began his private surveillance of Berdella. He sat outside Berdella's house, watching for anything suspicious. He went through Berdella's trash when it was put out on Monday mornings. He talked to most of Berdella's neighbors, asking them if they'd seen Jerry, telling them of his suspicions. No one had seen anything. The cops were getting nowhere. Several months later, in November 1984, the Howell family's frustrations finally overtook them. On Jerry's twentieth birthday, Howell's oldest son, Paul Howell Jr., walked into the Flea Market, marched up to Berdella, grabbed him from behind, spun him around and started punching him in the face. Berdella fell over some tables in the market, which collapsed beneath him. Howell Jr. shouted at Berdella, "I want to find my brother, motherfucker, you know where he is." Another merchant in the market pulled Howell off Berdella, and Howell stood up and stormed out of the store. When the case went to city court in January, both Howells began threatening Berdella again, and Berdella went to the police to file another complaint.

Three years later, Howell was finally starting to think he might get some answers about his son. But on this sunny, clear morning, they weren't coming from the police. What information he was getting was from reporters, who simultaneously pumped him for information about Berdella. Howell was glad to recount the story of his son Jerry, and how Berdella was the last person seen with him. With Berdella's house as a backdrop, he told anyone who would listen of the depressions and dead ends he'd faced since Jerry's disappearance in 1984. When Eikel approached him later in the day to ask for Jerry's dental records, Howell sneered and told him he'd turned those over to the police years ago.

At 9:30 every Monday morning, detectives from the Case Review unit go upstairs to the city jail and corral all the suspects who've been arrested over the weekend. The suspects are handcuffed and taken down to the adjoining garage for a short ride to Associate Circuit Court, where they are arraigned and appear before a judge for the first time. Most of the suspects don't have a lawyer, and the judge automatically enters a plea of not guilty. As the suspect stands handcuffed before the judge, the judge reads the charges quickly and monotonously. The judge normally asks the detectives if the defendant has a past record, asks the defendant if he can afford to hire his own attorney, then announces what the bond amount will be. The detectives then walk the defendants down a back corridor to the Jackson County Jail, where they either post bond or remain until trial.

When the Case Review detectives brought Berdella down from the city jail Monday morning, they emerged from the elevator into a phalanx of newspaper and television photographers. The cameramen swarmed around Berdella, backpedaling and circling as the detectives led him out of police headquarters into the adjacent garage. Berdella kept his head up, never looking at the cameras. Another defendant, handcuffed to Berdella, couldn't help but grin at all the attention. The rear door to an unmarked police car was opened for Berdella and the other man, who climbed in first. Berdella sat next to the window. staring straight ahead, as the cameras bore in on him one last time. With cameras banned in Missouri courtrooms, it would be the news media's only opportunity to photograph Berdella. The shots of Berdella walking to the police car, then sitting in the back seat, would be replayed repeatedly on television news shows over the next few months, providing most Kansas City residents with their only lasting image of Berdella.

Across the street, at the county courthouse, Paul Howell had arrived and decided what to do. He walked into the building's basement with a loaded .38-caliber pistol in his pocket. But as he neared the elevators, he met an unexpected obstacle: that morning, for the first time, metal detectors were being used to screen everyone who entered the building. "Fuck," Howell muttered, and stepped back to assess the situation. He noticed the courthouse regulars were bypassing the metal detector, stepping casually around it. As an elevator was about to close, Howell nonchalantly did the same thing. He entered the packed car and headed up, unsure where Berdella was being arraigned.

Howell stepped off the elevator on the seventh floor and happened to see his attorney, Jim McMullin.

"Jimmy, how ya doin'?" Howell said.

"Well fine, Paul, just fine," McMullin said, tugging on his trademark pipe.

"Listen Jimmy, where's Bob Berdella at?"

"They just took him in for arraignment," McMullin told Howell.

"Where?"

"Across the street, at 13th and Locust.

"Shit," Howell said. Another elevator opened up, and Howell hurried toward it. The weight of his gun made Howell's leather jacket swing heavily against his chest, and McMullin knew immediately what Howell was doing.

"Don't go over there with a gun, Paul," McMullin yelled, but Howell just looked at him as the elevator doors closed.

Howell walked quickly to the Criminal Justice Center at 13th and Locust Streets. The entrance there also had a new metal detector, and no one was circumventing it. Howell stepped back outside. He noticed this building had a garage, so he entered that and started trying to open several of the doors leading inside. All were locked. A building employee appeared, and Howell backed away from the garage. For now, at least, his plan to kill Berdella seemed foiled. He walked down the street and stashed the pistol inside his car.

On the second floor of the Criminal Justice Center, Berdella sat in the empty jury box of Associate Circuit Judge Charles Stitt's courtroom, still handcuffed to the other man, awaiting his arraignment. While other defendants were being arraigned, Howell entered the courtroom. I'll just go in and watch, Howell told himself, figure out a way to kill Berdella where nobody else gets hurt. Berdella, hearing the courtroom door open, turned his head and spotted Howell. A brief smirk crossed Berdella's face. Howell snapped. Without another thought, he raced down the aisle from the back of the courtroom and burst through the swinging door separating the audience from the lawyers. Diving headfirst over the jury railing, Howell began pummeling Berdella. Three police officers leapt off a nearby bench and grabbed Howell after he'd unleashed several shots at the curled-up Berdella, but Howell strug-

84

gled fiercely, and the officers wrestled him to the ground. At one point in the fight, one of the officers yelled, "Watch it, he's trying to get my gun." Finally, Howell stopped trying to wriggle away from the policemen, and they handcuffed him and led him out of the courtroom. No charges were filed against him.

Judge Stitt watched this brief drama with a concerned look on his face. All he knew about Berdella was what he had read in that morning's paper. But he wondered who else might be angry at Berdella. "We gotta get this guy out of here," Stitt said. Berdella was marched before him, a large red mark blossoming on the side of his face. Stitt read the charges very quickly, and asked Berdella if he could afford a lawyer. Berdella said yes. "OK," Stitt said. "Bond is set at $500,000."

Berdella asked the judge, "Could I be placed in protective custody?" He didn't know who else from his past might rise up in the county jail. Stitt told him the jail officials would handle that. The detectives hustled Berdella out of the courtroom and checked him into the jail.

About the same time that Berdella was being booked into the jail, police were beginning to excavate the backyard at 4315 Charlotte. Gary Howell of the crime lab had the yard divided into a grid of thirty-five squares, each six feet by six feet, and helped construct a set of sticks and strings to delineate each plot. He drew up a chart of the forty by fifty foot backyard, so police could keep track of where they recovered anything else they might dig up. Canaday arranged for a class of police recruits to be brought in from the Police Academy to do the manual labor. By midmorning, the digging had begun.

The first spot to be examined was the hole that had been opened the day before by the backhoe. Digging carefully, the recruits and investigators pulled up some more bones, along with some more white, decomposed material. Finnegan, the anthropologist, suspected the bones were human vertebrae that originally supported the head found in the hole. His later tests proved him right.

From time to time, a recruit's shovel would strike something hard, and those around him would draw a quick breath. The recruit would reach down and pull up what would appear to be a bone fragment—possibly the first sign of a graveyard. Finnegan would walk over, examine it, then toss it over his shoulder. "Dog bone," he'd snap, "squirrel," or "chicken leg." But in a plot not far from where the head had been found, the digging uncovered three glass jars. One of the jars had feathers inside, another had what appeared to be a bird skeleton. The third jar had some kind of dark liquid. Buried bird feathers? the investigators wondered. Was it another indication that Berdella was involved in some type of occult worship? No one knew. The digging continued until nightfall.

News photographers and reporters staked out the yard as well, and in midafternoon they were joined by Harriet Sanders and Bonnie Ferris. Occasionally breaking into tears, the two women told the reporters about Ferris's disappearance, and that Berdella was the last man seen with him, too. They didn't mention to the media the rumors they'd heard about Berdella injecting young men with Thorazine, or that Bonnie and James Ferris had had a falling out over James's drug use and homosexual affairs.

The women knew that Ferris was friendly with Berdella, but they didn't know how much time Ferris had spent with Berdella. Ferris met Berdella through Gene Shaw, a fellow drug addict who wandered into Berdella's shop one day in the summer of 1984 and shoplifted an expensive necklace. Several weeks later, Shaw walked back in while wearing the necklace, then panicked when he realized how he'd obtained it. Berdella noticed Shaw's anxiety, and asked him what the problem was. Shaw said he had high blood pressure. Berdella said he did too, and that he could sell Shaw some Valium after work. Shaw agreed, went to pick up his buddy Ferris, and the three of them began an occasional friendship, used mainly when Shaw and Ferris wanted dope.

Later that summer, Ferris and Shaw went to Berdella's house one night and bought shots of chlorpromazine, an animal tranquilizer. Both men needed a shot right away, so they injected the drug in Berdella's bathroom, while Berdella watched. They liked the buzz so much they bought the whole bottle for thirty-five dollars. But several days later, Ferris called Berdella and said the tranquilizer was no good. Could they trade it for some marijuana? Berdella was reluctant, but he agreed to take the chlorpromazine back and give them some wild marijuana that he'd found while horseback riding.

Not long after that, Shaw was arrested carrying hashish in Independence, Missouri, a city on the eastern border of Kansas City. The detectives said they would drop the charges if Shaw could set them up to make buys from some drug dealers. Shaw agreed. One night, when he and Ferris needed money for a fix, they called the detectives and told them about Berdella. One of the detectives accompanied them to Berdella's house and joined Ferris and Shaw as they asked to buy a half-ounce of marijuana. Berdella was uncertain about selling them the weed with a stranger around, but Ferris and Shaw convinced him their friend was cool. Berdella sold them the marijuana. Several months later, in early 1985, his car was towed from a no-parking zone, and when Berdella went to pick it up, he was arrested for questioning by the Independence police. By that time, however, the undercover officer had left the Independence police force. Berdella was never charged, and Ferris and Shaw didn't come around again.

But in September of 1985, Berdella saw Ferris hitchhiking along Gillham Road in midtown Kansas City. He stopped the car and let Ferris get in. Ferris was obviously high and drunk, and he was addicted to injecting cocaine. They drove to a nearby bar, and Berdella asked Ferris why he'd set him up with an undercover officer. Ferris said he didn't know the man was an officer. Berdella believed him, and later in the evening, when Ferris said he needed a place to stay, Berdella said Ferris could stay with him for a few days. Ferris took him up on the offer.

The next night, September 25, 1985, Berdella, Ferris and Shaw went to the same bar for a drink. Ferris asked if Shaw could stay over too, and Berdella said no. Ferris and Shaw got progressively more drunk, and eventually Berdella slipped out and went home without either of them. He double-locked his front door, disconnected his upstairs phone and went to bed. But at 3:30 A.M. that night, he heard pounding on the front door. He ignored it, and tried to go back to sleep. Five minutes later, his dogs began barking excitedly. Berdella put on a robe, went downstairs, walked into the kitchen and found Ferris crawling through a kitchen window into the house, with Shaw standing behind him. Berdella was not amused, but he let them in. They were both very high, and their energy levels kept them wide awake. Berdella went back upstairs to bed, but Ferris and Shaw kept awakening him. Finally, at 6:30 A.M., Berdella got dressed and told them he would give them a ride wherever they wanted, so long as it was out of his house.

That afternoon, September 26, Ferris called Berdella at home. He asked Berdella to meet him at the bar that night. Berdella said that if he got around to it, he would, then went out to run some errands. Ferris went to look for a bus downtown, but several minutes later, his wife, Bonnie, drove past where Ferris and Shaw were standing in front of a pay phone. Ferris asked her to drive him toward Westport, but his wife didn't have time to go that far; she had to pick up one of her daughters from school. Instead of Westport, she dropped Ferris off downtown at 13th Street, and Ferris then took a bus to 31st Street, and walked to the bar. Berdella met him there about 7:30.

Bonnie Ferris later remembered that her husband didn't say exactly where he was going in Westport, but she figured it was to see Berdella. There was almost no one else left who would let James Ferris stay with them, she said. Ferris had alienated everyone else by stealing from them for drug money; the final straw with Bonnie came when Ferris sold most of the couple's furniture for one hundred dollars. She moved out, though she was pregnant with her first child by Ferris. She was desperately hopeful that the new baby would convince Ferris to dry out and redirect his life. She felt sure that would happen, which is why she was so surprised when Ferris never called her again after she left him at the bus stop.

The search inside the house continued on Monday as well. Detective Bill McGhee read through dozens of scraps of paper, looking for names and phone numbers, more notes, any type of clue. In one upstairs room, he came across a sheet of yellow, lined paper. The only thing written on it were the words: "ONCE POLICE START DIGGING MUD, NO REASON TO CO-OP. . . ."

In the basement, the Crime Scene investigators were spraying Luminol, a substance which glows when it comes in contact with traces of blood. The investigators first had had to clear the basement of its massive clutter, no small task. But once they finished, in one corner of the basement, the fluorescent blue Luminol lit up in a round, pool shape. There were no wipe marks to indicate that anyone had tried to clean this up. Next, the investigators brought down two large plastic trash barrels and a smaller white plastic bucket, which had been stored in a gardening shed in Berdella's backyard. They brought the barrels into the basement because it was dark, and easier to see the Luminol. It was very easy to see the Luminol in all three of the containers once it was sprayed inside. There were no obvious bloodstains in the barrels or bucket, but the Luminol could be showing a residual film coating the inside of the containers. The investigators looked at each other in amazement.

Not far away, at Menorah Medical Center, Chris Bryson sat shivering in his hospital room, with the shades pulled and the lights off. Family members came to visit and to hear his incredible story. He still couldn't believe it himself, and he didn't know whether he should still fear Berdella — if the guy really was some sort of witch or Satanist, maybe he had friends who would come after him again, Bryson thought. A reporter sneaked past the nurses' station, ignored the sign reading No Visitors and knocked on the door. Bryson told him to come in, but he refused to answer any questions. The reporter gave him a copy of Hurn's probable cause statement, and Bryson read it anxiously. His sister sat next to Bryson, glaring at the reporter but saying nothing. Bryson still bore many of the scars of his ordeal, including red eyes, a raspy voice, marks on his wrist and mouth, and two round scabs on his shoulder blades. He had no idea how the scabs had gotten there. The reporter badgered him but finally left, and security outside his room was tightened considerably after that.

Driving back to Manhattan, Kansas, Dr. Finnegan carried the two skulls, along with the vertebrae that he theorized matched the skulls. He wanted to take the evidence back to his laboratory at Kansas State University to see if he could determine an approximate age, race and how long ago the person might have died. He would soon present some interesting findings to the task force.

At police headquarters, new detectives joining the squad flipped through some of the papers taken from Berdella's house, and scanned the photos. Cole kept answering the phones, did a couple of television and newspaper interviews and tried to read the reports his detectives and the crime scene investigators were writing. Officers from around the department streamed into the show-up room, and passed around Berdella's shocking Polaroids, gawking. They made jokes about cucumbers and homosexuals. The show-up room just wasn't working out.

Cole went to Winston's office and told him they'd have to find another place to hold this investigation. Winston told him to look around headquarters, and Cole began checking into various conference rooms. He found one on the third floor, in the budget department, and decided to move his squad up there the next day. The detectives went home about 7 P.M. Cole sat comfortably in front of his television that night to watch the Sooners, overwhelming favorites, lose to the Kansas Jayhawks. Not a good omen, Cole thought.

Chapter Five

"Mr. Kellogg?"

"Yeah?"

"I'm Detective Wilson and this is Detective Casebolt from the Kansas City Police Department. We're investigating this Bob Berdella matter and we'd like to talk to you for a minute."

Freddie Kellogg turned around and glanced at his girlfriend, who was watching with interest.

"OK," Kellogg said, lowering his voice, "but let's do this somewhere else."

The detectives had been looking for Kellogg for several days. His name was on numerous pieces of paper in Berdella's house: Berdella had sued him in Jackson County Circuit Court for reneging on various agreements, and Kellogg had jotted a page worth of his friends' phone numbers in Berdella's telephone directory. The detectives took Kellogg back downtown to get a full statement.

As police soon learned, Kellogg, twenty-four, was just one of many boarders who had stayed with Berdella in the last decade. Berdella's large house had spare bedrooms on both the second and third floors, and before they were overrun by clutter, most of the rooms had been inhabitable. Many of the boarders used Berdella's house as a temporary shelter and had little or no physical contact with

Berdella. But at least one housemate, Kellogg, was Berdella's lover. Once Kellogg began his tale, the detectives had little to do but sit back and listen.

Kellogg grew up first in a broken home, then in a series of group homes. When he was in his late teens, he landed at the Trailways bus station near 10th and McGee. A man there offered him fifty dollars if the man could perform fellatio on Kellogg. Kellogg went with the man to his house, where the man handcuffed him, then attempted to sexually assault him. While Kellogg was screaming for help, another man came in and stopped the encounter, and Kellogg ended up staying with him for a short time. That man introduced Kellogg to Bob Berdella sometime in early 1983. "Bob had told me that he had a three-story house all to himself, and I could live with him as long as I helped him out by paying him some money and helping him around the house until I got a job," Kellogg told the detectives.

"When I first moved in with Bob, we had sex, with Bob being the dominant one. The sexual activity between me and Bob took place in his bedroom on the second floor. There was never any bondage or handcuffs or anything physical other than the sexual activity."

Wilson and Casebolt listened intently, urging Kellogg not to edit himself simply because the squad's typist, Jennifer Cullen, was a woman.

Not long after Kellogg, then eighteen, moved in with Berdella, he introduced another friend, Foster Simmons, to Berdella, and Simmons moved in too. A third, older man, Phillip Bukovic, was already living there, and for a time four men were living in the house. But Bukovic, age twenty-eight at the time, soon moved out.

Simmons's agreement was the same as Kellogg's: pay rent by helping out around the house, or at the Flea Market. Both did odd jobs around the house, though Simmons never slept with Berdella. Berdella helped Kellogg finance a car, and helped Simmons find temporary work through employment agencies. Berdella liked to put things in writing, and he had the young men sign promissory notes and contracts, agreeing to exchange services or monthly payments for the goods or the housing Berdella provided.

One service Kellogg provided Berdella was as his liaison to the streets. "Bob had me drive him down to the Trailways bus station where he looked for tricks that he wanted to be with at his house," Kellogg told the detectives. "It was Bob's thing to pick up these guys and take them back to his house where he would shoot them up with drugs and have sex with them. . . . I would talk to the tricks that he wanted because they felt secure with me."

Kellogg didn't watch Berdella inject these hustlers, but he knew how it felt. He described a night when Paul Pankovits, the man who had introduced him to Berdella, came over, and the three of them went up to Berdella's bedroom. "Bob shot up me and Paul with these two drugs and the drugs rendered me totally helpless," Kellogg recalled, watching the two detectives for a reaction. They sat stone-faced. "I could see what was going on, but I was unable to move or speak. . . . I can't say whether or not Bob had sex with me while the three of us were on the bed because I was totally out of it."

The detectives showed Kellogg some of Berdella's Polaroid photos, and Kellogg identified himself in several of them. "I know for a fact that Bob always photographed everybody and everything at one time or another who he came in contact with at the house. He liked to photograph and he wrote everything down that happened in a diary. I never saw a diary he wrote on any person, all I know is I just saw him writing in a spiral notebook."

In the spring of 1983, Kellogg introduced another of his friends, Robert Sheldon, to Berdella, and Sheldon would stay with Berdella periodically over the next few years. But Kellogg had to move out. He had started dating a young woman, Kellogg said, and "Bob was obsessed with me and didn't approve of me having a girlfriend." Bob had helped Kellogg buy a used Camaro sports car, but had made Kellogg sign a contract agreeing to certain conditions and times of use, and now he tried to make Kellogg stick to the contract. Kellogg refused. He moved out in April 1984. He moved back in once more, for two months in 1985, then left for good, taking with him some wallets and cigarettes that Berdella had picked up in trade.

The detectives handed Kellogg a stack of Polaroids, and he identified several men, including Pankovits, Simmons, Robert Sheldon, a man named Greg Leinenkamp, and one he thought was Jerry Howell. When he was finished, the detectives gave Kellogg a ride back to his East Side house. Wilson thought he was very much like all the men who seemed to become involved with Berdella: thin, white, fair-haired, in his twenties, from a broken home, floating around with no real job or ambition, living from day to day, and bisexual. Some of Berdella's housemates were heterosexual. Simmons had told police when he found out Kellogg and Berdella were lovers, he moved out. But of the men the police had talked to, and the dozens of men in the Polaroids, the similarities were numerous.

On Tuesday, April 5, the circus atmosphere surrounding the Berdella squad only grew worse with the relocation of the detectives to a meeting room on the third floor. Officers from throughout the department streamed in to have a look at the near-legendary photographs. Veteran cops who thought they'd seen it all had a new story to take home to the wife that night. Some of the photos showed Berdella—or whoever was holding the camera—performing anal sex, or having fellatio performed on him. Some showed men with syringes and needles sticking out of their necks, or electrodes attached to their genitals. Dozens of the photos showed men tied to the bed, often with a gag around their mouth, always naked. Sometimes the men's eyes bulged with terror. In others, they had a look of defeated acceptance. The men's faces couldn't be seen in most of the pictures where Berdella was sodomizing them, shoving a cucumber inside of them, or pushing their legs up over their heads so he could have frontal sex with them. Berdella's face was only in one of the photos, a posed group shot. After a time, the photos became separated from the sets of notes they'd been found with.

Cole met with Lieutenant Colonel Jenkins, who asked how long the investigation was going to take. Cole told him it would be at least several weeks, and because it would be a drawn-out process, he didn't want to work his detectives sixteen hours a day and hamper their effectiveness. Jenkins agreed and told him to let him know if he needed anything else. Cole glanced at the crowd clustered around Berdella's photos, and said they might be needing a new location again. Jenkins just nodded.

By now, all eleven detectives had joined the squad, and Cole called the first of his daily briefings. "This is probably going to be the biggest case any of us has ever been involved in," Cole said, adding authority to his flat southwestern accent. "I can't stress enough how important it is to be thorough in your interviews, we can't overlook anything." Cole's biggest fear during the investigation would become the chance that he would miss a crucial detail that might cause a Berdella trial to be lost on a technicality.

"Our first concern is to identify the people in these photographs," Cole continued. "We need to establish who might be dead, and we've got to interview the ones who aren't. Also, I'm going to assign one of you every day to stay at Berdella's residence with the Crime Scene investigators to help with the search, and to write down all the names they come across."

The cramped room was silent. The seriousness of the case was fast erasing any jocularity about the photos or the house. Cole looked around to make sure he had everyone's attention. "This guy could be a serial killer," Cole said, "and the number of victims is anyone's guess. We already know of two people who were last seen with Berdella, and FAU (the fugitive/missing persons unit) thinks Berdella is good for them. Eikel, I want you and McGhee to go through those missing persons files and compare them with the notes we found with the photos, see if any of the dates or times match up. The rest of you, we've already got dozens of leads from stuff we found in the house and calls we've gotten. We'll have briefings every morning, and then I'll give out assignments, and we'll meet back here at the end of the day to talk about what we've got."

The detectives started to get busy, and Eikel and McGhee reached for the missing persons files on Howell and Ferris. While reading through the old police reports, they glanced at the folded sheets of lined stenographer's paper with handwritten dates and times on them. McGhee flipped through several sets, and came to one that had "7:30 Bar" at the top. Beneath that was written: "Ferris," and on the next line, "9/26 Drug." McGhee looked back at the top police report in the Ferris file. Ferris had last been seen going to meet Berdella on September 26, 1985. McGhee scanned down the page of entries, organized chronologically. He read:

9:00 Out
9:05 Shoes + socks off, move arms, snoring, no rea
9:10 Test need no react
    2$\frac{1}{2}$ cp left a "
    3 cp right a "

9:20 Photo, clothes off, no react
9:40 Turned over, slight arm movement
9:50 Fing F no reac
    1¹/₂ cc ket arm no rea
    Front F no react
10:15 BF no reac
10:30 Tied arms (Out)
10:50-11:00 Carrot F
    Slight resits
    1¹/₂ cc cp nk
11:00 2 cc cp vein
11:30-11:45 BF, cub F, slight react
    Regag
12:00 Fightin

The notes continued for two more pages. The top of the third page was marked "Fri," and the last two entries read:

11:45 Very delayed breathing, snoring
12:00 86

The whole thing started to make sense to McGhee very quickly. If Berdella had treated Ferris the way Bryson claimed he was treated, then the writer's abbreviations were easily deciphered. At 9:10 Berdella was poking a needle into Ferris, testing him to see if he really was unconscious. Then he injected him with 2¹/₂ cubic centimeters of something in his left arm, and 3 cubic centimeters in his right arm. At 9:20 he snapped a Polaroid of Ferris with his clothes off. The squad's detectives had already theorized that "F" was short for "fuck," which appeared for the first time at 9:50. If the notes were accurate, Berdella had inserted his finger into Ferris at 9:50, then had sex while facing Ferris ("FF") and at 10:15 had anal sex with the unconscious man ("BF"). These interpretations were based

98

on the premise that Bryson was telling the truth, that he really was injected with drugs and sodomized as often as he claimed. But what were the drugs? What was "cp" and "ket"?

Eikel was finding the same type of notations on two pages of Berdella's own stationery, which started with the line "JH 7/5/84." Jerry Howell had last been seen with Berdella on July 5, 1984. There were numerous lines with varying "cc" amounts of "cp," "ac" and "ph," as well as at least half a dozen "BF" entries. The final line, on the second page, read: "7/6 10:00 *DD.*"

There were other pages of notes, but these had no recognizable names or dates. Cole assigned Detective Albert DeValkenaere to go to the Fugitive unit to see what other cases they had on missing young white men. There were no other such cases.

After Cole gave assignments to the other detectives, he leaned back and took a deep breath. Looking around, he noticed some detectives not on his squad flipping through the stacks of Polaroids. Other interested police employees loitered just outside the meeting room door. The room next to his was the office for the reporters for the *Kansas City Star* and the *Kansas City Times,* the two daily newspapers. Cole figured they could probably hear everything through the thin walls, and just being so close gave them too-easy access. This location would definitely not work. Cole phoned Lieutenant Colonel Jenkins and asked for another office, and later on Tuesday Jenkins came up with a large conference room in another police building, away from headquarters. The squad would move to 1328 Agnes Avenue, the home for the traffic and administrative analysis divisions.

Berdella also was away from the crowds as he began his

99

first full day in the Jackson County jail. Every prisoner in the jail gets his own cell, but most of those are part of larger "pods" that open out into common areas shared by a dozen or so inmates. But jail officials were afraid Berdella might be hurt by a prisoner looking for notoriety, or simply because sex crimes suspects rank very low on the totem pole of respect in jails and prisons. Also, Berdella was plainly depressed, and was already on several medications for high blood pressure and hypertension. He might try to kill himself, the officials thought. So he was placed in the jail's medical unit, on the second floor, where he had no interaction with any other prisoners.

That suited Berdella just fine. The word "loner" popped into nearly every conversation about Berdella among people who knew him in Cuyahoga Falls, where the news of his arrest was just starting to spread. Although he hadn't lived there since 1967, he made an impression on those he spent time with. Art teachers at Cuyahoga Falls High School remembered him as highly intelligent, but hard to teach. He took nearly all of the classes offered by the school's art department, and showed such potential that one teacher placed him in an independent study program. Berdella was one of only three students to receive such a placement in the next twenty years. Although his project was never completed, Berdella earned excellent grades throughout high school, and ranked near the top of his graduating class of 803 students.

But there was another reason some people remembered Berdella: He could be arrogant, condescending. "Kids didn't like him, and he couldn't care less," said Ron Simon, one of his art teachers. Berdella liked to project the attitude that he knew more than both the students and the teachers. He read avidly outside of school, and was proud of his intellect. One fellow student remembered Berdella helping her with homework, and thinking that Berdella was more mature than the rest, that he was bound for big things. Another student, who saw Berdella as someone with few friends, recalled that "I always felt kinda sorry for the guy. But not sorry enough to hang out with him. He was kinda nerdy."

Part of that reputation may have come from Berdella's appearance: six feet two inches, with an average build. He was extremely nearsighted, and had worn thick-lensed glasses since age five. His hair was short, his clothes were conservative and he had a slight speech impediment. He *looked* older than the other students, though both friends and neighbors said he could not be described as handsome. He had no interest in girls, and began entering gay bars in Akron, but no relationships developed there either.

Neighbors perceived that Berdella's best friend may have been his mother, a homemaker devoted to her family. It appeared that Berdella's father preferred his brother, Danny, seven years younger than Robbie, in part because both Danny and his father were sports fans. Danny loved baseball in particular, and he and his father would drive to Cleveland for Indians' baseball games. Robbie had no interest in sports, but some thought that he still wanted desperately to win his father's approval. "I think Robbie was trying to prove to his dad he could do as good as his brother," one acquaintance recalled. Rather than sports, Berdella's passion was art. His paintings, entered in various scholastic competitions won several awards. When he wasn't in school, he did volunteer work at the city's Civic Arts Center and with the parks department, and he earned money by working in restaurants.

But Berdella also spent much of his time in his room, reading the "beat" writings of Kerouac and Ferlinghetti and biographies of Einstein and Gandhi. His world view expanded beyond Cuyahoga Falls, beyond his small-minded fellow students, beyond his disapproving father.

He wanted the intellectual challenge of college, in some place other than Ohio. His painting continued to improve, and one of his teachers, Dale Tener, helped him win a partial scholarship to the Kansas City Art Institute. This would really be a place to stretch his imagination, Berdella thought, to bat deep thoughts back and forth with other motivated students and professors. Maybe the life of a college professor was his calling. Berdella began to think he might enjoy teaching as a career. He enrolled in the fall of 1967, and majored in painting.

It took only about a year for Berdella to become heavily disillusioned with the academic world. Berdella found that in the late 1960s, many students went to college to avoid the draft, or only because college was expected of them. Many simply wanted to get high rather than study; some wanted to get high and *then* study. Marijuana's popularity was soaring, and its sedative effect hardly inspired ambition or achievement in an age of rebelliousness and cultural upheaval. Though Berdella continued to paint, his attentions turned elsewhere.

He fell in with a clique of students living along Warwick Boulevard, just north of the Art Institute, a strip notorious in the city as a haven for the local hippies. After a year of living in a dormitory, Berdella and two other students rented a house at 4106 McGee Street, one block east of Warwick. Though Berdella didn't particularly like to get high, he had a friend who supplied him cheap pot and pills, and he began selling them to other students. The money was not bad for a college student, and Berdella, now wearing shoulder-length black hair and a shaggy beard, started to buy loud, extravagant clothes. Friends recalled that his self-confidence grew and he liked to be theatrical, the center of attention. "He would dance outlandishly, not necessarily well," one friend said, and he hung out at a psychedelic nightclub in Westport that, years later, would become the Old Westport Flea Market.

As Berdella began to emerge from his shell, he developed an increasing sarcasm and an antiauthoritarianism that was almost expected of art students in the late sixties. He spoke disparagingly of organized religion and middle-class family values, friends remember. Where once he had been regarded as quiet and shy in Ohio, Berdella now was opinionated and gregarious. In one performance art piece at school, Berdella had his audience of students and teachers stand on chairs and place bags over their heads. He then screamed obscenities at them.

In January of his sophomore year, Berdella, nineteen years old, was arrested after selling amphetamines to a federal undercover agent. He posted a three-thousand-dollar bond and was released. Two months later, he pleaded guilty, and was given a five-year suspended sentence. But one month after that, he was arrested again, this time in Johnson County, Kansas, a suburban area west of Kansas City. Berdella and two other students were sitting in a parked car when police drove up and found what they suspected to be marijuana and LSD. This time, Berdella could not post bond, and he spent five days in the Johnson County jail before police dropped the charges against him and one of the other students for lack of evidence.

In both incidents, Berdella needed a lawyer. Now that he was effectively out of the drug-dealing business, he had to come up with some money to pay his attorney, so he got a job as a short-order cook at Sidney's, a midtown diner in Kansas City. "And very quickly found out I could make twice as much flipping hamburgers as I could as a college professor," Berdella later said.

He went to the Art Institute during the day, and worked at Sidney's at night, but Berdella was rapidly losing interest in college. In September 1969, at the start of his junior year, Berdella made a one-hundred-dollar down payment and bought a house at 4315 Charlotte Street, much farther away from the Warwick "hippie strip" and the Art Institute than he had been. Berdella was disappointed with the classes and the teachers in his third year at the Art Institute. "They were nothing more than professors reading out of books," Berdella would remark. He tried to create challenging projects, such as the maze with the chicken film, but no one seemed to understand. Curtis Shore, a longtime friend, recalled one afternoon when Berdella bought a live duck and took it to the Art Institute campus, then chopped its head off and danced around the corpse while chanting nonsense. He took the duck home and cooked it that night, but the college administrators were not impressed. At the end of the 1969 fall semester, Berdella voluntarily withdrew from the Art Institute.

Berdella stayed in Kansas City, and began to work fulltime as a cook. Eventually he moved up to some of the city's classier restaurants, performing various kitchen duties, and gradually became a chef or manager at several different restaurants, including the Carriage Club, the American Restaurant and the University Club. In the early 1970s, he began collecting and trading arcane artifacts, piling up items in the large bedrooms of his house. "He was very scholarly about this stuff he collected," recalled John Stith, a friend since the late sixties. "He evidently had taught himself." Berdella stayed in touch with his sixties clique, becoming even more outspoken as he grew older. In one-on-one situations, he was still fairly subdued. "But around other people, he'd start acting out," another longtime friend said, "until it reached the point where he tended to be left out of invitations to do group things." Others recalled the same thing, that Berdella seemed to enjoy being rude or gross, especially around people who didn't know him. "If he saw somebody who was new, he'd try to shock them," one man said. "It didn't shock us, it embarrassed us."

For years, some of Berdella's friends didn't know he was gay. He wasn't effeminate, and he didn't discuss his relationships openly. But by the mid-1970s, the closet was no place for gays to be, and Berdella started to acknowledge his homosexuality to his close friends. Soon, he became open about it, until it became another aspect of his attempts to shock people in mixed company. Acquaintances recalled that Berdella wasn't averse to making lewd remarks about young boys and their attractiveness.

But Berdella's actual relationships with men in their late teens or early twenties didn't begin until the early 1980s, and it was something he mainly hid from his older social circle. Sometimes a young man would accompany him on a trip to a friend's house or farm, but more often Berdella socialized alone. "He was embarrassed by them," one colleague believes. "They were inferior intellectually, people we wouldn't have tolerated. He just kind of lived in his own secret place."

Despite his secrecy, Berdella's arrest still shocked all of his Kansas City friends. Some refused to believe it was true: it must be a frame-up, they thought. The gruesomeness, and the publicity, kept many friends from visiting him in jail. Initially only one of his college friends and one Flea Market acquaintance went to see Berdella in the county jail. His mother and stepfather arrived, and they told Berdella they had arranged with a lawyer to sell some of Berdella's possessions, if necessary, to raise money for his defense. Berdella felt bad that he had to get his mother involved at all, and he was glad when she returned to Ohio, away from the hysteria his case was generating.

Usually, Berdella paced alone in cell number 3, in the second floor medical unit, a seven foot by eleven foot room with no outside windows and no bars. Just cinder block walls, it contained a long fluorescent light over the steel cot bolted to the wall and a metal mirror stationed over a combination toilet-sink unit. The steel door to his room had a narrow vertical window, but the only thing he could see through it was the medical unit attendant sitting at a desk, reading or making notes on a chart. He was allowed to leave the cell for his daily shower, and to meet with attorneys or visitors on the first floor. He was also allowed into the jail's gymnasium for recreation periods, but only when it had been cleared of other inmates. Denied access to television and radio, he devoured the daily *Star* and *Times,* clipping articles and growing infuriated at the one-sided way he was being portrayed. But all these daily routines were merely a diversion, as preparing his defense would soon become. Berdella dreaded the prospect of having to grapple with his actions in the past few years. So he didn't.

On Thursday morning, which happened to be his forty-fifth birthday, the Reverend Roger Coleman drove to work from his south Kansas City home to his office in the Westport Allen Center, just two blocks from the Flea Market. Coleman had met Berdella several times previously, and was well known in the Midtown area as both a minister and generally helpful person. He hadn't been much impressed with the way Kansas City had reacted to the Berdella case so far, mostly with bad jokes and insensitivity. A common joke that week was to leave a message with someone's receptionist, who would tell the person: "Bob Berdella called. Your photos are ready."

But Coleman wasn't thinking about that this morning. It was his birthday, and as usual, he had three million things to do. He flipped around the FM radio dial, and as he listened to the rock station KY-102, he heard the familiar strains of "Mellow Yellow" by Donovan. But it wasn't

106

Donovan singing, it was local disc jockey Skid Roadie, who had written and produced a full-blown parody.

I'm just mad about torture
The police are mad about me
Hitchhikers wearing dog collars
I give them jolts of electricity

They call me Bob Berdella
(Quite right, Skid)
They call me Bob Berdella
(Hitchhike, Skid)

The song continued, but Coleman was already completely disgusted. How can they joke about this? This is embarrassing. The people of Kansas City were handling this badly, thoughtlessly. Coleman wondered if he could change that. As a minister with the Christian Church (Disciples of Christ), he saw his role as a priest ministering to the entire city, not simply one church or congregation, to deal with larger issues. He wanted to enter situations of suffering and try to begin the healing process.

Knowing Berdella somewhat—he'd been present at the opening of Bob's Bazaar Bizarre years before—and watching the city laugh at Berdella, Coleman wondered how to make sense of the whole thing.

"I wanted to understand: what possibilities exist for a person who had committed what Bob committed?" Coleman said. "I wanted to believe there's some potential there, for new life and new understanding. If an individual can't change, then maybe society has no chance. Is it possible for someone to be possessed with evil? I never dealt with these issues [before]. Society making fun of Bob was not a positive step."

Coleman decided to try to help Berdella, if he could, if

he was allowed. He contacted the prosecutor's office, and offered his services. He told Albert Riederer, a friend for years, that he would like to visit Berdella "if you think I can fulfill a positive purpose." Then, some of Berdella's friends started calling Coleman, telling him Berdella wanted to see him. The process was set in motion to put the minister and the suspect together, so Berdella would have someone to talk to besides his lawyers.

A block from the county jail, on the seventh floor mezzanine of the county courthouse, prosecutors were beginning the first of their daily discussions over how to handle the Berdella case. Riederer wanted Rick Holtsclaw to handle the sodomy case, and if there was going to be a homicide case, Pat Hall would take that. But both were busy in trials at the beginning of the week, so Marietta Parker, a homicide prosecutor, and Donna Fischgrund, a sex crimes prosecutor, would handle the first task: getting Berdella's bond revoked.

As the assistant prosecutors and Riederer discussed what they knew about Berdella, they realized they didn't know very much. He owned a shop in Westport. Did it bring in lots of money? Was all that stuff in his house very valuable? Though Berdella's bond was set at $500,000 on Monday, if a bondsman wanted to post his bond, Berdella would only have to pay the bondsman $50,000. Did he have access to that kind of money? The prosecutors considered calling the jail and asking jail officials to alert them if someone appeared to want to post Berdella's bond.

The amount of bond is supposed to ensure that a defendant will return for future court proceedings. Berdella was charged with nine felonies, and he faced the possibility of a life sentence if convicted. Somewhere down the road, the prosecutors hoped, he might be facing murder charges. Why wouldn't he flee? He apparently had family in Ohio, they knew. Parker drew up and filed a motion asking that Berdella's bond either be revoked, or set at five million dollars. A hearing was set for Tuesday afternoon.

That morning, Parker met with Detective Hurn, who brought over a sampling of Polaroid photographs. They picked out some of the most dramatic to show to Judge Stitt, and discussed some of the points they would present to justify holding Berdella without bond. At the hearing, Stitt announced at first that denying Berdella bond was inappropriate. But after seeing just a couple of photographs, his mind and stomach quickly turned. Hurn recounted Bryson's story of torture and escape. Then Detective Bill Wilson took the stand and described the skull being dug up out of the backyard. He also testified about the picture of the naked man hanging upside down, apparently dead. Stitt revoked the bond of Berdella, who was not present for the hearing.

When Holtsclaw returned from his trial, he began preparing to present the sodomy case to a grand jury on Friday for an indictment, thereby saving the trouble of having an adversarial preliminary hearing, in which Bryson would have to testify publicly. When Hall finished his murder trial, a series of talks began among the prosecutors on the next step: how to prove in court that Berdella killed someone.

"We need a body," Hall said. "That would really help."

"An identity of those skulls is what we need," Riederer said. "According to the statutes, to prove homicide, we need an identity and proof that death was caused by 'criminal agency.'"

Holtsclaw and Parker joined in, tossing around suggestions about routes they might take that would convince a jury of murder. The house must have all sorts of physical evidence, they reasoned; traces of blood, of hair, fingerprints. We're really going to have to lean on the crime lab in this one, Hall thought. Maybe these victims died of drug overdoses, one theory went. Possibly the skulls could be examined for traces of drugs or poisons, and maybe those tests will show that a fatal amount had been ingested or injected.

The first task clearly was going to be placing a name with each of the two skulls. Each skull had a set of teeth, so dental records could be used to identify them. Having a name for a victim would then allow police to investigate in the way they were accustomed to, delving into the person's background, finding friends and enemies, determining whom they were last seen with. The prosecutors assumed that there would then be Polaroids of this victim, still alive and in Berdella's house, possibly being tortured or sodomized. Getting approximate dates of their disappearance might enable them to link some of Berdella's handwritten logs with the victim, as the police were already trying to do with Howell and Ferris. Someone would need to decipher the medical or drug abbreviations Berdella was using. They would need to prove it was Berdella's handwriting. The number of elements was accumulating rapidly. This case was going to be a monster, they all thought.

At midweek, Hall and Holtsclaw went to meet with Cole at the squad's new headquarters on Agnes Avenue. Hall glanced at the eight by ten inch enlargements of the Polaroids and was revulsed. Holtsclaw chatted with Hurn about preparing for the sodomy case. Hall reminded Cole to be sure the house was searched thoroughly and completely; the crucial murder clue could be buried in a sock drawer somewhere. Hall wanted the police to apply for separate search warrants every time they discovered something of value, if that something hadn't specifically been mentioned in any other search applications. He didn't want any evidence tossed out of court because of a bad search

110

warrant. Cole nodded, and the police eventually obtained close to two dozen search warrants for Berdella's house and possessions. Hall also told Cole to call him any time they had questions on anything. Cole said he would, and within days either he or one of the detectives was calling the prosecutor's office almost hourly.

As Hall and Holtsclaw left the squad, they passed by some television cameras, which had already camped outside waiting for any information from the police. Hall tried not to look at the reporters and photographers, but he could barely mask his irritation. The story was the lead of every newscast, every day. It was on the front page of the morning and evening papers, every day. The chance that a trial of Berdella would have to be moved, in order to pick an unbiased jury, was growing daily. Hall felt the newspapers in particular were sensationalizing the story, comparing Berdella with the nation's most prolific serial killers in one article, when he hadn't even been charged with one death. But all the media were running wild with the story, and it was the constant source of conversation at bars and dinner tables across the area. Finally, Riederer told the police they would simply have to stop giving out any more information. On Friday, the police held a press conference to announce there would be no more announcements, then rebuffed questions from news crews which had traveled to Kansas City from as far away as New York.

The "Berdella squad" settled into a routine. The detectives would arrive about 9 A.M., and Cole would brief them on what the others had learned the day before and what was in their reports. The days were so hectic that Cole would take the reports home at night and read for an hour or two, making notes on index cards about what

111

needed to be followed up or done differently. Cole then would hand out some of these cards to the detectives, and they would begin their tasks for the day.

At about 5 P.M., the detectives would reconvene, discuss some of what they had found, and talk about their theories of what went on inside 4315 Charlotte Street and how long it had been happening. Initially, some of the detectives thought Berdella might have been a devil worshiper or a witch: others discounted that immediately. If Berdella had killed people, they wondered, where were the bodies? Could he have fed them to the dogs? That was a persistent rumor, furthered by the discovery of some unmarked meats in Berdella's freezer. At the city dog pound, the detectives were told that the dogs wouldn't eat dog food. People who had lived in the house said Berdella told them to feed the dogs chunks of "mystery meat" from the freezer. Lab tests later showed that all the meat in the freezer was actually beef.

Still, the rumors sprung up continuously. Berdella, as a former chef, used to cook casseroles and curry dishes for neighbors' picnics and for "pot luck" lunches at the Flea Market. What kind of meat had been in there, his fellow merchants now asked. Berdella wasn't disclosing his recipes. Other rumors had Berdella linked to the disappearances of two missing Iowa newspaper delivery boys, and Iowa authorities sent the dental records of the youths down to Kansas City. Some detectives heard claims that Berdella was killing his victims in a satanic sacrificial ritual.

One of the detectives on the squad, Lin Cunningham, was brought in because she had attended numerous seminars on occult and satanic groups. The prosecutors wanted to make sure that the satanic angle wasn't overlooked, if there was one. Cunningham took her first tour of Berdella's house in the middle of the week, after detectives had already turned it upside down. She was disappointed that there hadn't been more care taken to preserve the original appearance. She made notes on things such as a ceramic devil's mask on a downstairs wall, and thought there might be something to this. Her task in the coming weeks would be to track down the origins of such items, and handle all the tips and information the squad was receiving on Berdella's supposed satanic interests.

The other detectives weren't so specialized. Their first tasks were to gather as much information as possible from the people who knew Berdella, and to try to put names with the dozens of men in the Polaroids. Detective Bennie White tracked down D.J. Blankenship, a nineteen-year-old hustler who had lived with Berdella in January and February of that year. Berdella had picked up Blankenship on the streets downtown the previous summer, took him back to his house and injected Blankenship with Valium. "That's all I can remember about that night," Blankenship said. "I passed out from the downer."

Berdella dropped him off the next day, and Blankenship didn't see him again until December, when he spent one night at Berdella's. In January 1988, Blankenship was arrested for burglary, and when he was released, he called Berdella for a place to stay. Berdella picked him up, and invited him to stay with him. Blankenship agreed. That night, in Berdella's bedroom, "he started talking about bondage," Blankenship said. "He asked me how I felt about it and I told him I didn't like it. He got pissed off and started to use force. That's when he tied up my hands. He tied up my left hand first and then rolled me over and tied up my right hand to the head of the bed." But Blankenship kept resisting, and Berdella didn't assault him sexually. Blankenship stayed.

The two had sex consensually several times over the next month, and possibly more when Blankenship was injected and passed out. Blankenship told White he didn't resist being tied up because he knew Berdella could overpower him. "He had told me that he would hurt me if I didn't go along with it." But in mid-February, Blankenship moved out and hadn't seen Berdella since. About six weeks after Blankenship moved out, Berdella captured Chris Bryson.

Eikel and Detective Dan Wilson located a more sedate former roommate of Berdella's, Phillip Bukovic, who had lived with Berdella for about a year in 1982 and 1983. Bukovic said Berdella had advertised a room for rent in the newspaper, and when Bukovic showed up on Charlotte Street, Berdella showed him a third-floor room for $150 a month. Bukovic asked if he could pay some of his rent by doing chores around the house, and Berdella agreed. Bukovic said he immediately asked Berdella if he was gay, and Berdella said he was, but Bukovic said Berdella never "hit on me" sexually during the time he lived there.

Bukovic estimated he saw six to ten young, white men in Berdella's house during that year, including Simmons and Kellogg, "all street kids." He never saw any drug use or sexual activity, but he suspected both. Bukovic told the detectives he thought Berdella "tried to control young people, primarily by loaning them money through rent and utilities, car loans, housing them when they were in trouble with the law. And he was so exacting in his business dealings; but I found it strange that he wanted no one in the neighborhood getting close to his personal life." He termed Berdella "very old-time hippie-ish," and very cheap with his money. "Thou shalt not pay retail" was Berdella's eleventh commandment, Bukovic said.

Bukovic told the detectives one other thing of interest: Berdella would visit a friend's farm south of the city, carrying trash bags that looked heavy because they sagged at the bottom. Bukovic went with Berdella on one of these trips, but he never knew what was in the trash bags. The detectives made a special note of this comment; the digging was continuing in both Berdella's front yard and backyard, but no bodies were discovered. Maybe he was burying them at this farm.

At the end of the week, Hurn picked up Bryson and took him to police headquarters to videotape his statement. The police wanted to record Bryson now, before his memory faded, and in case he should change his mind later about cooperating, a frequent occurrence in sex crimes cases. Before starting, Hurn told Bryson that they would run through the story chronologically, and then they would discuss the photos. He handed Bryson a stack of fifty-seven Polaroids. Bryson looked through them, eerie sensations flooding his body. Hurn asked him to put them in chronological order as best he could, and Bryson worked at that for several minutes. Then he shook his head, and handed them back to Hurn. "OK, I'm ready," he said.

Bryson recounted the meeting and first hour with a straight face, a blank stare, trying not to think about it. Even the sexual torture didn't seem to bother him much, Hurn thought. Is this guy experienced, is he a hustler? He thought Bryson made an insightful comment when he said of Berdella: "It seemed like he was not getting excited on the sex as much as he was the whole deal, me being there, powerless, for him."

But when Bryson talked about Berdella injecting him in the throat with Drano, or having a wet Q-tip gouging his eyes, or being shocked, his eyes would start to water and his normally steady voice shook. He discussed his constant thoughts of escape, saying, "I thought over and over in my head to kill him, kill him in the house, but I was too weak, he was too big." So he decided the best way was to wait until Berdella was out of the house, Bryson said, and he described in detail how he freed himself from the bed and

115

climbed out the window, actually falling to the ground when the window ledge collapsed.

Next, Hurn handed Bryson the pile of Polaroids, and they went through them individually, describing for the camera what was depicted in each one, and when it was taken, if Bryson could remember. When they were finished, Hurn asked Bryson if he wanted to add anything to his statement. Bryson said: "I would like to say that, you know, I have not been no angel in my life. I have not done nothing to deserve what had happened to me. The only thing I had to rely on when I was up there being tied, I kind of found God, and I think I've been spared for a reason, to help get this man off the streets so that he does not put anybody else through this, or maybe worse." Hurn thanked Bryson, and after two hours they were done.

The squad took the weekend off. When they returned, Dr. Finnegan had finished his findings on the two skulls. They were both white males. Using various chemical tests and measurements, Finnegan estimated the skull in the backyard was that of a man probably twenty-five to thirty-six years old at the time of death. He also noted the vertebrae found with the skull had knife cuts and saw marks. The person had been dead at least six weeks and as much as ten months. The skull inside the house was that of a man about twenty-one to thirty-two years old, and had been buried at one time and later dug up, Finnegan theorized. The teeth in the envelope went with this skull, as police suspected, and scrape marks indicated this skull appeared to have been scalped, Finnegan told them. The time of death might have been more than eighteen months ago. Finnegan could not determine a cause of death based on either skull. But his findings were a start. The detectives prepared to spend a long time in their new assignment.

Chapter Six

". . . for the last couple of weeks, all hell's been breaking out around here on a day to day basis, the difference being that I'm just not taking anyone's crap anymore."
— Letter from Bob Berdella to a friend, January 1983

Police officers continued to dig in, around and through 4315 Charlotte Street, finding papers that Berdella had written in school, copies of letters that he had sent to family and friends, and documents addressed to other people. Books on everything from sadism to sauces were scattered through the house, as were hardcore pornographic magazines, both heterosexual and homosexual. There was even a file folder of news clippings Berdella kept on serial criminals—murderers like Elmer Wayne Henley of Texas and Charles "Tex" Watson of California, and Kansas City's "Westport rapist" of the 1970s, James Maynard. Still, there wasn't much hard evidence that Berdella had killed anyone. The excavation of both the front and backyards had produced dozens of animal bones and the mysterious glass jars with bird feathers inside, but little else.

However, the police, nearly terrified that they would be accused of missing something or letting a serial killer slip through their fingers, brought in outside help. From the FBI's Kansas City office, they recruited Mike Napier, who had been trained in the study and profiling of serial killers. One school of thought in criminology is that, when a series of similar crimes occurs, learning as much as possible about the victims and circumstances will enable one to develop a "profile" of the unknown suspect, thereby narrowing the range of people to search for or interview. Another school of thought, widely subscribed to by Kansas City police, is that profiling is a bunch of crap. The profiles are so vague and general as to be worthless, some say. Besides, in this case, the suspect was already in custody.

But Cole didn't feel that he was in a position to say no to this suggestion from his commanders, not at an early phase of such a high-intensity case. In addition, the police had sent one of their own sergeants to Quantico, Virginia, to the FBI's National Center for the Analysis of Violent Crime (NCAVC), to be trained in profiling. The commanders decided to bring back the sergeant, Jon Perry, to assist the squad.

Perry had already spoken with Napier on the telephone, and Napier told him the case "had strong John Wayne Gacy overtones." Gacy had confessed to sexually torturing his thirty-three victims before killing them. However, Gacy also traveled throughout the Midwest, and the FBI felt Gacy could have been responsible for more murders, but there had been no coordinated, national follow-up. With the FBI's NCAVC, that was now possible. Perry discussed the case with Robert Ressler, his supervisor and a nationally known expert on serial sexual homicide. Ressler told Perry to act as a liaison with the FBI in case out-of-town leads needed to be investigated.

The animosity between the FBI and local law enforcement agencies stretches back for decades. Police and prosecutors see the federal agents as arrogant, aloof, inexperienced in the real down-and-dirty world of crime on the city streets. The feds see local police as small-town rubes and rednecks, bumbling and disorganized, unable to see the big picture. Entering this atmosphere, Napier and Perry were outsiders to Cole's squad, so they made their comments and suggestions gingerly.

After going through the house and looking at the photos, Perry diagnosed Berdella as a "sexual sadist," someone who gains sexual excitation from the pain and torture of others. In a study of twenty-six sexual sadists, Perry said twenty-three of them had meticulously recorded their criminal events, in ways similar to Berdella's logs. Most tended to have obsessive-compulsive personalities, the study found, resulting in the desire for orderliness, neat record keeping, and even the photographing of their acts, all in the name of completeness. The sadists also have strong fantasy lives, and gradually move from looking at sadomasochistic pornography, to practicing it with consensual partners, then to practicing it with unwilling victims, or sex slaves. On a cross-country trip, Ressler stopped in Kansas City one afternoon and toured Berdella's house. He noted Berdella's pattern, through his pornography collection, of deepening sadomasochism, and told Hall, the prosecutor, he would testify to Berdella's "sexual continuum." Hall thought Ressler's opinions were bullshit.

Perry presented an idea to Cole with more practical value. The hands, legs and belly of someone, apparently the person holding the camera, were in many of these

Polaroid photos. If the police took pictures of Berdella from exactly the same angles, the two sets of photos could be sent to the FBI lab in Quantico for scientific analysis and comparison. The police would hope for a match. Then, if one of the tortured men in the photos turned out to be missing, or was identified as one of the two skulls, Berdella possibly could be linked to them through some distinguishing marks or scars. Cole agreed, and after discussing it with Hall, told Detective Hurn to obtain a search warrant for permission to photograph Berdella's body.

The issue of interrogating Berdella remained unresolved. No one had tried to question him since Hurn and Cole spoke with him briefly on the morning of his arrest. In countless cases where police don't have the evidence for a conviction, they are able to convince a suspect that he'll really feel much better after he gets this off his chest, and the suspect confesses. The police try to supplement the case with physical evidence, but the confession is often the centerpiece. After being in jail for more than a week, maybe Berdella was ready to talk. It would sure put the puzzle together a lot quicker. Napier and Perry suggested questioning Berdella on the same day that he would be photographed in the jail. Take him down low, dominate him, possibly humiliate him, then build him back up, appeal to his ego. Show him the case is the top priority of this police department, and that the evidence is massive. "Overwhelm him," Napier said.

Cole was skeptical. Berdella's too smart for this, he thought. But Hurn liked the idea: High risk, high gain, he thought. Either Berdella is infuriated by the morning photo session, and won't cooperate at all, or he is bewildered by the photo session, psychologically leveled by the situation and weakened when he is brought to the squad room and shown what a big deal he is to the police. "Well, we've got to try sometime," Cole said. "Go ahead," he told Hurn, Napier and Perry.

On Tuesday afternoon, April 12, Hurn took the latest search warrant request to Judge Baker, who approved it. The next morning, April 13, Hurn and two technicians from the crime lab — Stephen Warlen and John Cayton — drove to the Jackson County jail to take samples of the hair from Berdella's scalp, mustache and pubic area, as well as to photograph him. The three men were led into the medical unit where Berdella was housed, and Hurn began to explain what was happening.

"Mr. Berdella, I'm sure you're wondering why we're all here today. I have a search warrant, basically, for your body." Berdella looked bewildered. "We're wanting to take photographs of your body, to be used in a comparison with body parts we believe to be you in a series of Polaroid photos."

Berdella said nothing. He listened calmly, but the jugular vein on his neck began pounding heavily. He began to rub his hands together, almost unconsciously. Hurn moved toward him.

"I have copies of these photographs, so there shouldn't be any problem with you getting into these positions in these photographs." He held out the photos so Berdella could examine them. "We're not doing this to embarrass you, and we're going to have a guard at the door, and the blinds will be turned down. But since we'll have to take shots of various parts of your body, many of the photos will require you to be naked."

Again, Berdella was silent. As he glanced through the enlargements of his original Polaroids, he swallowed heavily when he realized some of the positions he was going to have to take. Hurn told him to start undressing,

121

and Berdella complied.

For each photo, Warlen and Hurn would study the original closely, and then place Berdella's arm or leg at the same angle. Warlen then would stand directly in front of Berdella, to obtain the same shot as if Berdella was holding the camera. Berdella didn't seem embarrassed by the situation, but rather irritated that he could be forced to do this. He resisted only a couple of times. Once, he was asked to sit naked on a stool, his knees down, his legs spread apart, to recreate his position during anal sex. Another time, Hurn asked Berdella to grasp Cayton's gloved fingers with his palm up, to simulate the angle of someone shoving an object inside another person. Berdella knew what the detective wanted, but wouldn't hold his arm the same way it appeared in the original. Hurn told him sternly, "Mr. Berdella, recall what I told you earlier. If we're having trouble getting you in these positions, we will put you in these positions. We have these guards and you are not to resist us in any way." Hurn leaned forward and placed his hand on the back of Berdella's hand, turning his wrist to the correct angle.

The session lasted about an hour. As with many of the other detectives on the squad, Hurn had spent hours staring at these gruesome photographs, and he concluded that Berdella thrived on dominating other people. From their facial expressions, it was obvious the men in the pictures were not feeling similar gratification. Now the roles were reversed. Berdella was forced to do what someone else wanted him to do. It was a situation policemen rarely find themselves in, and Hurn paid close attention to Berdella's responses, first as he was photographed, then as Cayton plucked hair from various parts of his body. Then they thanked him and left.

More than a week after he'd been arrested, Berdella still did not have a lawyer. He'd been meeting with the attorney who had represented him in previous dealings with police, who in turn had referred Berdella to a second lawyer to help settle Berdella's finances and handle other civil dealings. The second lawyer, Sharlie Pender, suddenly moved center stage that Tuesday afternoon when the prosecutors filed a suit seeking to seize Berdella's house.

Riederer and two of his assistant prosecutors, Hall and Marietta Parker, had discussed the suit since the previous Friday, when they learned that Berdella, with Pender's assistance, had deeded the house over to his mother and stepfather in Ohio. The law the prosecutors considered using was enacted to seize cars and expensive property bought by drug dealers, presumably another tool provided by the state legislature to fight "the drug war." But the statute didn't specify that the defendant had to be a drug dealer, only that the property was used during a criminal act or bought with illicit proceeds.

The house was fast becoming a headache. Police had to guard it twenty-four hours a day, not only to protect the evidence but to fend off souvenir seekers and ghoulish teenagers. Already there had been one lapse in the guarding of the house, leaving open the possibility that any evidence found after the house was left unguarded could be challenged by defense attorneys. The around-the-clock protection was costing the police in both overtime payments and manpower on the streets, and police commanders worried about their liability if valuable contents inside the house were broken or stolen.

Seizing the house, and selling it, might possibly recoup some or the costs of guarding it, as well as cataloging, moving and storing the contents. The case probably wouldn't be heard until the criminal proceedings were finished, so it would eliminate the house as a nagging worry, the prosecutors reasoned. And it would give Berdella's lawyers one more dilemma to deal with.

But the suit changed the situation surrounding Berdella's representation. Though he had been meeting with a private attorney, Berdella also had applied to the public defender for a lawyer. The public defender's office, noting that Berdella owned a house, a shop and a car, decided that Berdella could afford his own lawyer, and had turned him down. Now Berdella's main asset was frozen. Without the house to sell or mortgage, Berdella probably couldn't afford the costly fees a private attorney would charge him. Then the public defender would reenter the picture.

The prosecutors were divided over this; some thought they would have a better chance of winning a case against the overworked, underrespected lawyers in the public defender's office, while others thought the trial experience and daily criminal work of the public defenders would be better for Berdella than a private attorney. Berdella could still sell his car and shop to hire a lawyer, so his options weren't completely closed. The prosecutors decided to file the suit.

Daily, informal discussions on the Berdella case were held in various offices of the county courthouse's seventh-floor mezzanine, sometimes in Hall's cramped cubicle, sometimes in Riederer's more spacious, paneled chamber. Early that week, Hall raised the topic of needing a "second chair" prosecutor to assist him in a possible murder trial. Was Parker interested? She asked for twenty-four hours to think about it, and soon realized that if Berdella were charged with murder, Riederer and

124

Hall would want the death penalty. Parker didn't believe in the death penalty, and the next day told the two men that she couldn't participate in such a prosecution. Riederer asked if she would be willing to handle the civil forfeiture suit, and Parker said she would.

The tasks were now clearly delineated for the prosecutors. Holtsclaw would take the sodomy case, Hall would prosecute the murder case (if there was one), and Parker would handle the suit seizing the house. Hall, as lead counsel, would be the clearinghouse for information on all cases, and would keep Riederer updated on new developments. Riederer reminded them not to rush into anything; this was one case where they had the luxury of time.

"What do we need to do next?" Riederer asked. The prosecutors talked about suggestions Hall could make to Cole the next time he visited the squad. With all the names police were finding in the house, had the detectives tried to collect mug shots of the names and compare them to the Polaroids? Had Berdella's personal phone book been thoroughly checked, phone numbers called, names run through the police computer? What about Bryson, had anyone seen him during the time he claimed to be in Berdella's bedroom? Were the police careful to get new search warrants every time they discovered something new? Were they investigating Berdella's collection of weird, seemingly satanic books and artifacts, and the rumors of Berdella's supposed devil worshiping? Over the next few weeks, Hall and Holtsclaw met with Cole at least two or three times a week, and spoke with him on the phone daily. The prosecutors made their suggestions tactfully—they had experience working with cops who didn't like being told what to do—and Cole accepted their ideas gladly. He was pleased to have someone outside the police department providing him with a neutral perspective on the investigation's direction.

Cole didn't tell the prosecutors of the plan to question Berdella that afternoon, mainly because he was dubious of its chances for success. Napier, the FBI agent, theorized that Berdella was an egotist, and thought the surroundings should appeal to Berdella's sense of self-importance. A large sign was printed and placed on the door to the squad room, announcing this was the Berdella Squad. The names of dozens of detectives were written on the large blackboard inside the room, all supposedly working on the case, most of them fictional. The photo enlargements were posted on the walls, and separate sets showing head shots of the young men, and scenes of torture in progress, were placed on two easels around the table in the center of the room. Selected books and papers from Berdella's house were brought in and carefully situated. A padded chair where Berdella would sit was placed between two wooden chairs, the padded seat slightly above the wooden seats, so Berdella would be looking down at his inquisitors.

Napier and Perry wanted Berdella to have the impression that this was a totally professional investigation, that he was taken seriously and was believed capable of many things. Build his ego by creating a sense of psychological worthiness, even supremacy, they thought. But at the same time, demonstrate to Berdella that the evidence was voluminous, irrefutable. Realistically, there was no way out. Hurn and Napier would do the talking, they decided. They would subtly inform Berdella of his Miranda rights to an attorney and to be silent, but without doing it Jack Webb style. Then they would try out various scenarios of what might have happened in Berdella's house, hoping Berdella would indicate that one was plausible, that they were on the right track, and then work on him from there.

Hurn made his second trip to the jail that day, along with Napier and Perry, about 2 P.M. Berdella was brought out to them, wearing the dark green clothes and plastic thongs issued to all residents of the county jail. He was handcuffed, placed in the backseat of the car and driven to the squad room. The policemen made small talk about the weather, and asked about Berdella's treatment in the jail. Berdella's answers were short and flat. Hurn couldn't tell how Berdella had been affected by the morning photo session. He told Berdella, "We're taking you to an office away from police headquarters, where we can conduct our investigation more easily, and hopefully provide less embarrassment for you." Berdella nodded.

When they arrived at the normally bustling Agnes building, no traffic cops or civilian employees were in sight. Hurn wanted to give the impression that this was a secure, tight environment, and he had asked the building's regular tenants to avoid the front entrance around 2 P.M. Berdella's handcuffs were removed, and he was led through several doors. At each door, a detective from the squad held the door open and said "Hello, Mr. Berdella," or "Good afternoon, Mr. Berdella." Napier thought this would provide another ego boost to Berdella, and that having detectives at each door would create the illusion of great secrecy.

Berdella saw the sign on the squad room door, with his name in large letters, and his mouth turned up slightly, as if pleased. He walked inside, and stared at the long list of detectives' names. The room was empty, and Hurn and Napier followed Berdella inside. Hurn began to walk around the table in the center of the room.

"You're welcome to look around," Hurn said. "This is where we've been doing our work. Would you like some coffee or some water?"

Berdella grunted "No" and continued to look straight ahead.

"I'm sorry, I didn't hear you," Hurn said, raising his voice to catch Berdella's eye.

Berdella turned and said no again. Hurn was standing by the easel which held the facial photos of the young men, and Berdella looked at them momentarily. As Hurn continued walking around the table, Berdella's eyes followed him until he reached the easel containing the torture photographs. Berdella turned his gaze down to his feet.

Hurn finished his circle of the table and invited Berdella to sit down in the padded chair. He took out a standard police form that detectives fill out, listing personal and biographical data about the subject being questioned. Hurn had already filled in Berdella's name, birthdate, address and social security number. He asked Berdella for his height and weight, and Berdella replied that he was six foot two and weighed two hundred ten pounds.

"Are you single or married?" Hurn asked.

"I'm single," Berdella said.

"Do you have any children?"

Berdella started to become angry. "That's not necessary," he said.

"I just have a few more lines to fill in," Hurn said, "about your marital status, your parents—"

"I don't care to answer those," Berdella said curtly.

Hurn decided not to press further.

Next, Hurn eased into the Miranda warning, in which all police suspects must be advised they do not have to incriminate themselves. "OK, Mr. Berdella," Hurn began, "I'm sure you're aware you've got the right to an attorney, and that you don't have to speak with us if you don't want to. But what we're looking for today is, we just want to share some things with you, run some ideas by you and see what you think."

Berdella was quiet, occasionally glancing around. Mostly his eyes were focused downward. Hurn finished, and Napier began. As Napier spoke, Berdella happened to look at Hurn's right hand. Hurn had done some research into witchcraft, and had spoken several times with an active practitioner. This "white witch" told Hurn that the horns of a ram had special significance in witchcraft, and that if the horns were curled upward, the positive forces would not flow out of the horns. Horns pointing down signified evil. Using upward-curled rams' horns could be a strong defense against a "black witch," Hurn was told, so he asked Detective Lee Floyd to make him such a ring. Floyd did, and Hurn wore it into the interrogation. When Berdella noticed the ring, his eyes opened slightly wider, one foot arched and he curled his toes underneath his feet. Hurn's expression didn't change, and Napier continued speaking to Berdella.

Napier told Berdella that anyone who might have been harmed on Charlotte Street was probably hurt accidentally, that things had simply gotten a little out of control. Berdella didn't make a sound. His gaze came to rest in the middle of the table in front of him.

Hurn started again. "It would be easy for someone who didn't know, who looked at these torture photographs, to make the assessment of this person to be an

129

animal, lower than life, a horrible person. However, the person that would make that judgment would not have had an opportunity to get to know the house where those photos came out of." Berdella remained still.

"Over the last several days," Hurn continued, "we've gone through virtually every piece of paper in your house, and I'm not certain that I see that type of man before me today." Berdella turned and looked at Hurn, saying nothing.

Napier resumed, noting that the investigation showed Berdella was active in his community, in the crime watch, that he had helped young men, that he obviously cared about humanity. Possibly some of the men he encountered were ungrateful, they couldn't accept that Bob was trying to introduce them to responsibility. Berdella was mute.

Hurn tried again. "We don't see you as an individual who would purposely go out of their way to do somebody harm. So there has to be some reason that some of these things happened." An inviting pause, but still no response.

"It's easy to see how someone would feel if he was in your situation. And in this individual situation, he wouldn't have wanted to hurt anybody more than he would want to hurt his own neighbor. Not somebody like James Ferris." They watched Berdella for a twitch, but there was none. He was looking down again.

"This individual wouldn't have wanted to hurt Jerry Howell." For the second time, Berdella's left foot arched, quivering, and he curled his toes in again. He turned to look at Hurn and started to talk, but Hurn cut him off.

"Don't you see what we're trying to do here?"

Berdella looked down and said, "Well you should know what you think you have."

130

Hurn started to respond, but it looked like Berdella wanted to continue. Berdella took a deep breath, then said, "Gentlemen, cut the chitchat. I can appreciate you trying to do your job, but I have no statement to make. I respectfully request my lawyer be present during this questioning."

It was over. No confession today. Hurn and Napier stood up, and Hurn replaced the handcuffs on Berdella's wrists. They walked him back outside to the car, and as they drove to the jail, Berdella was silent. When they arrived, Hurn told Berdella, "You know, you can ask to speak to us at any time, but now that you've requested an attorney, it'll have to be you that makes the contact." Berdella was impassive. "All we know is what we've uncovered. In order for us to conduct a fair investigation, it would be a lot better if we know what your feelings are." Berdella still said nothing, and Hurn turned him over to the jail officers.

Hurn got back in the car, and he, Napier and Perry discussed the session, searching for hints in Berdella's body language or expressions that a nerve had been touched. They agreed that the Howell comment had hit home.

"I think he liked the sign on the door," Napier said.

"Either that or he was sharp enough to recognize what we were doing," Hurn said.

"I think he had already made up his mind to remain silent," Napier said. "After he determined what we were going to do, he was going to invoke his rights."

"I'll be surprised if he calls us," Perry said.

The others nodded in agreement.

Captain Ron Canaday, the head of the Crime Scene

131

Investigations unit, had been placed in charge of searching and securing Berdella's house, and when he realized that it was going to be an enormous undertaking, he assigned two of his detectives—Mel Beverlin and Robert Dodds—to handle and process all the potential evidence. There would still be numerous investigators rummaging through the house, but at a future trial only two people would have to testify, rather than every member of his unit.

Still, no one could stay in the house long. Beverlin injured his leg when a step broke outside the house. Dodds was spooked by the house—he refused to go in alone—and also feared catching a disease. Eventually he asked to be reassigned. In addition, various officers developed what became known as "the Berdella cough," a niggling little half-hack that started in the lower chest. The combination of the dust, the decay and the chlordane seemed to cause the cough, Canaday thought, and so he had to rotate officers in and out of the house for health reasons.

One afternoon early in the search, Beverlin was walking out the back door past a small storage area on Berdella's deck, and he noticed a chain saw sitting on a table. He picked it up and looked at the blade, then peered inside the housing. It looks awful dark in there, he thought, darker than if it was just a lot of oil built up inside. He retrieved his lab kit and pulled out a hemostick. The stick can be a preliminary test for the presence of blood, if it is mixed with distilled water and turns blue. Beverlin poked the stick inside the saw, pulled it out and placed a drop of distilled water on it. Blue. Dark blue. The stick isn't a definitive test, so Beverlin made a note of what he'd found, and took the saw back to the crime lab at the end of the day.

The following week, Cole was sitting in the squad room after Berdella had been returned to the jail. With no confession to wrap things up, it was back to the drudgery of police work. The phone rang, and Cole began speaking with Beverlin's supervisor in the Crime Scene unit, Frank Booth.

"We took a chain saw out of Berdella's house last week. The tests on it shows there's all sorts of human blood, human flesh and pubic hairs inside the housing of the saw. A lot of it," Booth said.

"No shit?"

"No shit."

"This is one grisly son of a bitch, Frank," Cole said.

"Looks like it. Remember that electric transformer on the floor in the torture room?"

"The one that Bryson said he was shocked with?" Cole asked.

"Yeah. We tested it, turns out it puts out 7,700 volts of electricity," Booth said.

Cole whistled. "That's some voltage. Anything else?"

"That's it for now," Booth said.

A chain saw. In a way, it made sense, Cole thought. After completely excavating Berdella's property, the police weren't finding any bodies. Maybe victims had been cut into small pieces, furthering some detectives' theory that they became dinner for Berdella's huge Chow Chow dogs. But Finnegan's examination of at least one of the vertebrae had turned up knife wounds and saw marks, not the power blasting of a chain saw. Booth's revelation, startling at first, was now just another puzzle piece.

Cole called Hall to give him the new information, and they decided to get another search warrant to confiscate every knife or saw blade in the house. Then, possibly, a

133

lab technician could match the width of a particular blade to the width of a cut in the vertebrae. That might become a building block of evidence. The search warrant was quickly assembled, and by the end of the day, the police had removed a circular saw, two hedge clippers, a black ceremonial knife, a pair of scissors, three butcher knives, a set of steak knives, some hand shears, a circular saw, a dismantled saber saw, a hack saw, a miter saw, two box cutters, two wire saber cutters and fourteen saw blades. The building blocks would come slowly.

Meanwhile Cole's detectives were out in the field, trying to develop other building blocks. Families whose sons were missing were sending dental records to the squad, and the detectives were making regular trips to Dr. Ronald Gier's office. Gier, a dentist and professor at the University of Missouri—Kansas City, frequently assisted the police in trying to identify dead bodies through dental records. On this afternoon, Detective Lin Cunningham dropped off one set of records to Dr. Gier, and was informed of Gier's latest finding on two other sets: neither skull matched the dental records of Jerry Howell or James Ferris. Cunningham reported this back to Cole, who half expected it. It would have been too easy, he thought, too soon. Identifying the skulls was back to square one.

Cunningham also spent time that week phoning the recorders of deeds in numerous counties surrounding Kansas City, trying to determine if Berdella owned any land outside the city. He didn't. Cunningham also obtained a subpoena for Berdella's credit records from a local credit bureau, and the bureau turned over a computer printout of Berdella's bank accounts and credit cards. Nothing exceptional there.

Detective Bennie White was assigned to dig out every

police report that ever mentioned Berdella, and there were many. He'd called the police after someone tried to burglarize his house, and again after a Molotov cocktail was tossed at his front door. He'd been cited once for disturbing the peace of Freddie Kellogg, and he'd received summonses for violating dog ordinances. Someone had tried to steal some jewelry from him once. There was a report from the time he'd been punched by Paul Howell Jr. He had been stopped once at 11th and Main Streets in the company of Todd Stoops, "a known male prostitute in the downtown area." And in 1987, Berdella made an assault report from a hospital room after a man named "Larry Person" had bitten his penis during oral sex, causing a serious laceration. The report said Berdella didn't want to prosecute, which led Cole to wonder: Why would he call the police to make such an embarrassing report if he didn't want to prosecute? One of the newspapers had already gotten a copy of the report, and was having fun trying to describe the incident in family terms.

The name Larry Person was new, but Todd Stoops wasn't. He'd been interviewed by Fugitive detectives during the Jerry Howell investigation, and apparently lived with Berdella at one time. While showing copies of the Polaroids to a downtown hustler, one detective was told that one of the men was Stoops. Cole assigned Detectives Bill Wilson and Lin Casebolt to find Stoops, to see what he could add about Berdella, and whether he could identify any of the men in the photos.

Casebolt entered Stoops's name in the police computer and found he had a long record of misdemeanor convictions, including two for "soliciting for immoral purposes," as well as several warrants for failing to appear for various court dates. The computer listed three addresses for Stoops. The detectives visited each of them, with no success. They returned to the squad room, and started calling the few Stoopses listed in the Kansas City phone book. Eventually, they located two brothers of Stoops, and drove out to meet them.

The last time either brother had seen Todd Stoops was in June or July of 1986. This wasn't necessarily unusual. The men told the detectives that Stoops was an intravenous drug addict, and also may have been involved in some homosexual activity. Stoops had moved to Kansas City in the early 1980s from Oklahoma City, after being arrested for pimping and other prostitution-related charges, the brothers said. When he arrived here, he met and then married a young woman named Rachel DeKalb. Neither brother had seen her recently either.

Casebolt pulled out several photos, one of which had already been named by a hustler as Stoops. The men in the photos were naked, apparently asleep, in Berdella's house. The brothers unhesitatingly confirmed that one of them was Todd. Before the detectives left, they asked the men if Stoops had had any dental work done, and the brothers said they would check. If Stoops wasn't just missing, perhaps he was one of the skulls that had been found at Berdella's house.

Next, the detectives tried to locate Rachel DeKalb. They called in her name to a dispatcher, and received an address. They drove there, but got no answer. They left a business card, and went back to the squad room to report their findings.

The following day, Wilson and Casebolt located DeKalb's mother. She hadn't seen Rachel in four or five years, though she had gotten letters from her daughter, from Massachusetts, until about two years ago. Mrs. DeKalb said she would try to find the last address she had

136

for Rachel. The detectives then drove to police headquarters to pick up a mugshot photograph of Rachel, but her convictions were closed records, and under Missouri law the police records unit couldn't give the detectives a photo.

From Stoops's brothers, the detectives had gotten a phone number for Stoops's parents. Casebolt called them, and the parents agreed to drive down to the squad room the next day. Mr. Stoops had last seen his son in the spring of 1985, jogging in the midtown area. They'd last spoken by phone in the summer of 1984, and Todd said he'd been back to Oklahoma. That was about it. Stoops had little contact with his family. Mr. Stoops said his son had been in the army in 1981, and he would try to get dental records there. Then, the parents were shown the photograph that Stoops's brothers had identified as Todd. They agreed it was Todd. The detectives thanked them. Of all the men the squad had tried to locate so far, Stoops was the first one they couldn't track down.

The police would later learn that Stoops had met Berdella in the spring of 1984, at the corner of 10th and McGee. Stoops was muscular, attractive, twenty-one years old, and heavily hooked on "1 and 1s," an injected mixture of Ritalin and Talwin. He needed a fix badly that night, and decided to do a little hustling to raise the cash. Berdella drove up, and Stoops told him he'd do anything for thirteen dollars. Berdella took Stoops to a drug house. Stoops bought the drugs, then went back to Berdella's house and shot up. A few days later, needing a place to stay, Stoops agreed to provide his services in exchange for a room for himself and Rachel.

Berdella tried to encourage Todd and Rachel to find a job, to kick their drug habits, but neither did much

137

more than loiter around Berdella's living room watching television and smoking pot. Berdella would find them standing downtown late at night and try to get them off the streets, but Todd and Rachel were both addicted, and could see little reason to change their ways. About six weeks after they'd moved into Charlotte Street, Todd and Rachel moved out.

Three weeks later, in June 1984, Todd was arrested downtown for carrying a concealed weapon and scuffling with an officer. The next morning, in Municipal Court, he pleaded guilty. Before Stoops was sentenced, Berdella approached Judge Marcia Walsh and asked if Stoops could be released to his custody. Walsh looked over Stoops's record and sentenced him to one to three months in jail. However, she also added two years probation, with Berdella as the probation supervisor. Stoops was taken to the Municipal Farm for a month, and when he was released in July, he and Rachel moved back in with Berdella.

Stoops's probation officer, Betty Lincoln, made a note to herself to find out what type of drug counseling was planned by "Dr. Berdella," and later she sent a letter to "Dr. Berdella." By the time Berdella received the letter, he had already resumed feuding with the Stoops over their habits. He called Lincoln and told her that he was not a drug counselor, "only an interested person trying to keep Mr. Stoops off the streets," but that he had been unsuccessful. Berdella again had kicked the Stoops out of his house, and hadn't heard from them in more than a week, he told Lincoln. Several months later, at Lincoln's request, Judge Walsh removed her stipulation that Stoops receive drug counseling from Berdella.

Berdella didn't see Stoops again for almost two years, until June 17, 1986, when he spotted Stoops one morning at the Liberty Memorial Park, then a hangout for the city's young homosexuals. Stoops climbed into Berdella's car about 11:30 A.M., and when Berdella invited him home for lunch, Stoops gladly accepted. No one had seen Stoops since then.

While Casebolt and Wilson were interviewing Stoops's parents, Berdella was making his second appearance in court, to be arraigned on the grand jury indictment on several counts of forcible sodomy, one count of felonious restraint and one count of first-degree assault. He was surrounded by four jail guards, and a lawyer from the public defender's office stood next to him. Parker, the prosecutor, sat at the table behind him.

"Have you hired a lawyer yet?" asked Circuit Judge Alvin Randall.

"I've been trying, Your Honor," Berdella said, "but it's my understanding that my assets have been frozen."

Parker stood and said that wasn't true. He still had his car and his shop.

"How much is your shop worth?" the judge inquired.

"About fifteen to twenty-five thousand dollars," Berdella said, "but considerably less if it's liquidated quickly."

"Do you have any cash or savings?"

"No," Berdella answered. "All my money is tied up in inventory."

Randall decided to appoint the public defender to represent Berdella for three weeks, until the question of whether he could afford a private attorney could be answered. The judge scheduled a hearing on the prosecutor's motion to seize the house, and told the police to catalog everything taken from the house and give Berdella a receipt.

An assistant public defender, Kent Gipson, then asked

Randall to set a bond for Berdella. Parker opposed this and called Detective Hurn to the stand. Hurn testified about the skulls and the photographs, and Randall needed to hear little else before denying Berdella bond. Berdella returned to his cell in the jail's medical unit and decided he didn't want to be present for any more of these ceremonies. He wouldn't appear in the courthouse again for months.

Chapter Seven

Berdella couldn't sleep. With no opportunity to post bond, he realized he was going to be spending months, perhaps more than a year, in the county jail. Motions, depositions, hearings, trials. It could be endless. Berdella paced restlessly in his small cell, in an environment over which he had no control, and now he couldn't even control when he would or would not sleep. Sleeping pills were added to his regimen of medications. Still, when breakfast was delivered at 5 A.M., Berdella was ready.

Being taken to a first floor visiting room was one of Berdella's respites from the medical unit. His regular visitors were his lawyers: Pender for his civil matters, and public defenders Patrick Berrigan and Barbara Schenkenberg, who would finally represent him on the sodomy charges. Berdella also saw a jail chaplain, but felt the chaplain was judgmental of him, and was reluctant to open up. A social worker met regularly with Berdella, but seemed interested only in finding out about the crimes, Berdella thought. Another person he couldn't talk to.

Two people he looked forward to seeing were the Reverend Roger Coleman and Dr. William O'Connor, a psychologist hired by the public defenders to begin examining Berdella's mental state. O'Connor had done extensive research on violent behavior, and beginning in late April he met once or twice a week with Berdella, probing delicately into Berdella's childhood and adolescence. Berdella respected O'Connor's professionalism and intellect and answered the psychologist's questions honestly and candidly. Sitting in his cell for hour after silent hour, Berdella frequently wondered how he had gotten here. Intellectually, he was curious to see if O'Connor could provide some answers.

Also in late April, Coleman began visiting Berdella twice weekly, on Tuesday afternoons and Friday mornings. Berrigan laid out the ground rules before granting Coleman permission to speak with his new client: no discussion of the crimes or details of the crimes, and no talking about the meetings to his family, the police, the media, anyone. Coleman's role was to be more therapeutic than forensic, to provide Berdella with an outlet for his thoughts and fears.

When Coleman first saw Berdella in jail, Berdella was trembling, his eyes watering. He was anxious to convince Coleman that he wasn't a monster, but "a neighbor who had done some monstrous things." The media were making it seem like crime and satanic worship were his daily avocations, when actually he'd lapsed into certain actions only occasionally. Berdella was grappling internally to reclaim his identity as a good person, a difficult task in jail.

Coleman would write notes on a legal pad before visiting Berdella, a miniagenda of sorts, and then enter the jail through a back door to avoid attention. Berdella's moods varied drastically. Some days he was up, other days he was depressed. In their early meetings, Berdella wondered constantly about his future. The public defenders continued the battle to have a bond set for Berdella. He wasn't charged with Murder One, the only "no bond-able" offense, they argued. Could he get out on bond until the trial? If he did, where would he go? Coleman and his family considered letting him stay at their house. And what about the trial? It was Berdella's word against Bryson's. Maybe he could beat it. He was clever, Berdella thought, a hell of a lot more clever than the police. They'll screw it up somehow.

Coleman was more concerned with Berdella's spiritual status than his defense strategy, which he wasn't supposed to be hearing too much about anyway. He steered the conversations toward Berdella's self-esteem, his emotions. He found Berdella saw himself as a kind, helpful person. Someone who reached out to people, only to have them take advantage of him. He talked about the positive things he'd done, the places he'd visited, his family in Ohio, his schooling. He was sensitive, aware. There just wasn't any way he saw himself as capable of what they said he'd done, or what crimes the papers were implying he'd committed. No way.

The urge to confront Berdella, to challenge him, occurred to Coleman. But Coleman decided that wasn't his role. He was there as a minister, to help Berdella as he struggled along. Berdella could be indignant one moment. But, if Coleman offered a supportive response, he would suddenly become emotional, his eyes watering. Berdella also was concerned about his survival, his day-to-day jail existence, his drastic shift from freedom to regimentation. The social worker had told Berdella to control the things he could, and leave the rest alone. Coleman endorsed that idea.

But not having control of all the elements in his life disturbed Berdella. Friends and business associates knew that Berdella liked things to be orderly, that he expected people to keep their word. He was punctual and fair with those who treated him the same. They knew he was cynical, with a sardonic sense of humor, to be expected of a college student from the late sixties. He enjoyed stimulating conversation, and could be condescending or arrogant with those he felt were beneath him intellectually. That arrogance could extend to a lack of courtesy or respect, many said. "He was lacking in social skills," said Douglas Mac-Farlane, another longtime acquaintance. But how lacking? Lacking like a felon? A murderer? The friends and neighbors discussed it, horrified, for months. Berdella knew it was all a surprise to his associates; he had done an excellent job of concealing certain aspects of his life. Now he also wanted to know why those aspects existed. The scientist in him wanted someone to develop theories or write scholarly papers. He would have to be studied, he thought, perhaps for years and years. He was a sociological mutation. Berdella was ready to assist in the research.

The drab suits and conservative haircuts wordlessly announced "police" as the two detectives entered one gay bar after another. Detectives Albert DeValkenaere and Guy Livingston would walk to the bar, ask for the manager, then slowly glance around, squinting in the darkness. Invariably, the bars were windowless, clean, decorated with photos or drawings of muscular, sweaty men. A manager would emerge and take the investigators to a back office, where DeValkenaere and Livingston would pull out a sheaf of Berdella's photographs for possible identification. Sometimes the manager would call in an employee or regular customer for assistance while perusing the photos. Though some recognized Berdella, and all had heard of him by now, each manager handed the photos back apologetically. When the detectives reappeared in the bar area, the customers had cleared out. The pattern continued through the night.

DeValkenaere and Livingston also approached the hustlers at 10th and McGee, and later at the Liberty Memorial. Where normally the sight of police in these areas caused the young men to scatter, the opportunity to see some of these highly publicized photos drew a small crowd. But on this night, no one could match any names to the faces.

The photos on the wall of the police squad room no longer repulsed any of the detectives. Actually, they were growing weary of being surrounded by them. Names were placed beneath the enlargements of the men who had been identified, but several had more than one name, when different witnesses provided different identifications. Officer Steve Warlen at the crime lab had spent more than a week just staring at the photos, trying to place them in groups or figure out now many different individuals there were. One group of photos had dates from "6/22" to "7/2" written on the back, some with times as well. Warlen put those together. By using the Polaroid coding numbers on the back, he figured that certain other shots also were taken about the same time. Warlen also tried to find tattoos, scars or other body markings to match photos of the same person.

Shuffling through a total of 334 Polaroids and 34 snapshot prints, Warlen theorized that there were twenty different men who appeared to be unconscious, asleep, or dead. He sorted these into envelopes. A twenty-first packet contained people who were awake or posing for the camera. Since some of the men in the photos had identifiable scars or tattoos, Cole had parts of those photos enlarged, to see if the same marks could be found in other pictures.

Reading Warlen's memo, Cole thought Berdella was very well capable of close to twenty murders. "These son-of-a-bitches are dead," Cole told his squad one morning, surrounded by the gallery of photos. "We've just got to find out where they are. We've got to identify every single one of these guys, that's our number one objective right now. Positive IDs for every photograph." The detectives took several approaches: simply showing the photos to people on the streets and in gay bars, as DeValkenaere and Livingston were doing; locating someone whose name was scrawled somewhere in Berdella's house, and showing the photos to them; or showing the photos to people who were definitely friends or former roommates of Berdella. Men such as Kellogg, Simmons and Bukovic had already provided some names. Finding those people, in turn, often produced more identifications.

To find some men, the detectives had to travel. One name that had popped up several times was Lamar Rich, who appeared to be posing for Berdella in several shots. Detective Clarence Luther typed Rich's name into the police computer and found he'd been arrested in Council Bluffs, Iowa, for attempted murder. Rich seemed to be about the best-known of the street hustlers, so Cole sent Luther and Detective Bennie White to Iowa. The detectives made the four-hour drive, and Rich agreed to talk so long as the room wasn't "bugged." Rich said he supported himself by hustling, and if he was going to the penitentiary, he didn't want the word out that he was "a faggot."

Rich had met Berdella about five years earlier. Berdella was cruising the downtown strip, picked up Rich and took him back to his house for sex. Rich made several subsequent visits, and also posed for photos, for which Berdella paid him. He never injected any drugs at Berdella's house, Rich said, and was unaware of any torture or killing going on there, though he said Berdella once wanted him to kill Freddie Kellogg. He added that there were several hustlers he knew that were missing from downtown, and he named Jerry Howell, James Ferris and Todd Stoops.

Luther brought out a set of photos and showed them to Rich. He correctly picked out Stoops, Kellogg, Blankenship and several others he knew as hustlers, but not by

146

name. Rich told the detectives he hadn't seen Berdella in about a year, ever since Berdella tape-recorded a phone call Rich made from Berdella's house to a Kansas City narcotics detective, "snitching off" a drug dealer. Berdella then spread the word that Rich was a police informant, Rich said. Because of that, Rich said he would gladly provide information on Berdella too.

Rich's voice speaking to a narcotics detective was on one of the many audiotapes that police had found in Berdella's house. Berdella had apparently taped many phone conversations over the years, and Hurn now spent hours listening to them for hints about activity in the house. As often as not, an unfamiliar male voice was as likely as Berdella to be on the tape, calling a girlfriend or a parent. Twice, Hurn found, angry customers who had bought something from Berdella called his answering machine to claim they were ripped off.

One live conversation Berdella had was a discussion with a man about attending a pagan festival. Hurn passed this tape on to Detective Cunningham, who recognized the voice on the other end. It was a man she'd investigated in the past, an acknowledged witchcraft practitioner, who had his own shop in the Westport area. Cunningham had already visited the man one afternoon at his shop, and he flatly denied knowing Berdella or ever speaking with him.

Cunningham returned to the shop, and the man renewed his denials. Cunningham played the tape for him. The man reluctantly admitted it must be his voice on the tape, but he said he didn't know whom he was speaking with. The man told Cunningham he was a witch, and if Berdella were a witch, he would know about it. Cunningham decided not to pressure him further, and left the shop.

Back at the squad room, Detectives Eikel and Dan Wilson were talking with Hamp Reichler and his girlfriend. Reichler's name appeared on a strange police report Berdella made in May 1987, in which Berdella complained about having some jewelry stolen, and then included a typed, signed confession of the theft by Reichler. The detectives thought Reichler might be a candidate for the list of missing people last seen with Berdella, but they located him by phone and he volunteered to come down and talk.

While the detectives waited for Reichler, Eikel started working on another name from a Berdella police report, Larry Person, the man Berdella claimed had bitten him last August during oral sex. Eikel sat at a police computer terminal and tapped in Person's name. No record. He tried "Larry Pierson." Nothing. He entered "Larry Pearson." The screen flashed back. A Larry Pearson was arrested last June at the Liberty Memorial for indecent exposure, and he had missed his court date in August. There was no address listed for Pearson, and no Larry Pearson in the phone book. Eikel then entered a "pick up" for Pearson in the computer; if any officer encountered Pearson, he was to be invited to the Berdella squad for questioning.

Reichler arrived, and Eikel and Wilson began another interview. Reichler said he met Berdella in April 1987 through his brother, Russell, to do odd jobs around Berdella's house, such as cleaning out the dog pens. "See anything unusual in the pens?" Eikel asked. Just bones and dog feces, Reichler said. "What kind of bones?" Eikel wondered. Just dinner bones, Reichler replied. Reichler continued, saying Berdella frequently asked him if he'd like to stay the night, or be tied up for sex, but Reichler refused. Berdella, in turn, stalled on paying Reichler for his chores, so Reichler stole some of Berdella's jewelry. Berdella found out, and typed up a confession, which Reichler signed. With this in hand, Berdella demanded Reichler move in with him, or he would turn the confession over to the police. Reichler moved in, but con-

148

tinued resisting Berdella's advances.

Reichler often would flee to his girlfriend's house in Independence, where Berdella would later show up and threaten to press charges for the stealing. Several weeks later, Berdella did go into a police station and file a complaint, and Reichler was arrested in June. Reichler ended up being sentenced to time in the municipal farm, and hadn't seen Berdella since. Reichler looked at a stack of photographs, but didn't see his brother Russell or anyone else he recognized.

Reichler's girlfriend told much the same story to Wilson. She said Berdella was jealous of her, that he "wanted Hamp for himself." Berdella told her he would call the state's Division of Family Services and have her children taken away if she didn't leave Reichler, she said. When Wilson pulled out the photos, the woman identified Lamar Rich and said several others looked familiar, but didn't know their names. She said her brother, Greg Schayes, was a former hustler and he could identify them.

Two more people to track down: Greg Schayes and Russell Reichler. It seemed like every person they found gave them two more people to find, the detectives thought. Wilson and DeValkenaere eventually located Russell Reichler at a trailer park near Fort Smith, Arkansas, and drove down to interview him. Reichler said he used to hustle at 10th and McGee, but never was picked up by Berdella. He said he would sometimes call Berdella and ask for a ride or some money, but would never give Berdella anything in return. Reichler said he couldn't pick out anyone in the photos, and DeValkenaere glared at him suspiciously. This guy's holding back, he thought. Or lying.

Hamp Reichler said his brother was a friend of Berdella's; Russell Reichler said he didn't know him that well. It was obvious that neither man wanted to be associated with such a high-profile criminal case. If Berdella really was a devil worshiper, they feared what he might do to them. If he was a serial killer, but was never convicted, he could seek revenge on them for providing information. Similar thoughts passed through the minds of nearly every witness police interviewed. It was up to Cole and Hall to sift through the various stories the detectives were told, and try to pluck out the strands of truth.

DeValkenaere received another travel assignment after locating Greg Schayes in the state penitentiary at Jefferson City, Missouri. DeValkenaere made the two-hour trip to the prison, and learned that Schayes was assigned to the AIDS ward. Before he was let out of his cell, his entire floor was locked down. DeValkenaere, picturing a withered, helpless inmate, was puzzled. He watched a strong, angry-looking inmate ask a guard, "Why you locking us down?" The guard said, " 'Cause we're letting Schayes out." The inmate instantly darted for his cell without another word. The entire ward cleared quickly.

Two guards walked Schayes out of his cell. He was one of the largest human beings DeValkenaere had ever seen, about six feet six inches tall and weighing maybe 275 pounds. Schayes was cooperative with DeValkenaere once they sat down, though he didn't know much. He remembered Berdella, and that Berdella had threatened his sister and her children. Schayes, in turn, went to the Flea Market and told Berdella if he made such a threat again, Schayes would blow his head off. DeValkenaere showed Schayes a pile of Berdella's photos, but Schayes couldn't come up with any names.

The mundane detective work of gathering more information on Berdella was producing stacks of reports, but no real answers. Cole continued to take the reports home at night, spending hours in his basement reading them, making notes on what needed to be done next. Then the reports were photocopied and passed on to the prosecutors, who were astounded by the volumes of paper the police were generating.

Dozens of tasks had to be performed which led to dead ends. One detective was assigned to obtain Berdella's long distance phone records over the last several years, to see if any patterns could be discerned. None could. Citizens who bought skulls from Berdella were bringing them in for examination, and every one had to be taken to an expert. One turned out to be real, but was a relic. More acquaintances of Berdella were interviewed, including a man who told of Berdella's membership in the local culinary association, and Berdella's familiarity with boning and slicing up large sides of beef. Anxious parents of missing men brought in dental records, which were then taken to Dr. Gier's office for comparison with the two skulls. Included in this group were the parents of Todd Stoops, who had located Stoops' dental charts. Gier ruled him out too.

Locating men who had once lived with Berdella was important, the police thought. Some had been found, such as Kellogg and Simmons, who told of other boarders. For several weeks, the squad had been unable to find one of these housemates, Taylor Gallup. In late April, Gallup suddenly appeared on television—in Las Vegas. Gallup had moved there, and when the news reached him in Nevada, he approached a television station and presented himself as a survivor of Bob Berdella. After the interview aired, the Las Vegas police questioned Gallup, but Cole thought he should have someone more familiar with the case try to work something out of Gallup, so he dispatched Detective Luther to Las Vegas.

By the time Luther had flown to Las Vegas, Gallup had given another television interview, speaking mysteriously about the chain saws Berdella owned. Gallup's story was less sensational when he told it to Luther. He had never actually seen anyone killed or cut up with a chain saw. Gallup spoke of living with Berdella sporadically since 1983. Another man, Hunter Gill, also lived there at one time, but he tried to slit his wrists in Berdella's house, was taken to a mental hospital, and never seen again, Gallup said. Berdella told Gallup that Gill had run off with a circus. Gallup also said he'd seen young gay men being injected with drugs by Berdella, and that more than a dozen gays were "regulars" in Berdella's house. Gallup said he was last kicked out of the house by Berdella in August 1987.

Luther brought out his set of photos, and Gallup found himself in several. Luther asked Gallup about the track marks on his arms, clearly visible in the photos. Gallup told him Berdella must have injected him while he was sleeping. Luther inquired why, if people were being tortured or killed while Gallup was there, wouldn't Gallup know about it? Gallup said he was an alcoholic, and was prone to "memory lapses." Later, Gallup allowed that he was holding back his most important information to make "big money" on a book he was planning to write. Gallup's credibility suddenly plunged.

Gallup was both helpful and obstinate, and when Luther returned and compared notes with the squad, it turned out Gallup was at least partly accurate. Kellogg had mentioned a Hunter Gill living with Berdella in the early eighties and when Hurn located Gill several days later, it turned out he had joined a circus. Gill remembered Berdella as temperamental, but someone who seemed truly interested in helping young people get back on their feet.

Cole's squad was slowly working its way through the long list of names linked to Berdella. The detectives were finding most of them, though a few were proving difficult. The fact that many of Berdella's younger friends had regular contact with the law, and thus had updated addresses entered into the police computer, was useful. The next two subjects were Greg Leinenkamp and Robert Sheldon, both former friends of Kellogg's. Kellogg was positive Leinenkamp was the man hanging upside down in Berdella's basement, and Sheldon was another ex-housemate of Berdella's. Cole handed both tasks to Detective Lin Casebolt, nicknamed "Pappy" both for his senior status in the robbery unit and his deliberate manner.

Casebolt couldn't find Leinenkamp in the police computer, the phone book or the city directory, and Leinenkamp didn't have a state driver's license. He asked Napier to use the FBI's national resources to see if he could come up with a location for Leinenkamp. Napier came back with a printout showing that Leinenkamp had a police record in Louisiana dating back to April 1984, with arrests for vehicular homicide, driving under the influence and burglary. The most recent arrest was in October 1987.

Napier tracked down Leinenkamp's father in Pennsylvania. The father hadn't seen his son in three years. He gave Napier a current phone number and address. Napier then called the FBI field office in Louisiana, and asked them to contact Leinenkamp. An agent later visited Leinenkamp, who said he hadn't been to Kansas City in years, and had never lived with Berdella. He also had never been hung upside down by his ankles in Berdella's basement. Kellogg's identification was wrong.

Casebolt and Detective Bill Wilson also started trying to find Robert Sheldon, who had met Berdella through Kellogg. Sheldon had two Kansas City addresses listed in the computer: 4315 Charlotte and 4245 Locust. The Charlotte entry had been made in February 1985. 4245 Locust did not exist. Sheldon had made two police reports, one for robbery and one for assault. Casebolt pulled copies of the reports, and found that Sheldon listed a "friend" named Merrick Villaj. Casebolt tried her name in the computer. Again, two addresses. The first was a used car lot. The

153

second was 4201 Locust.

Casebolt drove to the apartment building at 4201 Locust, where no one named Villaj was listed. Casebolt jotted down the phone number of the building manager, and called it when he got back to the squad room. An answering machine. The detective left a message, and the next day, the building manager called. Villaj had lived at 4201 Locust, and Sheldon was one of her roommates. They had moved out in July 1984, still owing rent, the manager said. The manager did, however, keep some papers he found in the apartment, including a health card issued to Sheldon for a job at a restaurant in Las Vegas, and a receipt for emergency treatment from the University of Kansas Medical Center. The receipt listed a "Kim Bland" as Sheldon's "closest relative," and a phone number for Bland. Casebolt called the number; the person answering had never heard of Bland.

Casebolt finally located Merrick Villaj, in Springfield, Missouri. Villaj wasn't talkative, but she said she hadn't seen Sheldon in more than two years.

In fact, no one had seen Sheldon during that time. The same day Casebolt found Villaj, he interviewed Jeb Marcus, a veteran hustler who was in jail on an unrelated case. When Casebolt showed Marcus the standard group of photos, Marcus recognized Sheldon's face. Though he didn't know Sheldon's name, he said he had last seen him at 10th and McGee with Bob Berdella, and hadn't seen him since.

Marcus also said his brother, Geoff, used to live with Berdella, and had warned Jeb to stay away from Berdella because he'd become "dangerous," though he didn't explain why. Geoff later told Jeb he'd seen Berdella performing sex acts on unwilling young men who had been injected with drugs, though the men were never beaten or injured. Jeb Marcus then related his own story of encountering Berdella in a bar, and leaving to take a ride with him. When the two men reached Liberty Memorial Park, Marcus claimed that Berdella started to try to tie him up inside the car. Marcus fought him off and leapt from the car, and Berdella reportedly yelled, "I'll see you again." Casebolt was growing dubious of Marcus by now, and sent him back upstairs to the jail.

Running out of leads on Sheldon, Casebolt decided to visit the apartment manager who had kept Sheldon's health card and hospital receipt. As he drove toward the manager's office, Casebolt pondered what steps he might take next. Few people in Kansas City seemed to really know Sheldon. As it turned out, that was because Sheldon grew up in California. When he was eighteen, he left home. He worked for a time at the Frontier Hotel and Casino in Las Vegas, then moved to Kansas City in the spring of 1983. Looking for a way to make some money, Sheldon entered a thirty-day program at the Quincy Research Center, which sought volunteers to participate in medical experiments.

At the same time, Berdella told Freddie Kellogg and Foster Simmons about Quincy, and they enrolled in the program. Kellogg and Simmons met Sheldon, and introduced him to Berdella when Berdella came to visit. After the thirty-day program ended, a group of participants decided to celebrate by staging a party at Berdella's house. Though Berdella didn't know everyone there, he agreed to inject some Thorazine into anyone who wanted to try it. Kellogg apparently had been advertising it to the guests, and Sheldon was willing to experiment. The shot knocked Sheldon to his knees, and he was carried to a bed to sleep the rest of the night.

Sheldon ended up staying at Berdella's house for the rest of the week, sometimes hanging out with Greg Leinenkamp, another volunteer from the Quincy program.

Sheldon moved around the city after that, sometimes living with girlfriends such as Villaj, but occasionally staying with Berdella for brief periods. Sheldon never had a sexual relationship with Berdella, and Berdella never pursued one. But when Sheldon was drinking, Berdella would become impatient and annoyed with him, usually asking him to move out. Sometimes, Berdella and Kellogg would see Sheldon hustling at 10th and McGee, but when they stopped to talk to him, Sheldon was so high that he barely made sense.

After Sheldon met Villaj, he began to settle down somewhat. In the winter of 1985, he got a job doing manual labor at a manufacturing plant in Kansas City, Kansas. His supervisors gave him satisfactory evaluations so long as he showed up on time. The supervisors wrote that incidents outside of work, such as a bar fight which caused Sheldon to be hospitalized and miss some work, needed to be reduced. Still, Sheldon had started to establish a future for himself. He worked steadily through March and April, then suddenly didn't show up for work on April 11 or April 12. A paycheck for the previous work period awaited him, but Sheldon never picked it up.

Detective Eikel thought he had something. During an interview with a college friend of Berdella's, the friend mentioned that Berdella would sometimes visit her at her farm south of Kansas City. Maybe this was the farm where Berdella was burying his victims. Eikel asked if she would show the detectives the farm, and the woman agreed. Eikel and Dan Wilson drove there one afternoon, and toured the mostly undeveloped acres on foot. While walking along a dry creek bed, Eikel spotted several bones sticking out of the mud. He moved closer. They looked human. Wilson agreed. Eikel hurried back to the farmhouse to call Cole to notify the crime scene experts.

In addition to notifying Gary Howell at the crime lab, who rounded up an evidence technician, Cole told Captain Winston that this could be the breakthrough they were looking for. Winston notified his boss, Major Elmer Meyer. A caravan of unmarked cars soon was speeding south, hopeful of the biggest development in the case since the skull in the backyard was found nearly three weeks before.

When Cole and the others arrived, Eikel was waiting for them. So was a large, mud-covered dog who lived on the farm. Apparently recognizing the highest ranking officer, the dog raced past Cole and Winston and immediately leapt on Meyer, badly soiling his freshly pressed suit.

As the group walked toward the creek bed, they could see Wilson's arm, holding a stick, thrashing up and down. Another dog was tugging away at the new evidence, and Wilson was trying desperately to scare the dog away. Howell and Beverlin from the crime lab climbed down into the creek bed and started digging around the bones. After a couple of minutes, Howell glanced up at Eikel. He dug some more, then abruptly pulled out a large chunk of bone.

"Tom, I think you've found us a cow.

Cole burst out laughing, and Howell could no longer keep a straight face either. Eikel had discovered the pelvis of a cow. Cole scooped up some of the bones, and the next day hung them on the squad room wall, where they stayed for the rest of the investigation.

However, the squad had located two more farms in the same general vicinity. Since Berdella visited all three, all three would have to be checked out. First, Dan Wilson took a ride in the police helicopter, taking aerial photos of the farms. Then Cole sought out the best body-sniffing dog he could find. The farms were too large to simply start digging around haphazardly, and dogs specially trained to detect the scent of human remains might give the police a starting point. After speaking with several local animal experts, Cole found that "Junior" was the dog he wanted. Junior, who lived in Texas, was legendary for sniffing out corpses through deep water and thick soil, Cole was told.

Cole phoned the Texas Department of Corrections, and spoke with Sergeant Billy Smith. Smith said he'd be glad to come up to Missouri if his expenses were paid. Unfortunately, Smith couldn't fly to Kansas City because no airline would allow Junior to ride in the passenger cabin with Smith. Smith also could only stay in hotels that would allow Junior to sleep in the same room with him. Cole's eyebrows raised, but he told Smith to come ahead.

Smith actually brought two dogs, but Junior was his ace. When Cole told Smith there were about forty-five total acres to be searched, Smith asked that other dogs be brought in to help, so Cole located two more dog handlers in Kansas. On April 26, the dogs crisscrossed the three farms, through woods and open fields, around the houses and barns. Still nothing.

The next day, Smith and Junior were taken to 4315 Charlotte Street. Junior seemed more excited than the day before, and as Smith followed his dog up the steps to the house he said grimly, "Junior smells death. The smell of death is strong around here." The policemen looked at the portly dog handler with "LOVE" and "HATE" tattooed across his knuckles, as if he were a voodoo doctor. When Smith pulled out a small Tupperware container with human flesh inside, to remind Junior what he was looking for, the police were truly unnerved.

Outside Berdella's main chimney, Junior began yelping ferociously. In the backyard, around Berdella's toolshed, Junior again detected traces of humanity. The Kansas dogs were brought in to provide a second opinion, and they too "alerted" on the chimney and the toolshed. The next day, the police completely excavated the chimney, both inside and outside, and opened up a huge crater where the toolshed once stood. Some teeth under the shed, later determined to be old dentures, were the only discovery.

The squad's frustration was increasing. They'd been at it almost four weeks and still hadn't identified either skull. The case file was four volumes thick and still growing, but they didn't have a single witness who'd actually seen Berdella hurt anyone, or anyone who even had any solid knowledge that Berdella was doing so. The physical evidence of murder was purely circumstantial—the blood and flesh on the chain saw, the photos of men who were missing—and would prove little in court. Hurn and several other detectives were having trouble sleeping some nights, discouraged that they hadn't made a murder case, anxious that they might never.

At times, the case felt hopeless to Cole, especially after Howell and Ferris were ruled out as the two skulls. "If this guy's killing people, where are the bodies?" he asked the squad one afternoon.

"I still think the dogs got 'em," Eikel said. "He used the chain saw to cut 'em up, and fed 'em to the Chows." Several other detectives nodded in assent.

"Then why didn't we find anything in those pens?" Cole asked. No one could answer that one.

"What's our cause of death?" Cole said next. "The lab said the cut marks on the vertebrae came after death, so he couldn't have killed them by cutting their heads off."

"Maybe they overdosed on Thorazine," one detective volunteered.

"Maybe he strangled 'em, that wouldn't show up on the bones," said another.

"Maybe he stabbed 'em, and we'll find the stab wounds on the body."

159

"A defense attorney is going to tear a bunch of 'maybes' to shit."

"Yeah, they'll say anybody coulda put that skull in the yard."

"Or else Berdella bought 'em from someone at the Flea Market."

"We don't have a motive either."

Cunningham, brought in expressly to investigate the satanic aspect of Berdella, thought the motive could be linked to ritual or witchcraft killing, but she was reluctant to join the discussion. She felt the others had discarded that option, and they didn't want to waste any more time with it. Cunningham wondered, Why would Berdella have all that satanic stuff in the house if he wasn't at least dabbling? She called an expert in Florida and told him about the buried bird feathers, and the expert said it sounded like Berdella was mixing-and-matching his evil rituals. Hurn, separately, agreed but also didn't say anything aloud.

Cole wanted to focus on proving a murder first, regardless of what Berdella had done before or after the crime. After talking with Pat Hall, he told the squad, one possible trail would be to have the skulls and tissue chemically analyzed. A laboratory might be able to discern the presence of a lethal amount of one of the drugs Berdella had in his house. If the detectives could then identify that skull, determine that Berdella had pictures of this person being tortured, and get friends to identify the pictures, there might be a case. Might.

At the prosecutor's office, the frustration was growing also. Hall was beginning to think that the sodomy case would be the only case the police could make against Berdella. He met with Gary Howell of the crime lab and discussed ways to develop physical evidence of a homicide. Howell suggested sending the skulls and tissue to the St. Louis crime lab, which has one of the most extensive forensic toxicology units in the country, and Hall told him to do so. Cole sent along copies of Berdella's logs, and a list of the drugs found in the house, in case Berdella's abbreviations correlated with the drugs. Howell also mentioned DNA testing, in which cells could be genetically typed from different sources to see if a match could be made. Perhaps matching blood cells from the chain saw and bone cells from the vertebrae would provide a link.

The pressure was starting to mount on the prosecutors as well as the police. Holtsclaw, Parker and Hall were constantly asked about Berdella. The most frequent question was: "When are you going to charge him with murder?" The prosecutors pondered a dilemma; with such a heinous criminal in their midst, should they file murder eventually, even if they weren't sure they could prove it? Riederer decided no. He told Hall not to hurry, but to bring him a murder case as soon as he could.

Hall disliked the pressure of high profile cases, and he especially disliked this one. Normally, he was presented with a gang member who had taken a shotgun blast in his stomach, several witnesses, and a young suspect with easily traced motives. He had none of that here. He also had to deal with the public defender's office, which had already begun its counteroffensive on the prosecutors by appealing Berdella's "no bond" situation to the state appeals court. It was only Hall's second appearance before the appeals court in seventeen years as a prosecutor, but it was the first of many side battles he would fight with Berdella's lawyers in the coming months.

So Hall dug in. His tenacious nature was well-known around the courthouse, and his trial preparation was even more meticulous than usual. He stayed in his tiny office many nights until midnight, sifting through police interviews and lab reports. He answered calls from the squad at all hours, both at home and in his office. He curtly fended off the news media. Still, the furious pace never slackened.

Hall, thirty-seven, was a Kansas City, North native who went to St. Pius X High School and then the University of Missouri-Kansas City for both undergraduate and law school studies. He first joined the prosecutor's office in 1973 as a law school intern, then was hired as an assistant in 1975. He left prosecuting for a year in 1985, but was back working for Riederer in 1986. Policemen liked Hall because they knew he was intense, highly disciplined, always well-prepared. Defense attorneys and witnesses were sometimes less admiring. Hall's courtroom manner was stern, unrelenting and humorless. He argued even the smallest motions with an almost vicious fervor. He was also very successful.

Riederer inevitably turned to Hall to handle the toughest murder cases. Hall was reliable. Riederer knew Hall would devote himself utterly to each case, whether it was a stabbing in the projects, or a serial killer. Except that Kansas City had never prosecuted a serial killer before. Everything about the Bob Berdella case was new to Hall. He didn't like that either.

Chapter Eight

As April drew to a close, there were still roughly six or seven men in the photos from Berdella's house who hadn't been identified as anyone, alive or missing. It seemed like the squad had shown the photos to everyone who might have any clues to their identities. But some remained anonymous. The man hanging upside down was still nameless, though detectives weren't showing that photo to anyone. But they noticed the man had a scar on his leg, and that he appeared in other photos, lying in Berdella's bedroom. That photo was shown to various people, also without success.

Cole decided to seek the public's help. The police could crop the photos so they would only show the men's faces, then release the pictures to the news media. Seven photos were selected, including a different shot of the "upside-down man" with the scar on his leg, and on April 27, the pictures were given to the television stations and the newspapers. Each photo was assigned a letter, and people who thought they recognized someone were asked to call the squad and refer to each photo by its letter. Cole knew this would create a deluge of calls. Because the Polaroid shots, cropped and reproduced by police cameras, were somewhat fuzzy, no doubt dozens of people would identify the same person as their son or husband. But the squad needed new names to work with, to try to link someone to either of the two skulls.

The seven photos aired for the first time at 5 P.M. and 6 P.M. on the local news. Paul Howell and his family were watching the news, and they scanned the photos to see if they recognized anyone. Howell had already been shown some other photos, and had identified his son Jerry in some of them. It appeared to him, though, that Jerry was only sleeping in the photos. Because he knew Jerry's photo wouldn't be shown, he wasn't watching the screen as closely as his children.

"There's Jerry!" screamed Howell's twelve-year-old son. "That's Jerry!" Howell swung his head around instantly, and saw enough to know his young son was right. For some reason, the goddamn cops had put Jerry's photo on the news. Why would they do that? Howell figured Cole was pissed off at him for calling the squad regularly, or for talking to the media. Cole probably just put it on there to get back at us, Howell thought.

The families of Jerry Howell and James Ferris were living a nightmare that far surpassed the sorrow they felt when the young men first disappeared. Now, they felt even more sure that the men were dead, but they couldn't be *absolutely* positive. There still were no bodies. Their sons weren't the skulls that had been found at Berdella's house. If anything, there were more questions now than before. Reporters called constantly, expecting the families to have answers. Both Paul Howell and Bonnie Ferris were honest and open with the press, and for that they were shut out by the police and prosecutors. Hall and Cole felt they couldn't tell the families anything new or sensitive, for fear it would be in the newspaper the next morning.

Cole hadn't put Jerry Howell's picture in with the unidentified group to raise Paul Howell's ire. The photos of his son Paul Howell had picked out several weeks earlier

164

did not appear, to police, to be the same person as the one put on TV. The photo he saw that night, photograph "F," was the cropped head shot of the man with the scar on his leg. The same man who was hanging upside down, apparently dead. Jerry Howell was the man hanging upside down.

Paul Howell charged down to the squad room the next morning and confronted Cole. Howell's temper was bubbling, and Cole did his best to soothe the upset father. Cole apologized, and told Howell it was a mistake. They hadn't meant to give Jerry's picture to the media, they just didn't realize he was the same person as the one Paul Howell had picked out previously. Howell stalked away, unconvinced. Cole didn't tell him about the connection to the upside down photo. There was no definite proof that the upside down man was dead. He just looked that way. Jerry Howell could still walk in the door tomorrow and say he'd been back out to California, or somewhere. It was a Polaroid, not very well lit, slightly out of focus. No need to alarm Paul Howell unnecessarily. And no need for the media to start another one of their frenzies, either.

When the photos were published that morning in the *Kansas City Times,* where people had more time to study each picture, the expected barrage of calls began. One woman called and said photograph "G" was positively her ex-husband. The ex positively denied it.

One man phoned, sounding very upset, and said photograph "C" was him. He came down to the squad room and identified himself as Homer Roloff. He had befriended Berdella at the flea market, and sometimes when Roloff was depressed and drinking, he would call Berdella at home. Berdella occasionally would pick him up, take him back to Charlotte Street and provide him with some Valium, whereupon the young man would pass out. Roloff said he did jobs around Berdella's house when he needed money, and remembered telling Berdella once that he was afraid to climb a ladder because he feared falling and killing himself. He said Berdella commented, "Well, I know how to get rid of the parts."

Meanwhile, Detective Casebolt was still on the trail of Robert Sheldon. He'd met with the apartment manager from 4201 Locust Street and gotten Sheldon's receipt from the University of Kansas Medical Center. Now Casebolt was headed to the hospital, situated on the Kansas side of the state line. Maybe the hospital would have dental records of Sheldon, which would give them another person to compare with the skulls for a possible identification.

When Casebolt explained his reasoning to hospital officials, they checked their records. Yes, there were dental charts for Sheldon. But no, he couldn't have them. The officials were leery of violating a patient's privacy and possibly being sued. But they also wanted to cooperate with the police. If they received a subpoena they'd comply with it, they told Casebolt.

Casebolt drove hurriedly back to the squad and told Cole of his latest lead. Cole called Pat Hall, and Hall drew up a grand jury subpoena, requesting the hospital officials to appear before the grand jury with Sheldon's dental records. The officials could forego the appearance simply by turning over the records to the police, the subpoena stated. Casebolt took the subpoena to the hospital that afternoon and the hospital officials handed over their dental x-rays of Sheldon.

The next morning, Casebolt was busy with an interview, so Detective Bill McGhee took the x-rays to Dr. Gier's office for a comparison. Gier knew what he was looking for, since he'd already done numerous other comparisons. He took about ten minutes. Then McGhee called Cole to tell him that Sheldon's charts matched.

McGhee could hear the roar through the phone when

166

Cole told the squad. The detectives yelled and exchanged high fives, smiling broadly. Though the fact that Robert Sheldon was dead was not something to celebrate, the identification of one of the skulls was a hugely important break in the investigation. Now the police could do at least part of their work in the standard fashion: demonstrate the links between the suspect and victim, discover any motive the suspect might have had for killing the victim, and show when the victim was last seen with the suspect.

When the news came about Sheldon, Detective Bennie White was in Springfield, Missouri, looking for Merrick Villaj. Cole had already decided they needed more information about Sheldon, and sent White out to interview her. Villaj identified photos of Sheldon, either sleeping or dead, in Berdella's house, and told White that Sheldon had lived there with Freddie Kellogg several years ago. She also said Sheldon was from Los Angeles, and that she hadn't seen him in at least two years.

In Kansas City, Kansas, Detectives McGhee and Luther found another former girlfriend of Sheldon's, June Ford. Ford was more talkative than Villaj and provided more background on Sheldon's past. Ford said she and Sheldon argued in November 1984 and broke up, and she hadn't seen him since then. Ford also thought Sheldon's parents lived in North Hollywood, California. This brought up another necessary, if distasteful, aspect of any murder investigation: Notifying the relatives. Dan Wilson called the North Hollywood Police Department and asked them to find the Sheldons, and an officer informed Connie Sheldon on May 2. Mrs. Sheldon had called the squad for more details, and told them she hadn't seen or heard from her son in seven years. He originally planned to go to Chicago, and Mrs. Sheldon didn't know how he ended up in Kansas City.

Connie Sheldon had a lot of questions for the police,

for which they had almost no answers. Who killed her son? They weren't exactly sure. She wasn't told Berdella's name, only that her son's head had been found inside a man's house. Where was his body? No one knew. Why was he killed? There was no reply for that one either. Two days later, Sheldon's father called Cole and asked if the family could at least get the skull back for burial services. No, he was told. It was needed as evidence. Now a third family had been brought into the Berdella ordeal.

The same day the Sheldons learned about their son, two men phoned the squad with a positive identification of another of the photos. They provided a name the detectives hadn't heard before, Mark Wallace. A high school classmate said photograph "E" was Wallace, and later that morning, another man also said Wallace was the man in "E." Wallace didn't show up in the police computer, so McGhee was assigned to find him.

Two days later, McGhee located one of Wallace's older sisters. She told McGhee that Wallace was born in Ohio, and the family moved to Kansas City when Mark was seven or eight years old. He attended and then dropped out of Southwest High School, and entered the Marine Corps when he was seventeen. After a few months, he went AWOL from the service for more than a year, returned and was dishonorably discharged. Wallace came back to Kansas City, moved in with his sister for several months at one point, then moved out. She hadn't seen him since 1985. McGhee asked if Wallace had any dental work done, and his sister provided the name of a local dentist.

McGhee continued to search for Wallace, but couldn't find him. He spoke with an old girlfriend of Wallace, but she hadn't seen him since 1984. Wallace's dental records were located and taken to Dr. Gier, but they didn't match the skull taken from the backyard. Not only did no one know where Wallace was, there was no indication he'd ever met Berdella.

What police didn't know was that in the summer of 1985 Wallace had been making money helping a friend cut lawns in the midtown area. He met Berdella when they mowed his front and backyards. On the night of June 22, 1985, Wallace had been drinking and was walking through the south Hyde Park area when a heavy rain began to fall. Wallace remembered that Berdella had a toolshed in his backyard, and that he and his friend hadn't locked it the last time they'd been to Berdella's house, several days earlier.

Wallace found Berdella's house in the downpour, and ducked into the toolshed for cover. But Berdella's dogs saw Wallace trespassing and began barking. Berdella yelled at the dogs to shut up, but they kept yapping. Finally, Berdella got out of bed and went to see what was causing the noise. He noticed the door to the toolshed was slightly open, checked it, and found Wallace inside. Berdella invited the shivering, soaked Wallace inside to dry off. After that, Wallace never showed up at his friend's house to cut lawns again.

While McGhee hunted around Kansas City for Wallace, other members of the squad were on the road once more. Cole sent Eikel and White to Oklahoma to find Todd Stoops and T.R. Holub, a former downtown hustler who'd been identified by other hustlers in one of Berdella's photographs. Holub had already been located and interviewed by the police in Chickasha, Oklahoma, but Cole felt Holub was holding back, and wanted his own men to try him again. No one had found Stoops yet, but his family felt it possible he was back in Oklahoma City, so that was the detectives' second stop.

In Chickasha, Holub said he had met Berdella while

hustling in 1984. He would call Berdella periodically when he needed money or drugs, and would do tricks for Berdella in return. Once, while drinking beer at Berdella's house, Holub said he passed out. That was weird, he thought, since he hadn't even been getting high that day, and he never passed out from beer. When he awoke, he was naked in Berdella's bed, but he didn't think he'd been sexually abused.

Eikel asked Holub if he knew Jerry Howell. Holub said he did, but Howell never mentioned Berdella to him. After Howell disappeared, Howell's father told Holub that Berdella was responsible, and Holub and several other hustlers decided to stay away from Berdella after that. Looking at Berdella's photos, Holub picked himself out, and also identified Lamar Rich, as many people had. Holub didn't know anything about Berdella torturing or killing people, and the detectives thanked him for coming down.

The next day, Eikel and White drove to Oklahoma City and picked up a police report and mugshot of Stoops from his April 1985 arrest for prostitution. A local officer guided the detectives to several bars and areas where gay men gathered, but no one could recall seeing Stoops. They went to the county jail and interviewed the woman who'd been arrested with Stoops in 1985. She said she hadn't seen Stoops in eight months. Eikel and White headed back to Kansas City.

One person Cole felt could be crucial was Geoff Marcus. Marcus's brother said Geoff had lived with Berdella and had warned that Berdella was dangerous. Detectives found a friend who had gotten collect phone calls from Geoff Marcus, and the originating phone numbers were in Miami. Cole told Detective Bill Wilson he was going to Miami. "Find this guy," Cole said. "I don't care if it takes a day or a week."

170

With the help of Miami police, Wilson spent several days scouring the city's lesser areas for Geoff Marcus, leaving his business card everywhere. He returned without finding Marcus, but several days later, Marcus called, denying he'd ever known Berdella or told his brother to stay away from him.

One of the few known housemates of Berdella who still hadn't been located was Larry Pearson. Before he left for Oklahoma, Eikel had gone down to the police records unit and obtained a copy of the summons that Pearson had been given for indecent exposure. The fingerprint on the back of the summons was assigned a classification number, and Eikel found it matched the number of a Larry W. Pearson in Wichita, Kansas. According to the National Crime Information Computer, the Pearson in Wichita had been arrested for robbery in 1985, convicted, imprisoned and paroled in April 1987. Eikel called the Wichita Police Department, and learned that Pearson was wanted for a 1987 parole violation. The Wichita police agreed to send Eikel a photo and police record of Pearson.

While Eikel was in Oklahoma, the package from Wichita arrived. Dan Wilson picked it up, opened it and saw immediately that the police mug shot looked very much like photograph "D," which had not yet been identified. Photo "D" was a picture of a young man looking sadly at the camera, sitting naked in a bathtub, wearing what appeared to be a dog collar. Wilson then checked to see what had happened with Pearson's indecent exposure case. Pearson, free on bond, had never shown up. Wilson called the bonding company to see who had posted the bond. It was Robert Berdella.

Next, Wilson called Pearson's parole officer in Wichita. He learned that Pearson was one of seven children, all of

171

whom were taken from their mother when Pearson was four years old because she was a prostitute. As a ward of the court, Pearson lived in several different foster homes while growing up, and told one doctor he'd been physically abused when he was small. The state required Pearson to have regular medical and dental examinations, so Cole sent Wilson and McGhee to Wichita to see if they could find some dental records.

The two detectives drove to the offices of the Social and Rehabilitation Services in Wichita, about three hours southwest of Kansas City. After picking up dental x-rays of Pearson, they showed the photo of the naked man in the bathtub to social workers and Pearson's foster father. All were certain the man in the picture was Larry Pearson.

The police also learned that several months after Pearson graduated from high school, in the summer of 1985, he was arrested and charged with aggravated robbery for holding up a Domino's Pizza delivery man. In December 1985, Pearson pleaded guilty and was sentenced to five to twenty years in prison, but was released on a five-year probation term in June 1986. He was directed to participate in a ninety-day counseling program at a Christian ministry in downtown Wichita. He completed that, but began missing meetings with his probation officer. In April 1987, the court placed the twenty-year-old Pearson in the custody of the Salvation Army, and ordered him to enroll in a vocational training program.

Instead, Pearson was disruptive at the Salvation Army, refusing to follow minor house rules, such as properly dressing and keeping a positive attitude. On May 4, Pearson's counselor told him he was going to be terminated from the program, which could result in Pearson going back to prison. Pearson stalked out of the building immediately, leaving his belongings behind. He headed for Kansas City.

Pearson, who had told his various counselors he was disturbed about his mother's prostitution, took up the profession when he arrived in Kansas City, strolling at 10th and McGee and also Liberty Memorial. In his regular drives through those areas, Berdella began to recognize Pearson as a new face. One day in late May 1987, Pearson happened into Bob's Bazaar Bizarre, and Berdella mentioned he'd seen Pearson downtown. Pearson shrugged. After Pearson browsed for a time, Berdella took him to lunch at a fast-food restaurant on Main Street. With little else to do that afternoon, the two men went back to Berdella's house and chatted. Pearson explained that he was new in town, and had left Wichita after a fight with a girlfriend. Later, Pearson admitted to Berdella he was probably wanted for a parole violation, and maybe it wasn't such a good idea to be hustling downtown.

Over the next several weeks, Berdella occasionally would see Pearson walking alone downtown, and offer him a ride. Pearson would end up spending the night in one of Berdella's spare bedrooms, but they did not have sex. He helped Pearson get copies of his Social Security card and his birth certificate, so Pearson could have identification when he applied for a job.

In early June, Pearson asked Berdella if he could stay at his house regularly, in an attempt to stay away from the streets. Berdella agreed. But about 2 A.M. on Friday, June 5, Pearson was arrested at Liberty Memorial for exposing himself to passing cars. He spent the rest of the night in jail, and when he appeared before a judge in the morning, his bond was set at $150. Pearson didn't have it, so he was sent back to jail, where he spent Friday and Saturday night.

On Sunday morning, Pearson called Berdella and asked if he would post the $150 bond. Berdella was preparing to drive to Ohio to visit his mother, but if he didn't help Pearson now, he knew Pearson would have to stay in jail until Berdella returned later in the week. Berdella said he'd post the bond if Pearson would accompany him on the drive to Ohio. Pearson, anxious to get out of jail before someone discovered he was wanted in Kansas, said sure. Pearson met and stayed with Berdella's mother and stepfather, then returned with Berdella to Kansas City and moved back in. Now, ten months later, no one could find him.

Wilson and McGhee took Pearson's dental x-rays back to the squad. The next morning, May 11, McGhee carried the x-rays to Dr Gier, who by now was very used to the routine. Since he'd identified the skull in Berdella's closet as Robert Sheldon two weeks ago, the police had brought him even more dental records, trying to identify the skull from the backyard. None matched—until that morning. Gier quickly determined that it was Larry Pearson's head which was buried in Berdella's backyard.

Cole sent Dan Wilson back to Wichita to gain more biographical information about Pearson, and see if anyone there had ever heard of Berdella. The sergeant assigned Bill Wilson to trace Robert Sheldon locally, find any more girlfriends Sheldon might have had, and obtain Sheldon's work records. The detectives were also told to go through Berdella's logs and see if any of the dates correlated with the approximate dates on which Sheldon or Pearson were last seen. In Sheldon's case, he took a medical leave of absence on April 10, 1985, according to his work records. One of Berdella's logs began on "4/10." For Pearson, he was last seen either in June, when he was bonded out of jail, or August, when he ostensibly bit Berdella's penis. One of Berdella's logs started with "6/23." Maybe he bit Berdella while he was being held captive, the detectives theorized. Why, then, would Berdella make a police report?

Other questions persisted. There were eight separate sets

of notations. If three of the logs referred to Bryson, Howell and Ferris, and these two latest logs chronicled the stays of Sheldon and Pearson—to whom did the remaining three logs refer? Todd Stoops and Mark Wallace were the only two people the squad hadn't accounted for, and the detectives had no real idea when they were last seen. Even if the logs referred to Stoops and Wallace, there was still one unknown victim, if all the logs related to men who were killed.

Despite the continuing mysteries, the detectives finally began to feel they had accomplished something. The secrecy surrounding the squad meant they couldn't publicly celebrate yet, though the news would soon leak to the press about the identification of the two skulls. But a month's worth of frustration had been erased at last. From his bunker in the prosecutor's office, Hall realized he was going to have a murder case after all.

By May of 1988, Sergeant Tom Moss had been rotated out of the Fugitive Apprehension unit, where he once tracked Bob Berdella, and was now assigned to the East Patrol division. On a warm night that spring, Moss was working off-duty, in uniform, at an East Side apartment complex that had been overrun by crack dealers. Crack had established an imposing foothold in Kansas City, introduced first by Jamaican posses, and then by Los Angeles gang members. Though the police had pushed most of the Jamaicans and "L.A. boys" out of the city, the visitors had made lasting business connections that would continue the pipeline well into the future.

Moss had rousted some crack vendors from a second-floor apartment earlier in the evening, and now stood guard outside the unit to ensure that it wasn't reopened that night. In such situations, police are amused to find that addicts still will stomp right up to the door, sometimes even pushing a cop aside, in their singleminded pursuit of that quick dope rush. Two young, red-eyed men approached Moss now, one with a slight limp. Moss flashed his toothy smile, renowned among the city's dopers since heroin's heyday, a smile which always said: I know what you're up to, shithead.

"Sorry boys, closed tonight," Moss said.

"Closed?" one said. "What're you talkin' 'bout man, we're just looking for a friend."

"Oh I see, I see," Moss said, as the men leaned against a stairwell railing. "Your friend wouldn't happen to stay in this apartment right here now, would he?"

"Might, don't know," one man mumbled.

"OK, well you boys oughta get on home now," Moss told them.

One of the men stepped up to Moss and leaned closer. "Hey man," he said, "you know Bob Berdella?"

"Well, yeah, I think I've read about it in the paper," Moss said, casually. "I'm not sure I remember."

"You know man, the guy jumped out the window, the guy had two skulls at his house, over there by Westport?"

"Yeah, I think I know who you're talking about."

"I'm the one who jumped out the window and he held captive and did all those things to," Chris Bryson said. And Bryson proceeded to convince Moss that he had been inside Berdella's house for four days, and that horrible things occurred on Charlotte Street. Moss was sympathetic; if he'd been tortured like that, he didn't know how he'd respond. Perhaps he'd be looking for some crack now too.

As the only known witness to the crimes of Bob Berdella, Chris Bryson was a priceless commodity to the prosecution. While in the hospital, Bryson told the doctors he'd taken drugs by smoking, snorting, swallowing and shooting them. Soon the defense attorneys would know this. Hall needed Bryson to be an unshakable witness, physically clean and mentally alert. On April 30, Cole handed Hurn a lead card that said, "Make periodic contacts with Bryson." Cole added, "Stick close to him as best you can."

At first, Hurn checked in with Bryson by telephone about once a week, through mid-May. Hurn could tell Bryson was having trouble handling the stress that followed the realization of what he'd survived, but nothing seemed too unusual to Hurn as late as May 21. But on May 30, Bryson clearly was depressed. He was having doubts about going through with a trial, about taking the witness stand in public, about reliving what horrific moments he could remember. Hurn called again two days later, and Bryson wasn't home. Bryson's mother said Chris was extremely depressed, possibly suicidal. Immediately, Hurn dialed Bryson at work. He hadn't shown up.

The next day, Bryson's wife called Hurn. She was crying, apologetic and scared. Her twenty-two-year-old husband was on the verge of cracking up. He had just disappeared for eight days, and he was using cocaine heavily, she said. Bryson would tell her he was going to work, but when she would call him, he wasn't there. She was getting ready to move out, and take their infant son with her, until Bryson could get cleaned up. Bryson had even mentioned suicide, his wife told Hurn. Hurn left several messages for Bryson at his job, but they went unreturned. Hurn reported the situation to Holtsclaw, the prosecutor on the sodomy case. They decided that when Bryson surfaced they would try to put him in a drug rehabilitation program. That night, Hurn looked for Bryson downtown at 10th and McGee, at Joseph's Lounge, at the Liberty Memorial, at his mother's house. Nothing.

The following morning, June 3, Cole told Hurn to

change into plainclothes, so he wouldn't look too much like a detective, and talk to Bryson at work. Hurn changed, but again, Bryson didn't show up for work. Hurn called Bryson's apartment three times, but got no answer. On the fourth call, Bryson picked up the phone.

"Hey Chris, it's Ashley Hurn from the police department, how're you doing?"

"Yeah man, what's up?" Bryson croaked, his raspy voice barely audible.

"Heard you hadn't been around in a while, just wanted to check in with you," Hurn said.

"What's the deal?" Bryson asked, sounding irritated. "They didn't like me on tape?" he said, referring to his videotaped statement.

"No, we just wanted to see where your head's at," Hurn answered. "It's me talking, Ashley, not a policeman."

"Yeah, my old lady told me you called."

"We just want to help you," Hurn said. He wanted to treat Bryson as carefully as possible.

"Shit, I need help," Bryson said softly.

Hurn suggested that Bryson try to clean out in a drug program. He knew Bryson had been in such a program before, and that Bryson would resist the idea. "It's not that long," Hurn coaxed. "It'll be a kick for you. You get to kick back, get some rest. And not only does the state pay for it, they'll also match your salary at work."

"I don't know, man," Bryson said.

"I'm trying to work something out for you," Hurn said.

"You'll never get it done."

"I'll fix things up at work," Hurn said. He had already spoken to Bryson's boss, who agreed to rehire Bryson if he entered a drug program.

"Don't call my work," Bryson said anxiously. "I don't want anybody there to know." Hurn assured him that everything was being handled confidentially. Bryson finally relented, and Hurn and Holtsclaw picked him up that morning. After stopping at his mother's house to explain the situation to her, Bryson went with his new guardians to Research Psychiatric Center, where he checked in under the name Dale Branson.

Hurn called Bryson daily, and Bryson's mood seemed to improve steadily. Hurn and Holtsclaw also visited regularly, including one occasion when they couldn't remember Bryson's pseudonym. The psychiatric center staff wouldn't let them in. "I'm with the prosecutor's office, we're paying for this," Holtsclaw reminded them indignantly, but he and Hurn were not admitted that day.

Though in protective custody, Bryson still gave Hurn and Holtsclaw heartburn. "They're wasting their money," Bryson told them on one visit. "It's a cakewalk. These people in here don't have their shit together." Not only was the treatment ineffective, but Bryson confided that he'd figured out a way to escape. Hurn alerted the center's security staff. Still, when Hurn called several days later, Bryson wasn't there. He'd been released on a temporary pass to visit his family. Hurn grew alarmed at the prospect, but Bryson returned to the center that night.

At the courthouse, Holtsclaw was enmeshed in a flurry of motions, some of which he filed, others filed by the public defenders, who were now officially appointed as Berdella's lawyers. One of Holtsclaw's moves was to have Bryson's testimony videotaped "in the event of his unavailability as a witness." The defense attorneys opposed this, saying Berdella had a right to confront his accuser in the courtroom. A hearing was scheduled for June 9, and Holtsclaw tried to keep Bryson from having to appear there too, but Circuit Judge Gene Martin denied that motion.

Hurn picked up Bryson at the psychiatric center, and drove him to the courthouse that afternoon. It was his first public appearance, and he was understandably nervous. Berdella was not in the courtroom. Defense attorney Barbara Schenkenberg asked Bryson if he planned on moving any time soon, or if Bryson had any trouble recalling the events he claimed happened on Charlotte Street. Bryson said no. Schenkenberg asked Bryson, "When was the last time you saw a doctor for a physical problem?" Bryson replied, "Shortly after I jumped out of Bob Berdella's window." The defense attorneys didn't know, and Bryson didn't volunteer, that Bryson had been hospitalized for psychiatric treatment. Hurn returned him to the center after the hearing.

The lawyers fought other battles, each side dividing up the victories. The defenders' motion to have a bond set for Berdella was upheld by the Missouri Court of Appeals, which then placed Berdella's bond at $750,000. The prosecutors sought to get a handwriting sample from Berdella, to prove that he had written the logs found in his house. Berdella refused to cooperate and was sentenced to six months in jail for contempt of court.

Berdella fought back on other fronts too. With his civil attorney, Pender, he filed a countersuit against the prosecutors who had seized his house, claiming the seizure was simply an attempt to deprive him of his property and thereby from hiring the lawyer of his choice. Pender wrote in the suit that if the courts upheld the prosecutors' "perverted and nonsensical argument" that the house was "somehow an instrumentality of a crime," the homes of all but a few Missouri residents could be seized by the state.

The public defenders unleashed their first set of motions, seeking first to have the trial moved because of the heavy publicity. Then, Schenkenberg and Berrigan charged Hall with abusing his powers by issuing a subpoena to the

University of Kansas Medical Center for Robert Sheldon's dental records. The subpoena's jurisdiction was limited to the state of Missouri, the lawyers noted. Hall responded by issuing another subpoena, to Menorah Medical Center, in Missouri, for the records on the injury inflicted by "Larry Person" last August. A judge quashed that subpoena, and the defense motion for a change of venue was also rejected.

The lawyers on both sides were quite familiar with each other; in contrast to private lawyers who represent criminal defendants occasionally, the public defenders and the prosecutors are in the courtrooms almost daily. Each side refers to the other on a first-name basis, though not genially. Some prosecutors thought Berrigan was obstinate — not necessarily to serve his client, but "just to be difficult." When Berrigan accused Hall of being unethical for issuing a subpoena to a Kansas institution, Hall was infuriated.

It angered Hall in part because in several discussions with Riederer, he found himself practically arguing on behalf of the defense counsel. The conversations concerned the huge amount of police reports that were still piling in. As part of the usual criminal process, the defense attorneys had made their "discovery" motion for all the information the prosecutors had about the sodomy case. Hall thought the best thing would be to just turn over everything to the defenders as it was received. Riederer disagreed. "They're not entitled to the murder stuff until we file murder charges," Riederer said. The top prosecutor pointed out that very few of the police reports being generated by the squad had anything to do with the sexual assault on Bryson. The police were trying to prove a murder, and until they did so, the defense lawyers weren't entitled to see the work product in progress.

Holtsclaw argued that the two types of cases were commingled, and that much of the information about Berdella's background, his penchant for cruising downtown and injecting young men was relevant to both cases. Hall, ever cautious, didn't want to be accused of withholding anything, and giving the defenders a technical toehold by which to overturn a conviction. When a murder charge was filed, Hall wanted the defense attorneys to be current on the police investigation, so they wouldn't have to start from scratch in researching a new case. After several such discussions, Riederer finally agreed, and the flow of documents to the public defenders' office began in earnest.

As the papers piled up in Berdella's cell, he recognized that the police, inept as they were, had the makings of a serious case against him. His obsession with how the outside world saw him was slowly dwindling, and his meetings with Berrigan and Schenkenberg helped him focus on assisting their preparations for the sodomy trial.

Berdella continued to meet with both the Reverend Coleman and Dr. O'Connor, both offering therapy of different sorts. Coleman was more sympathetic, more willing to simply listen than O'Connor, who was more analytical and more curious. He discussed his life all the way back to childhood with both men. But in Berdella's eyes, it was simply a matter of putting his life in context, painting the complete picture. He was determined not to blame his parents or his upbringing for where he was now. His past was not responsible for what he had become. But Berdella also didn't accept the responsibility himself. In part, society and its twisted morality had pushed him to this precipice, he told one visitor. He also felt as if he'd been possessed, possibly by anger, during certain periods. He could be very angry, he told Coleman, and perhaps took that out on other people.

O'Connor wanted more specifics. One of his specializations in psychology was predicting violent behavior in mental patients, and he had published studies in which patients' backgrounds were examined for indications of future tendencies. After the early sessions established a rapport, O'Connor explored Berdella's relationship with his father. Berdella told the psychologist that he wasn't particularly athletic as a youth, and that his father valued sports and athletic activities. Sometimes, his father would launch into fits of anger, Berdella said, and become violent. In these episodes, Robert Berdella Sr. was both physically and emotionally abusive, and would beat his oldest son with a leather strap.

Berdella told O'Connor that he was close to his mother and to his aunts, on both sides of the family. However, he said his mother was essentially ineffective or passive when her husband would fly into these recurrent rages, which Berdella said occurred throughout his childhood. In a report which O'Connor prepared about these conversations, there is no discussion of why Robert Berdella Sr. became violent. Those who knew Berdella's duties at the Ford Motor Company plant said his job as a die-setter was not an assembly line task, and was not particularly stressful. Berdella was a World War II veteran, but friends did not notice him to be suffering from any postwar syndrome. He liked to drink now and then, neighbors said, but he was not thought to be an alcoholic. Occasionally, he might sneak off to "the supper club," code for the neighborhood bar, for a nip, and he was a member of the Knights of Columbus, a Catholic men's organization that served alcoholic refreshment at its functions. But to friends and neighbors, there were no signs that Berdella was a dysfunctional parent.

Berdella Jr. told O'Connor that he was aware of his homosexuality during adolescence, and that he was never interested in girls. He was not sexually active through high

183

school, he said. However, at the age of 16, he was the victim of a homosexual rape by a man who worked with him in an Ohio restaurant. There is no indication of what immediate effect this had on the young Berdella, but he told O'Connor that even after he moved to Kansas City, he was rarely sexually active up through the 1970s, until he was past the age of thirty.

Around 1982, Berdella said, he became seriously emotionally involved with a Vietnam veteran who had multiple emotional and substance abuse problems. O'Connor wrote in his report that the man was apparently bisexual, and that "in general, Mr. Berdella has never been comfortable with homosexual individuals and has some significant degree of ambivalence about these relationships."

When O'Connor made occasional forays into Berdella's current mental state, he found confusion. Berdella could not say how he felt about what he'd done, or explain why. He was still unwilling to face it. If Berdella felt guilt or remorse approaching, he blocked it out. He refused to become overwhelmed by emotion. Still, through the various therapy sessions, Berdella felt he was making progress in overcoming this phase of his life, and moving on to the next.

To the police, Berdella was no more a human being now than he had been the day he was arrested nearly two months before. He was a suspect, possibly a suspect of historic proportions, and he had the potential to embarrass them if he wasn't handled just right. Berdella was still the talk of the city, his house a continuing tourist attraction. Charlotte Street residents knew better than to park their cars on the street after watching assorted rubberneckers crash into parked cars while gawking at the house. Tourist buses, even the city-run trolley bus, detoured past

Robert A. Berdella Jr. in his Westport shop, "Bob's Bazaar Bizarre," in December 1986.
(*Photo by Bob Travaglione*)

The house in Cuyahoga Falls, Ohio, where Berdella grew up.
(*Photo by Tom Jackman*)

Berdella's high school, Cuyahoga Falls High School.
(*Photo by Tom Jackman*)

Berdella working as a volunteer during a benefit auction for public television Channel 19 in Kansas City, April 1982.
(*Courtesy of Kansas City Star*)

Berdella with two friends during a party at his house, date unknown. Police found this photo among Berdella's collection of Polaroids.
(*Courtesy of Kansas City Police Department*)

After being arrested in February 1985 for selling drugs to an undercover officer, Berdella was questioned but never charged.
(Courtesy of Kansas City Police Department)

4315 Charlotte St., Berdella's home, as it appeared when police first began searching it in April 1988.
(Courtesy of Kansas City Police Department)

The bed where Berdella tortured all his victims, and where five of them died. This was taken shortly after Chris Bryson escaped.
(*Courtesy of Kansas City Police Department*)

The washcloth and cord used to gag Chris Bryson.
(*Courtesy of Kansas City Police Department*)

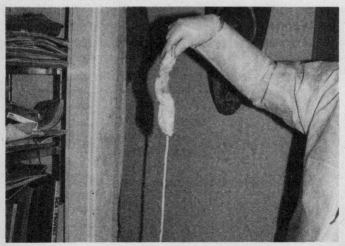

Berdella's police mugshot, taken minutes after his arrest in April 1988.
(*Courtesy of Kansas City Police Department*)

Detectives found a bag of Berdella's torture photos, and his logs, underneath the bed in the "torture room."
(*Courtesy of Kansas City Police Department*)

One of Berdella's "torture logs," detailing his sex acts, his methods of torture, and the drugs he injected into his victims.
(*Courtesy of Kansas City Police Department*)

The "artifact room," Berdella's gallery of exotica displayed in an upstairs bedroom. The skull found in this room was not genuine.
(*Courtesy of Kansas City Police Department*)

Berdella's cluttered dining room, where police found files Berdella kept on some of his victims.
(*Courtesy of Kansas City Police Department*)

The skull found in one of Berdella's closets, later identified as that of Robert Sheldon.
(*Courtesy of Kansas City Police Department*)

Detectives uncover a human head in Berdella's backyard, later determined to be that of Larry Pearson.
(*Courtesy of Kansas City Police Department*)

After discovery of the head, the backyard is sectioned off and fully excavated.
(*Courtesy of Kansas City Police Department*)

Sgt. Troy Cole supervised the squad of eleven detectives assigned to investigate Berdella.
(*Photo by Alison K. Barnes*)

Berdella being led into court for a hearing, July 1988.
(*Courtesy of Kansas City Star*)

Jerry Howell, Berdella's first victim, killed in July 1984.
(*Courtesy of Paul Howell Sr.*)

Robert Sheldon after being drugged into unconsciousness by Berdella, April 1985.
(*Courtesy of Kansas City Police Department*)

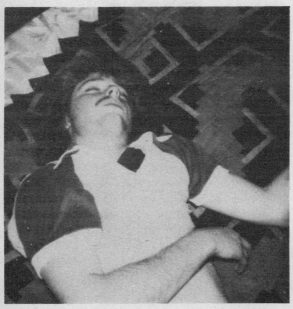

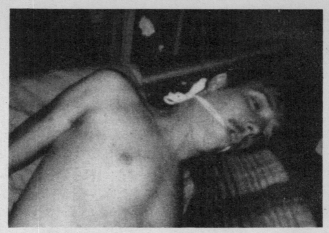

Mark Wallace, shortly after his capture in June 1985, in one of Berdella's Polaroid photographs.
(*Courtesy of Kansas City Police Department*)

James Ferris, in a portrait taken just months before his death.
(*Courtesy of Harriet Sanders*)

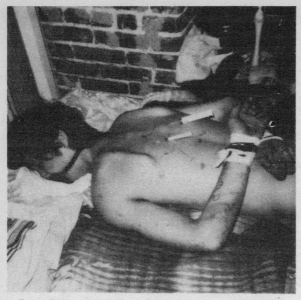

James Ferris, bound, gagged and injected, September 1985.
(*Courtesy of Kansas City Police Department*)

The midtown gay bar "Midnight Sun" where Berdella met James Ferris for the final time in September 1985. It has since changed its name.
(*Photo by Alison K. Barnes*)

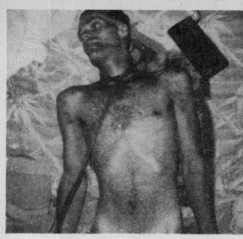

Todd Stoops after two weeks as a hostage, June 1986. His appearance had changed so dramatically police did not recognize Stoops from Berdella's earlier photos of him.
(*Courtesy of Kansas City Police Department*)

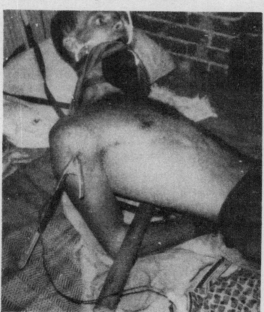

Stoops receiving a 7,700-volt jolt of electricity from Berdella.
(*Courtesy of Kansas City Police Department*)

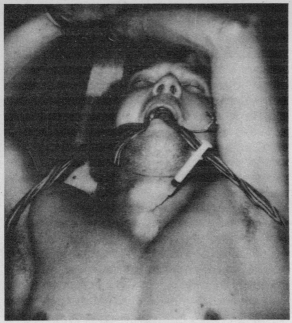

**Larry Pearson, shortly after being captured by Berdella in
June 1987, handcuffed, gagged with piano wire and in-
jected with a hypodermic needle.**
(Courtesy of Kansas City Police Department)

**Pearson some time later, his face battered and his
right hand broken.** *(Courtesy of Kansas City Police Department)*

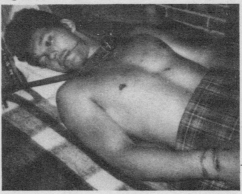

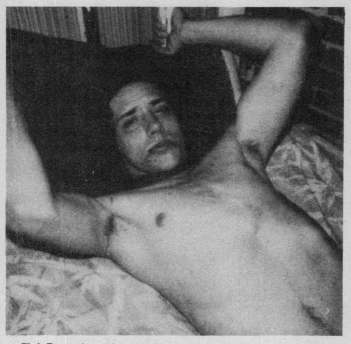

Chris Bryson in captivity, as photographed by Berdella, April 1988.
(*Courtesy of Kansas City Police Department*)

4315 Charlotte St. as it appears today. *(Photo by Alison K. Barnes)*

Berdella on the witness stand at his sentencing in Jackson County Circuit Court, December 1988.
(Photo by Sam Harrel)

the house. Sometimes, passengers hopped out and photographed each other in front of the macabre landmark. Activity inside the house ended in early May, when police finished emptying all the contents and placing them in storage until the seizure suit was resolved. After that, the windows were boarded up, the excavated yards reseeded, and the empty hull left for the sightseers.

The news media didn't lose interest in the case either. In mid-May, the Howell family received another shock when the *Kansas City Times* reported that the man in the oft-described "upside down picture" was thought to be their son Jerry. The police had not shown the photo to the Howells, but Paul Howell Jr. went down to the squad and asked to see it. Yes, it was his younger brother. This spurred a new round of speculation on how many people Berdella might have killed.

Cole's detectives continued their own daily round table of speculation, though that hardly helped build the case. They needed hard evidence, and the Regional Crime Lab was starting to weigh in with some notable findings. A complete spraying of the house with Luminol, to discover blood traces, glowed positive in several locations. A comparison of the cut marks on the vertebrae found in the backyard, of Larry Pearson, showed the marks were consistent with the 7¼-inch circular blades found on two electric power saws in Berdella's house.

Hurn traveled to St. Louis one afternoon to meet with Dr. Christopher Long, the St. Louis University pathologist who'd received the Pearson skull, hair and tissue for analysis, along with copies of Berdella's logs. The chemical analysis wasn't completed, Long said, but he had reached one conclusion from looking at Berdella's notes: it appeared "CP" was short for chlorpromazine, an animal tranquilizer, and whoever was being injected in the notes beginning on "4/10" had received a toxic dose. If Berdella truly had injected this person—Sheldon—this frequently with this drug, Long said, and the logs were accurate, the accumulation could be toxic. When Hurn asked whether the dosage could cause death, Long said he wasn't prepared to go that far. Hurn was frustrated, but figured that Long's testimony was another piece of circumstantial evidence to add to the growing pile.

Hurn also continued the tedious task of listening to all of Berdella's audiotapes, to see if Berdella had recorded any of his crimes. Similarly, DeValkenaere was awarded the job of watching all of Berdella's videotapes and films. DeValkenaere did discover the film Berdella made in college of a baby chick being shot to death, but little else.

One of the tapes Hurn monitored opened his eyes one evening. For one thing, it wasn't a telephone conversation. A man was moving about, shifting things around in the room, occasionally talking to a second person. "You going to come up here baby?" the first man says. After some loud thuds and scraping sounds, the sounds of bed springs squeaking and hard breathing are heard. A second voice whispers "Why?" After a few minutes, the first man says, "Bitch," then, "I'm going to have to kill you, motherfucker, I'll kill you." Something falls onto the floor, and the first voice says, "You son of a bitch," then begins laughing. The sequence continues to the end of the tape, and then resumes on the other side.

Hurn was sure the first voice was Berdella, and the second voice was one of his victims, possibly being moved while bound and gagged. In early June, he sent the tape to the FBI's electronic surveillance unit in Virginia and asked them to enhance the tape electronically, for possible use in a trial. But the FBI was unable to improve its intelligibility, and sent it back in July.

The squad had finished. They had identified everyone in all of Berdella's photos, and found all but six of them.

Two of those six were Pearson and Sheldon. Many of the detectives felt Berdella had probably killed more than six, but there were no photos, no skulls, no evidence of any more, just one brief, unexplained page of a log. There was no solid proof of any ritual or cult activity, Cole thought. And so on June 10, after hundreds of interviews and thousands of miles, Cole disbanded the squad and sent the last of the ten-volume case file over to the prosecutors' office. It was their ballgame now.

Chapter Nine

The great drought of 1988 enveloped Kansas City early in the summer and baked it dust dry. The relentless, moistureless heat further damaged the already depressed farming industry surrounding the city in both Missouri and Kansas. Day after day, Midwesterners plodded through the stagnant, heavy air. Pat Hall often said the Berdella case brought out the worst in everyone: prosecutors, defense attorneys, cops, reporters. Maybe it was just the damn heat.

Added to the mix that summer was the quadrennial election for county prosecutor. Riederer, a former county legislator and two-term prosecutor, had begun a run for county executive in 1986 but had to withdraw due to illness, so he reupped for a possible third term. In the August 2 Democratic primary, Riederer's top two opponents were Leonard Hughes II, a retired municipal judge, and Carol Coe, a lawyer and Jackson County legislator. Coe loved the spotlight. She had worked for the city's law department before being appointed to the county legislature to fill the slot of a man who had pleaded guilty to embezzling money from a scholarship fund. Upon taking office, Coe announced that she would proudly uphold her predecessor's legacy. Reporters flocked to Coe after that, in their search for good quotes. Coe's sharp mind and rapid-fire tongue never disappointed.

Beneath a blazing July sun at the height of the prosecutor's race, Coe staged a news conference on the front steps of Bob Berdella's house, to accuse Riederer of exploiting the case for his political benefit. She said Riederer's news conferences and "handling of this case" had "tortured the justice system as well as the families of Robert Sheldon and Larry Pearson as surely as the alleged torturing which occurred in this house."

Riederer had held several news conferences for the benefit of the local television stations, who complained that they weren't getting the information that was appearing in the morning newspaper. Riederer was certain the police were leaking details to the paper, such as the identities of the skulls, when he had ordered them not to discuss the case, and he told police commanders he didn't like it. Then, to appease the rest of the media, he would confirm what had appeared in the paper. Coe said this situation demonstrated that Riederer lacked control over the police and the case. She also criticized Riederer for prosecuting the sodomy case too slowly, and for using the case to "build up media hype before the August 2 primary." Coe also claimed she'd heard from police sources that Riederer had no plans to ever indict Berdella for murder.

Riederer, a political veteran, responded the same day with his own press conference. The idea that he might never charge Berdella with murder, and that the police told Coe this, tickled him. "There isn't anybody in the police department likely to share information with Carol Coe," Riederer quipped. Are you calling Coe a liar? a reporter asked. "What I'm saying is that she does not know what she is talking about. . . . As far as I know, she is the first person who has tried to use this case for political advantage or manipulation." The exchange made for lively sound bites on the news that night. Berdella read about Coe's press conference and told his lawyer to send her campaign a bill for the use of his house.

The following week, Coe announced that she intended to crack the Berdella case right away. She was going to visit him in the Jackson County jail. "I want to get him to confess, like Perry Mason, so we can put him away," Coe told the *Kansas City Star*. A short time later, she said she was still discussing the idea with other lawyers, and wasn't certain whether she would try to see Berdella. If she did, she said she would urge him to ask for a special prosecutor to handle his case. Berdella might agree to see her out of curiosity, Coe said, and then confess to her. Barbara Schenkenberg, one of Berdella's lawyers, said Coe would only see Berdella "over my dead body."

The same week, Riederer made a speech to the Young Lawyers section of the Lawyers Association of Kansas City entitled "The Upcoming Prosecutor's Race and the Berdella Case." His appearance, or the topic, drew the largest crowd in the group's history. Riederer complained that the case had increased tension between police and prosecutors and put more political pressure on him. He said his attempts to limit pretrial publicity had been circumvented by the police, and that police and prosecutors often disagree about when charges should be filed. "If you want to have fun sometime," Riederer said, "sit down with a police officer or a detective who has been a police officer for fifteen years and try to talk to him about the meaning of the word *justice*. It's a difficult thing to do, and one that we have to do on a daily basis."

Riederer likened his situation to that of the prosecutor running for reelection in the novel *Presumed Innocent* by Scott Turow, in which the murder of assistant prosecutor Carolyn Polhemus becomes a central campaign issue. "Some people say that the Berdella case is my Carolyn case," Riederer said. However, Riederer's suspect was not another prosecutor but a sadistic shopkeeper. And while there was only one victim in Turow's novel, the number of Bob Berdella's victims was still a mystery.

The shadow of the prosecutor's race added another intangible, albeit an unmentioned one, to the deliberations of Riederer, Hall, Holtsclaw and Parker on the Berdella case. Riederer didn't want to be seen as using the case for political purposes, but he also didn't want to fumble the prosecution and blow either the primary or general election. He sat in on case discussions, was kept updated by Hall and handled all media inquiries. But he let Hall continue to manage the daily details of the case, knowing that the normal pace of criminal prosecutions in Jackson County would take the start of Berdella's trial past both voting dates.

The prosecutors frequently gathered to discuss how to build a murder case against Berdella that would stand up in court. The first step, obviously, was filing a murder charge. For several reasons, the prosecutors decided to take the case before a grand jury. Grand juries, composed of twelve citizens who meet regularly in secret sessions, hear witnesses and evidence presented by the prosecutor and the police, without rebuttal from the defendant or his attorney. If the grand jury decides to file charges, it issues an indictment. If an indictment were handed down on Berdella, the prosecutors reasoned, it wouldn't appear politically motivated since it wasn't filed by the prosecutors. An indictment also automatically negated the need to hold a preliminary hearing, with its public testimony and cross-examination by the defense. When prosecutors file charges, a preliminary hearing is held by a judge to determine if there truly is enough evidence to warrant a trial. When a grand jury files charges, the case is "bound over" for trial without further hearings.

There were two possible murder cases to present to the grand jury: Larry Pearson or Robert Sheldon. Without skulls or other physical evidence, putting together a murder case on Jerry Howell or James Ferris would be impossible. Riederer would continue to bluff his way through questions about how many murder cases he might file, but both he and the police privately knew that the maximum was two.

The first major obstacle the prosecutors faced was proving the cause of death. Dr. Long in St. Louis had finished his analysis of the skull hair and tissue of Pearson and reported that he had found traces of acepromazine and chlorpromazine in the hair. But Long told Gary Howell he couldn't say how much of either drug had been injected into Pearson, and he couldn't testify that the amount had been toxic or lethal. Hall and Cole had been hoping desperately that the chemical tests would provide the crucial physical evidence to prove the cause of death. Now that avenue was closed too.

The prosecutors pondered whether they even had to have a cause or death when presenting the case to the grand jury. Possibly they could devise different theories of murder, based on the available evidence. Hall, Parker and several law interns researched the question, and found that there was no requirement that the grand jury specifically state a cause of death. Hall thought he might be able to convince the grand jury by negative evidence; that is, that the men didn't die by natural, accidental or self-inflicted causes. That left only the criminal means committed by another person.

Then there was the issue of *corpus delicti,* the victim's body. Where was it? Can you prove murder without it? In recent years, the courts seemed to be saying yes. In 1976, the U.S. Supreme Court wrote that, because of the number of procedural safeguards protecting the rights of defendants, "the *corpus delicti* rule is supported by few practical or social-policy considerations." Advances in forensic science and technology also seemed convincing to authorities. While the prosecutors debated the Berdella case, prosecutors in Connecticut were trying to prove the so-called "woodchipper murder" of Helle Crafts based on less than three ounces of fabric and human remains, including a capped tooth that experts said belonged to the victim. And elsewhere in Missouri, prosecutors filed murder charges against a man whose wife's bloodstained car was found with spent shotgun pellets and bone fragments. The wife was never found.

Hall reviewed the stack of circumstantial evidence, and decided the Larry Pearson case would be the first one to try. The sheer cumulative weight of what the police had uncovered should be enough to at least obtain an indictment, the prosecutors thought. In addition, the crime lab had come up with more supporting evidence that helped indicate, if not flat-out prove, that Berdella had killed Pearson.

By mid-July, the case against Berdella included the following:

A) *Pearson's skull*. Positively identified by dental records. There was no chance that Pearson, unlike Howell or Ferris, was still alive.

B) *Photos of Pearson*. There were at least sixty Polaroids of Pearson in Berdella's house, both dressed and undressed. There were pictures of Pearson being sodomized, sexually abused and tortured. People who knew Pearson had positively identified him in the photos. In addition, Warlen at the crime lab had put together a montage of enlarged photos of Pearson which showed a scar on his right leg. The same scar is visible in two pictures of a naked man with a plastic bag over his head. Suffocation was a possible cause of death.

C) *Berdella's logs*. The notes police figured Berdella kept on Pearson began on "6/23/87," and continued for more than two weeks, past "Wed 7/8" to "Fri," which would have been July 10, 1987. In more than twenty pages of a spiral notebook, and also three loose-leaf pages which started "6/23," Berdella detailed the times and amounts of every injection he administered, every instance he had sex, every occasion of torture, every time he gave food or drink, as well as the subject's reactions. "Master Bob" he quoted the person calling him once. The final entry read, *"10:00-11:00 All Fr + Photo Fever Down."* However, there was no clear indication that the person, Pearson or whoever, had died.

To help decipher the abbreviations in the logs, Gary Howell at the crime lab had enlarged the small pieces of paper to ten by twelve inches, and started making notes between the lines in red pen. Comparing the notes with the photos, with the drugs found in Berdella's house, and with what Bryson had told them about Berdella's preferences, Howell theorized that Berdella's abbreviations were logical and consistent.

"ACE," "KET" and "CP" referred to acepromazine, ketamine and chlorpromazine, three injectable drugs found in Berdella's torture room, and invariably listed with a "2 cc" or "3 cc" amount in the logs. Acepromazine, often known by the brand name "PromAce," is a tranquilizer used on animals, particularly dogs, to calm them down before examinations or car trips. Chlorpromazine is the generic name for "Thorazine," long used as a tranquilizer for human mental patients, and sometimes as a preanesthesia on pets. Ketamine, with the brand name "Ketalar," is an anesthetic used mostly on animals, sometimes in combination with acepromazine, and is a derivative of PCP.

Howell also translated "Pen" in Berdella's notes as penicillin, which Berdella told Bryson he was injecting to fend off infections. "F" meant fuck, "BF" meant back-fuck or butt-fuck, "CF" meant carrot-fuck or cucumber-fuck, and "FF" meant fist-fuck or front-fuck. "EKG" was probably a reference to the neon-light transformer found near the bed, with alligator clips attached to it. In the logs, "EKG" was usually followed by a number and sometimes a body part, indicating how long the shock was administered and where, such as "8:53 EKG 10 sec, eyes." "86," Howell noted, was sometimes used as slang meaning to get rid of or destroy something. "86" was the last entry in the Jerry Howell log.

D) *Berdella's handwriting.* Although Berdella had defied a court order and refused to provide a handwriting sample, there were plenty of Berdella's writings in the numerous lawsuits he'd filed over the years. Berdella's writing was legible and consistent, and would link him to the logs. Also, during trial, prosecutors would be allowed to tell the jury that Berdella had refused to provide a handwriting sample, implying Berdella must be hiding something.

E) *The cut marks on Pearson's vertebrae.* The lab had matched the blades in two of Berdella's saws to the marks on the vertebrae. Though tests indicated the cuts were made after Pearson was dead, if Berdella hadn't killed Pearson, someone had used one of his saws, or one with a very similar blade, to cut Pearson's head off.

F) *The chemical tests.* Even if Dr. Long couldn't say the amounts were lethal, Pearson definitely had acepromazine and chlorpromazine in his system. An overdose of the various tranquilizers was another possible cause of death.

G) *The oral sex incident*. If Pearson had bitten Berdella badly enough so that he had to go the hospital, that might have provided a motive for Berdella to kill Pearson. Berdella made that police report last August 5. Later in August, Pearson didn't show up for court on his indecent exposure arrest.

H) *Berdella paid Pearson's bond*. Records showed that when Pearson was arrested in June, Berdella went to a bonding company and paid them a $30 fee, and the company in turn posted Pearson's $150 bond. When Pearson missed his August 21 court date, the bonding company's $150 was forfeited and a warrant issued for Pearson's arrest. Several days later, Berdella paid off the $150 with a money order. It was one more link between Berdella and Pearson. Tests indicated Pearson had been dead from six weeks to ten months. Pearson's skull was found eight months after the oral sex incident.

I) *Bryson*. Bryson could testify not only to what had happened to him, to give indications of Berdella's behavior, but also that Berdella told him he had killed other people, and had threatened to kill Bryson. A living survivor made a much better witness than bond records or lab technicians.

While lawyers around Kansas City debated how to prove Bob Berdella committed murder—or how he might beat the rap once it was filed—Hall, in early July, began presenting witnesses to the grand jury for the purpose of obtaining a murder indictment. Hall told the grand jury he didn't know the exact cause of death. Probably, Pearson either died by asphyxiation after a plastic bag had been placed over his head, or by a drug overdose, or both. If the case went to trial, Hall could focus on one theory then.

196

* * *

In mid-July, Chris Bryson was released from the Research Psychiatric Center. Not long after that, he disappeared again. By this time, Hurn had taken a genuine interest in Bryson and his family, recognizing the suffering they'd endured, and the troubles still ahead. Hurn spoke with Bryson's wife frequently about what was happening in their household, what was happening with the investigation, what step was next in the prosecution and how to cope with all of it.

Hurn was convinced almost from the beginning that Bryson had gone to Berdella's house to make some money. During Bryson's first night in the hospital, it was Hurn who had asked him if there really was a woman in the car with Berdella, and Bryson admitted there wasn't. But that didn't mean Bryson was not a rape victim. Though some people, including many policemen, believe prostitutes cannot be raped, Hurn did not agree with that thinking. Even if Bryson was hustling that night, he didn't deserve what Berdella had done to him. Hurn felt that no one else in the police department cared about Bryson as a person. Hurn saw a savvy yet vulnerable young man, and wanted to help him.

However, Hurn and the prosecutor Holtsclaw were starting to get discouraged. Bryson's "rehabilitation" had cost the state of Missouri twenty thousand dollars, Holtsclaw thought, and we still can't control him. Hurn told Bryson's wife to call him as soon as Bryson resurfaced. When Bryson did return home, he convinced his wife not to call Hurn. "They're done with me," he told her. "They don't need me, they're using me." And again he vanished.

Several days after that, Bryson's wife phoned Hurn. Her husband was at his mother's house. Hurn sped over to the East Side house, growing steadily angrier at Bryson, who had been gone for more than a week. He pulled up to the one-story house, got out of his detective's car and slammed the door. He walked up the concrete steps and knocked on the glass storm door. The mystery man appeared.

"Hey Ashley," Bryson said calmly.

"Chris," Hurn said, pausing to cool down, "you need to shoot straight stick with me. What the hell's the deal?"

"I was on the streets."

"What streets?"

"Down by Joseph's," at 10th and McGee, Bryson said. "People saw me. Just cruising around."

"Cruising in what?"

"I know some babes," Bryson replied, raising Hurn's temper again.

"You're back on the shit," Hurn accused him.

"No man, I'm straight, I'm straight," Bryson said. The two men stepped inside.

"You're treating your wife like shit," Hurn told Bryson. "You've got a new baby boy, you can't just leave them."

"Yeah, you can say that," Bryson said frustratedly. "You can say that. You've got it all."

Hurn considered correcting Bryson, but decided against it. Actually, due largely to troubles with his fiancée, Hurn's personal life was disintegrating, and he was concentrating on the Berdella case to distract him from his own troubles. He resumed his attempt to set Bryson straight.

"Why aren't you working?" Hurn asked. "Don't leave your old lady hanging. At least send them some money."

"This is fucked," Bryson said tensely. "This is *fucked*."

"Well yeah, there are some problems, it is fucked," Hurn said, trying to mollify Bryson. "But don't let it get you. I know you, and I like you, and you can handle this."

"You weren't there, you don't know."

"Yeah, you're right, I wasn't. I know what the mother-fucker did," Hurn said, using the word that Bryson always used to refer to Berdella. "And I appreciate you staying in. I know you could have gotten out."

"Damn right I could have."

"Don't let it affect you," Hurn urged him.

Bryson slammed his fist down on the table. "I think about it every fucking day."

Hurn let that thought hang there. Bryson's physical scars may have healed, but his psychological scars were deeper, far more lasting. It didn't seem likely that Bryson would be able to face Berdella in a courtroom anytime soon, yet he was the only person who could assure that Berdella went to jail. If the situation came down to Bryson's psychological well-being, or Berdella's freedom, Hurn did not want to be the man to make the choice.

Berdella's outlook on life was improving, and Coleman observed that he was having more "up" days than "down." This may have been because, after three months in jail, he began to believe that the sodomy case would be the only one filed against him. Just his word against Bryson's. A Westport businessman and neighborhood crime fighter against a downtown street hustler. In April, he was emotional and fearful. In July, he was determined and prepared.

Berdella grew more expansive with Dr. O'Connor, discussing his recent relationships with young men, his attempts to help people such as Freddie Kellogg, or D.J. Blankenship, or Jerry Howell. Berdella told O'Connor that he sometimes had several men living in his house at the same time, and he would assist them with their personal problems, help them find jobs and provide emotional support for them. These men, in turn, broke promises to him, refused to repay debts, flouted him. Increasingly, Berdella began to feel victimized, humiliated, that he was being manipulated in these relationships. But as Berdella's older friends drifted away, these men provided his only real source of personal contact and involvement. Professionally, Berdella immersed himself in the development of Bob's Bazaar Bizarre, though that still allowed him plenty of freedom to pursue his activities on Charlotte Street.

O'Connor reached some conclusions about Berdella based both on his subject's voluntary autobiography and the clinical tests he administered, including the widely used Minnesota Multi-Phasic Personality Inventory, or MMPI. O'Connor wrote that Berdella "clearly demonstrates three of five specific predictors or subsequent violent or dangerous behavior": parental violence, injury and a lack of adequate protection, and relatively early parental loss. However, Berdella was not a violent individual, and did not exhibit antisocial behavior. O'Connor wrote that "this pattern is typical or classic for individuals who are not antisocial and not psychotic, but who develop a pattern in adulthood which leads to well encapsulated or specific serial assault with a very narrowly defined class of victims."

The tests showed Berdella was above average intellectually, a "bright and well-educated individual." An index which measured accuracy and candor of responses indicated Berdella was being open and truthful. Other tests showed that Berdella was depressed, had a tendency to convert emotions into physical symptoms (thus his hypertension and other health problems), was sexually ambivalent or confused, and had a "somewhat disorganized thought process."

Numerous scales, however, were "clearly indicative of the long-standing, internal conflicts which Mr. Berdella has experienced," O'Connor found. "Each of these involve conflict or discord related to the family, to close interpersonal or sexual relationships, and to cognitive or thought process controls." O'Connor wrote that one test was particularly significant, showing that "Berdella's personality organization is one in which hostility or anger is internally directed or directed at self. . . . His general personality organization is that of an individual who handles emotional pain or anger in a self-destructive or self-punitive fashion. While he is clearly not psychotic or schizophrenic, such individuals may develop well-encapsulated or highly specific areas in which aggressive behavior occurs. These are individuals who are not generally delusional, but operate in a specific area as if delusional thought process were present but translated into actions which are not well-rationalized or clearly understood."

O'Connor summarized Berdella's test results as "characteristic of an individual who has experienced harm or violence in childhood, but who did not engage in poorly socialized or antisocial behavior. The test findings are . . . typical of individuals who handle post-traumatic stress by assuming a hyperresponsible, conventional social role, who internalize anger or aggression, but who develop a highly encapsulated or well-controlled area of illogical thinking which is emotionally driven and may lead to symbolic violence with a highly selected target population. Such individuals have an extreme sense of fairness, may identify with any even minor injustice or victimization, and high needs for control and for rational behavior. If such individuals are placed in a victimization circumstance, they may behave in a very self-destructive fashion," O'Connor concluded.

O'Connor continued to see Berdella regularly, in therapy sessions that lasted about ninety minutes each, until mid-September. Coleman also visited Berdella, though his frequency was reduced from twice to once a week. Coleman also spoke regularly with Berdella's mother, who was still having difficulty comprehending what her son was accused of. Some friends in Ohio shunned her, and reporters still called her. She tried to provide support to her oldest son by phone, but the thought of what his arrest had done to her bothered Berdella, and he became irritable when she called.

While Berdella unburdened himself to Coleman, the minister began to wonder if this was a confessional, if he was bound to secrecy. He felt there were times he knew more than the police did, and that troubled him greatly. "I wasn't worried about having to testify," Coleman recalled later, "it was just sitting there, with this person across from me, the emotional intensity with him. I took on his suffering. I was someone who saw what he had been, and knew this was not what he wanted. He saw himself as a good person who'd done certain things anybody could do. It was almost, 'Thank God it's over.' Then it turned into, 'Why didn't the police catch me sooner?' "

Leaving the jail each week, Coleman sometimes felt breathless. There was no one he could unburden himself to, because almost no one knew he was seeing Berdella. The visits began to affect him physically. His appetite diminished, he had difficulty sleeping, he couldn't make love to his wife. His weight dropped from 128 to 116 by the end of the summer. He knew he was helping Berdella, but he wasn't sure he was finding any larger answers.

Berdella was oblivious to this. He concentrated on his case, digesting the police reports stacked in his cell. He worried that the public defender's office had too many cases, that they weren't spending enough time on his. And from the first week of his incarceration, he worried about the death penalty. It had been reinstated in Missouri in 1977, and Berdella feared it above all else. His survival instinct revved into high gear at the thought of the state's method of execution, lethal injection. If a murder charge was filed against him, Berdella predicted, Riederer in an election year would certainly press for the death penalty. When Berdella's lawyers told him that the prosecutors had begun submitting a murder case to the grand jury, his preoccupation grew. At all costs, he must avoid the death penalty.

Rather than present all his evidence in one sitting, Hall brought in about fifteen witnesses on two separate Fridays to explain to the grand jury what they knew about Berdella and what evidence there was that he had murdered Larry Pearson. In the third session, on July 22, Hall presented records and paperwork for the jurors to examine, such as the bond papers for Pearson signed by Berdella, Pearson's medical records and the confirmation that it was his skull and neckbones in Berdella's backyard.

At 2:30 that afternoon, eleven days before the prosecutor's primary, the grand jury indicted Bob Berdella on one count of first-degree murder. The indictment charged that "between the dates of June 7, 1987 [when Berdella bonded Pearson out of jail] and April 3, 1988 [the date Pearson's head was uncovered, but one day after Berdella had been arrested] . . . Berdella, after deliberation, knowingly caused the death." No cause of death was alleged. The only available penalties to those convicted of Murder One in Missouri are life imprisonment without parole or death by lethal injection.

Riederer held a press conference that afternoon, and once more denied using the case for political gain. He wouldn't say what evidence had been presented to the grand jury, but said most of it had already been made public by the news media. Would he seek the death penalty? a reporter asked. "I see no reason to ask for a life sentence,"

Riederer replied, but added, "I'm not going to discuss trial strategy." Asked whether he would charge Berdella with Sheldon's murder, Riederer said that investigation was continuing, and that prosecutors might seek another indictment later.

The indictment was almost anticlimactic in Kansas City. Berdella was finally past the stage of being a sick joke. His constant media presence had become an irritant, and as the details of the police investigation began to seep out, those with weak stomachs decided they didn't want to hear any more. Veiled references in the newspapers to cucumbers and chain saws, once a curiosity, were now merely tiresome. For the police, the indictment was a vindication of sorts, though Cole and his squad had long since returned to their daily detective duties. For Hall, it was simply an early step in the long climb to a potential conviction. He continued to work exhausting hours, researching, writing, looking to plug any holes in his attack scheme. He called Gary Howell at the crime lab periodically, seeking more evidence, making more requests to have items scraped, tested or retested.

Howell was used to this, knowing from previous trials Hall's predilection for scrupulous preparation. Even though the detectives had completed their investigation, the lab would continue working on the Berdella case, in some fashion, for several more months. During one of Hall's phone calls, Howell was able to tell him about another photo montage Officer Warlen had put together for possible presentation at the trial. This one matched the photographs that Warlen and Hurn had taken of Berdella at the jail in April with Berdella's own photographs of himself involved in sex acts or torture with other men. The nearly identical angles showed Berdella's forearm extended, his hairy stomach protruding, his stubby hand reaching out. Berdella's Polaroids were enlarged to eight by ten inch size, and cropped for easy, side-by-side comparison. Though the FBI lab in Quantico had done much the same thing and decided the comparison was inconclusive, Warlen thought the photos would still be an effective tool in front of a jury.

As Election Day, August 2, arrived, Holtsclaw faced a significant step of his own in the sodomy prosecution. Circuit Judge Gene Martin had upheld Holtsclaw's motion to videotape Chris Bryson's testimony, in case Bryson became unable to testify. Berdella's lawyers, Berrigan and Schenkenberg, appealed this ruling to the Missouri Court of Appeals, but had heard nothing. Martin set the videotaping for Thursday, August 4. But the judge also scheduled a meeting between Bryson and Berdella's lawyers for August 2, so that the defense attorneys could prepare for the Thursday session. Holtsclaw, Berrigan and Schenkenberg were present and ready at 9 A.M. that morning. Only Bryson wasn't ready. He didn't show.

Hurn couldn't find Bryson anywhere. He wasn't at his apartment. He wasn't at his mother's house. He wasn't at work. He wasn't downtown. Again, he'd vanished. Hurn left messages everywhere, but none was returned. As the day wore on, a mounting panic gripped the prosecutors. For most of the office, the mood was euphoric: Riederer was trouncing Coe and Hughes at the polls, well on his way to a third term. But, with each of Bryson's disappearances, the prosecutors' frustration grew.

At the end of the afternoon, Berrigan and Schenkenberg filed a motion with Judge Martin to exclude any further testimony by Bryson in the sodomy case, for refusing to comply with the subpoena ordering him to the morning questioning. Martin took it under consideration. On the other side, Hurn and Holtsclaw decided to make another late-night search for Bryson. They visited his mother's house, they stopped in the downtown bars and showed his photograph. In Joseph's Lounge, the bartender told them Bryson had been in but was gone.

The rest of the night was spent sitting and waiting outside several drug houses in Bryson's old East Side neighborhood, including the apartment complex where Sergeant Moss had seen Bryson in May. Hurn and Holtsclaw watched shadowy characters stumble in and out of cars and dilapidated houses all night, but none of them was Bryson. Finally, after 2 A.M., the surveillance team decided to go home and sleep, hoping that Bryson's wife or mother would hear from him soon.

The prosecutors realized gloomily that if Bryson was gone for good, a major turning point had been reached. Bryson was their ace in the hole, the entire foundation for an unshakable sodomy and kidnapping case. A conviction on the murder case would always be questionable. At least with the sodomy, Berdella would be assured of getting some hard time. But Bryson had disappeared even before being videotaped. Without him, the sodomy case would have to be dismissed. The opening Berdella needed was now there.

Chapter Ten

The elusive Chris Bryson was still nowhere to be found as Pat Hall and Marietta Parker entered the courtroom of Circuit Judge Alvin C. Randall the next morning, August 3. If Bryson didn't want to cooperate, the murder case took on even greater significance. Today's hearing was the very first stage of the case, the arraignment, in which the defendant is read the charges and enters a plea. Even if the defendant plans to plead guilty, he customarily pleads not guilty at the arraignment, then waits to see what evidence the prosecutors have before beginning plea bargain negotiations. The most significant event of the arraignment often is the first appearance of the defendant's lawyer.

Though preoccupied with Bryson, two things made Hall's antennae twitch. First, Pat Berrigan of the public defender's office was here. Were they going to defend Berdella in this case too? Some judges, and Randall was one of them, didn't want the public defenders handling so many cases; it slowed down the docket. Hall thought Randall was going to appoint a private lawyer to represent Berdella on the murder charge. Second, Berdella was here. He hadn't made a court appearance since a bond hearing in early April. Hall thought something was up. Are we going to have another battle over Berdella's bond? Hall wondered. Are the public defenders going to fight to keep representing this guy? Are we already going to argue over evidence? Hall had turned over everything he had. It looked like a hearing which would normally take less than five minutes could take up much of the morning. Hall could feel himself becoming impatient with Berrigan again.

Judge Randall entered the Division Four courtroom, sat down in his high-backed brown leather chair, and nodded to Hall to start the proceedings. "I noticed that Mr. Berrigan is seated by the defendant," Hall told the judge, then turned to face Berrigan. "Does your presence mean that the public defender's office has volunteered to represent him?"

Berrigan ignored Hall's gaze and looked up at Randall. "We have an entry of appearance ready to be filed, Judge."

"The court did not plan to appoint your office," Randall said.

"I see," Berrigan said.

Randall explained that he had been appointing private attorneys to lessen the burden on the public defender, and to keep the court dockets moving. Berrigan asked the judge for a hearing, to determine if it was appropriate for the public defender to volunteer to represent someone. Randall said no. "You do not need to have a hearing because I will not appoint the public defender," the judge said.

"All right, I would like to represent Mr. Berdella today, Judge," Berrigan responded.

"All right," Randall said. "The public defender is voluntarily entering his appearance, by provision of the court, for the purposes of the arraignment only." Turning to Hall, he added, "You may proceed, Mr. Prosecutor."

One issue resolved, Hall thought. Still standing, Hall picked up the murder indictment off the prosecutors' table. He looked at Berdella, dressed in his dark green jail

208

uniform, his black hair combed straight back, seated next to Berrigan. "Mr. Berdella, in cause number CR88-3495, you are present in the court with your attorney for arraignment only, Mr. Berrigan, and I wish to inform you at this time, Mr. Berdella, that you have been charged by the Jackson County grand jury, by indictment. This indictment charges you with murder in the first degree, a Class A felony."

Hall handed the indictment to Berrigan. Berrigan in turn handed his own paperwork to Hall, making a routine "request for discovery," which seeks a list of all the prosecution's evidence and asks whether they intend to seek the death penalty. Berrigan then gave the indictment to Judge Randall. The law requires that the judge read the charges to the defendant, but defense attorneys usually waive the reading. However, Berrigan asked Randall to read the charges. Randall did so, formally accusing Berdella of killing Larry Pearson sometime in 1987 or early 1988.

"Does that complete the arraignment then?" Randall asked the lawyers.

"Your Honor," Berrigan said, "is that the only document that has presently been filed in this case, that is, is there any notice of aggravating circumstances presently before the Court?"

Randall said, "Why don't you look at the file and you tell me?"

"Thank you," Berrigan said, and Hall handed him the case file, which contained only a couple of standard documents. While Berrigan paged through the papers, his defense partner, Barbara Schenkenberg, was trying to get into the courtroom. Randall had ordered tight security, in case someone wanted to take another swing at Berdella. Schenkenberg was motioned toward the judge's chambers, then entered the courtroom and sat down next to Berdella.

"Thank you Judge," Berrigan said. "At this time,

209

it's the defendant's intention to enter a plea of guilty, as charged, to murder in the first degree."

Hall's jaw dropped involuntarily. So did Randall's. Hall was stupefied. He thought he was on the way out the door, the arraignment was over. Now this. The courtroom spectators began whispering, asking each other if they'd heard Berrigan correctly. Hall stared at Randall. Randall stared at Berrigan. Berrigan stood firm. The bomb was dropped. Finally, Randall plunged ahead. "All right, we'll have to make a record," the judge said. "Go around to that chair," he told Berdella. "Raise your right hand and be sworn."

Berdella stood up and shuffled over to the witness stand.

"Would you state your full name please, Mr. Berdella?" Berrigan began.

"Robert Andrew Berdella Jr."

"What is your date of birth sir?"

"1-31-49."

"Now Mr. Berdella," Berrigan said, "I realize that the copy that Mr. Hall just handed me this morning is the first time you have seen this particular copy of the indictment, is that correct?"

"That's correct."

"But you have, on prior occasions, seen a copy of this same indictment, have you not?" Berrigan asked.

"Yes." Berdella's answers were flat, emotionless, his lisp slightly evident.

"Do you understand that it charges you with the offense of murder in the first degree?"

"Yes."

"Do you understand that the punishment for that offense, unless the state has requested the death penalty, is life imprisonment without parole; do you understand that?"

"Yes."

The lightbulbs flashed on in Hall's and Parker's minds instantaneously. Berdella was trying to plead guilty today before the prosecutors filed notice of their intent to seek the death penalty. He must have thought he could avoid death by pleading quickly, Hall figured. Fairly tricky. Hall prepared to respond.

Berrigan continued with a standard list of questions that defense attorneys ask every defendant who pleads guilty, to assure that they know what they're doing. Did Berdella understand he wasn't obligated to plead guilty, that he could have a trial by jury, that he could call witnesses, that he could cross-examine prosecution witnesses, that he could testify or not testify, that he was presumed innocent until proven guilty. Berdella answered yes to every question.

"Do you understand, Mr. Berdella, that there is no plea agreement in your case?" Berrigan inquired.

"Yes."

"The only thing left to do, if the judge accepts your guilty plea, is to sentence you to life imprisonment without the possibility of parole," Berrigan said. "Do you understand that?"

"Yes."

"Just a second, Your Honor," Hall said, rising to his feet, the irritation palpable in his voice. "The state is not waiving the death penalty in this case."

"Your Honor," Berrigan responded, "the state has not filed its request for the death penalty, as they're obligated to do. There's no notice of aggravating circumstances filed with the Court, and they're not able to obtain the death penalty without having done so."

Hall was ready. "Your Honor, pursuant to Chapter 565, we are not entitled to file notice of aggravating circumstances until request is made by the defendant and we are given a reasonable amount of time in which to file the notice of aggravating circumstances. We were not given that request until approximately five minutes ago, Judge. I hardly consider that to be a reasonable amount of time. If this plea goes through, I want it understood that the state is not waiving the death penalty in this case, and the state is seeking the death penalty."

Berrigan pressed on. "The state has had ample time to prepare this case for trial, Judge. This indictment was two weeks ago. The investigation has been going on—"

Randall interrupted. "But that wasn't his point. I don't know what you mean by preparing for trial. There was no trial set today."

"I didn't say anything about a trial, Judge," Berrigan said. "I meant, prepare to file this aggravating circumstances."

"I think you said prepare for trial," Randall said. "But, in any event, his [Hall's] statement was that under the law they are not required to file a notice of aggravating circumstances until it is requested by the defendant."

"It is requested in the request for discovery, Judge," Berrigan said.

"Well, does the statute also say that they have a reasonable time to file it?" Randall asked.

"Not that I know of," Berrigan answered.

"Well, we'll have to check that out then," Randall said.

Hall remained mute, but satisfied. He was right. Missouri Revised Statute 565.005 states, "At a reasonable time before the commencement" of a first-degree, death-penalty murder case, the state, upon request, shall provide a list of "aggravating or mitigating circumstances" which necessitate the death penalty. Hall had made his objection on the record. Now he would see what else Berrigan had planned.

"Well, you go ahead with the plea," Randall told Berrigan.

212

"I'm not going to proceed and have the defendant make a factual basis unless it's clear, Judge, that the possible sentence in this case is life without the possibility of parole," Berrigan said.

"All right," Randall said. "We'll take a recess. Take him [Berdella] back to the cell."

The lawyers filed into Randall's chambers and began arguing heatedly, loudly enough that their voices filtered through the closed door. Several times, Berrigan and Schenkenberg left the chambers to speak with Berdella, who sat handcuffed and chained in a holding cell.

Hall and Parker went upstairs to the prosecutor's office, met with Holtsclaw, and got Riederer on the phone. Riederer was at home, having celebrated his primary election victory the night before. Schenkenberg had called him just as the arraignment began to inform him of the plea. Now the prosecutors had a decision to make.

With Bryson's disappearance still foremost in everyone's minds, a guilty plea by Berdella would eliminate the need for Bryson's participation. Berdella would get life in prison without parole—truly without opportunity for parole. No better sentence could be imposed in the sodomy and kidnapping case. If all else fell through, this would be a perfect back-up, Holtsclaw thought.

The public wanted the death penalty, though. Badly. Local sentiment against Berdella had galvanized in such a negative way that even people who once knew him now were afraid to admit it.

But the prosecutors still had the Robert Sheldon case, the skull found in the house. They could seek the death penalty on that one, with this plea bargain as insurance, Riederer said. In that trial, or any other trial, the prosecutors could use this guilty plea against Berdella.

This whole maneuver is so sneaky it must be Berdella's idea, Riederer thought. Even Berrigan wouldn't do this,

213

Parker said. Hall, who had provided Berrigan with every document that came his way, was simply angry.

They could still get the death penalty on the Pearson case, even if Randall proceeded with the plea, the prosecutors decided. They could easily appeal the fact that they didn't have a "reasonable" amount of time to file their intent to seek the death penalty. Or they could simply dismiss the murder charge against Berdella. He was still in jail on the sodomy case. They could just have Berdella reindicted, and file the death penalty notice then.

In front of a jury, however, the murder case wasn't a sure thing. It was circumstantial. Even if a jury convicted Berdella, would it be willing to assess the death penalty based on a circumstantial case? A guilty plea was a sure thing. Not only that, but Berdella couldn't appeal a guilty plea.

The discussion returned to Bryson. The prosecutors had been planning to use him as a witness in the Pearson murder trial as well as his own sodomy trial. If Berdella pleaded guilty, the prosecutors could plea bargain the sodomy case away, and Bryson wouldn't have to testify in either one.

What was their real responsibility to the public? Parker asked. At the least, it was to protect people from Berdella. Rolling the dice for the death penalty, and going to trial on Berdella, could result in Berdella being acquitted and going free. Accepting this plea would eliminate that possibility. The prosecutors agreed. Take this plea, and go for the death penalty on Sheldon. If the public protested, so be it.

About two hours after the recess was called, the lawyers returned to the courtroom. Berdella took the stand again. His right hand was unchained so he could be sworn in again; Berrigan stood before him. Hall and Parker sat expectantly in their chairs. Word of the plea had spread rapidly, and the courtroom benches were full.

214

"Mr. Berdella," Berrigan started, "I'm going to now ask you some questions pertaining to what it is that occurred on August 5, 1987, in Jackson County, Missouri. First of all, on that particular date, August 5, 1987, where were you living, sir?"

"At 4315 Charlotte," Berdella said.

"Did you at that time know a person by the name of Larry W. Pearson?"

"Yes."

"Was he present in your house on that date?"

"Yes."

"Did you, after deliberation, knowingly cause Mr. Pearson's death by asphyxiating him?" Berrigan asked.

"Yes."

He *did* suffocate him, Hall thought. The courtroom was utterly still. "Could you tell the court briefly what occurred sir?" Berrigan said. Without pausing, Berdella said calmly: "I put a plastic bag over his head, secured it with rope and allowed him to suffocate."

Berrigan continued his list of standard questions. "Prior to doing that, did you realize what you were doing?"

"Yes."

"Did you deliberate about what you were doing and think about it?"

"Yes."

"Did you know that it would result in the death of Mr. Pearson?"

"Yes."

"And, in fact, it did, did it not?"

"Yes."

"Did you know at that time that what you did was against the law?"

"Yes."

"And all of this occurred on or about August fifth at your residence at 4315 Charlotte, Kansas City, Jackson

215

County, Missouri, is that correct?"

"Yes."

Hall asked Berdella a few questions about whether Berdella was mentally unstable at the time of the murder, and Berdella said he wasn't. And then it was over. Without so much as an evidentiary hearing, Robert Berdella had pleaded guilty to murder. The plea happened in time for the noon television news shows to broadcast the bulletin, and the afternoon *Kansas City Star* printed a huge banner headline across the top of its front page: BOB BERDELLA PLEADS GUILTY TO MURDER.

Riederer held a press conference that afternoon to explain what he could. He said waiving the death penalty was proper because Berdella would "be off the streets forever. He cannot appeal, and he can't ever do this to anyone again." Someone asked if Riederer would seek the death penalty on the Sheldon case. "That is something that will have to be decided down the line," Riederer answered, playing his cards closely, though he knew what his intention really was.

Still, dozens of questions remained. Why did Berdella kill Pearson? What did he do to Pearson before he killed him? Did he have any accomplices? What did he do with Pearson's body? Why did he save the head? How many more victims were there? A trial offered at least the promise that some of those questions would be answered. But the guilty plea was tightly controlled. Berrigan and Schenkenberg had told the prosecutors that Berdella would give only the briefest details of the killing, and that's all he gave. Judge Randall told a reporter later, "We never unnecessarily extend the plea. It was simply a matter of confining it to just this one case."

Paul Howell was furious. He still had learned nothing about what happened to his son. "I would like to be able to bury my boy," Howell told the *Kansas City Times*.

"What do they have to bargain with now? They threw my chance away." The families of James Ferris and Robert Sheldon felt the same way. How would they ever find out what Berdella did to their sons? The last chance seemed to be to obtain an indictment on the Sheldon skull, and work backward from there.

The next step, however, was resolving the sodomy case. Bryson resurfaced shortly after Berdella's guilty plea to the murder charge, and Hurn told him the pressure was now off. The prosecutors didn't want to drop the sodomy case altogether, but they were willing to dismiss some of the charges in exchange for another guilty plea, however symbolic, from Berdella. In mid-August, Holtsclaw began meeting with Berrigan and Schenkenberg to discuss terms of a plea agreement.

Even though any sentence Berdella might receive would be redundant, Riederer wanted Holtsclaw to be careful in his negotiations. Berdella had surprised them once already with the murder plea; Riederer wanted no more surprises. The final outcome of the cases were likely to be scrutinized for a long time, Riederer thought. Let's handle every step carefully.

Holtsclaw's initial offer to Berdella was that he would drop six of the seven sodomy charges and the assault charge, leaving one count of sodomy and one count of felonious restraint. If Berdella pleaded guilty, he would receive a life sentence on the sodomy and seven years on the felonious restraint. Berrigan and Schenkenberg took that offer back to Berdella.

Several days later, in another meeting, the public defenders presented Berdella's additional conditions: if the prosecutors would drop their civil suit to seize Berdella's house, Berdella would drop his own countersuit against the prosecutors. And Berdella had one more request. He wanted Bryson to sign a waiver stating that he would not

217

sue Berdella after the case was resolved. This was a highly unusual request in a criminal prosecution, and Holtsclaw sure wasn't going to approve it without presenting it to the other prosecutors.

Holtsclaw took Berdella's offer back to Riederer, Hall and Parker for group discussion. It appeared to the prosecutors that Berdella was concerned with keeping his "fortune" intact. No one knew exactly what his house and its contents would bring at auction, but what could Berdella do with the money anyway? He was spending the rest of his life in prison. Did he have something up his sleeve? Was this the next phase of some grand plan to have the murder plea overturned? This guy must think he's getting out, Parker thought.

Beside a nagging suspicion, Parker had no real objection to dropping the civil suit. It looked like it might drag on for years, with lawyer upon lawyer piling into the fray. That would negate any profit the county might receive if it won the case. If Berdella was going to insist on protecting his property as a condition of the plea, he could have it, Parker said. Riederer agreed. This would clear up two issues at once, and not keep his office involved in protracted civil litigation.

Riederer also had no problem with including a waiver for Bryson to sign, but he knew that decision was entirely up to Bryson. If Bryson wanted to sue Berdella when this was all over, the prosecutors could do nothing about it. They would go back to Berdella's lawyers and say they agreed to the exchange of dropped suits, but Bryson wouldn't take part in the deal.

Holtsclaw had misgivings about getting the prosecutor's office involved in a civil waiver, but he called Bryson and asked him to come down to the courthouse for a meeting. Riederer and Holtsclaw met with him, and explained what Berdella was demanding.

"Berdella says he won't plead unless you agree not to sue him," Riederer told Bryson. "If you want us to try the case, we'll try it. It's your call."

Bryson did not have a burning desire to go through with a trial. Because he was a rape victim, his name had been kept out of the news media, except for one mention by a local television reporter and one mention in the *Chicago Tribune*. But the longer he was involved with the Berdella mess, the more likely his identity would become known. More important, the prospect of a trial meant reliving the ordeal over and over, both before and after his testimony. Concluding the case now would help Bryson put it all behind him.

"No problem," he told Riederer and Holtsclaw. He said he didn't want to sue Berdella, he wanted the whole thing over with. Holtsclaw went back to Berdella's lawyers and told them the deal was done.

The night before Berdella was scheduled to plead guilty to the sodomy charge, the prosecutors put Bryson in a downtown motel to ensure he would be available the next day. Police officers were assigned to guard Bryson, including Detective Hurn. Bryson still had questions about the plea bargain. Hurn knew that Bryson wanted to get back at Berdella, not necessarily with a lawsuit, but somehow, some way. Hurn disagreed with the waiver, but he didn't want to tell Bryson that.

"You're doing the right thing, man," Hurn reassured Bryson. "Berdella's only going to talk about what he's done if he can plead. He'll never testify in a trial. And for him to talk, we need you. Everyone's counting on you, Chris—the parents of Howell, of Ferris." Hurn played to Bryson's brief experience as a father. "If it were your kid, wouldn't you want to know? The only way to go forward is if you continue to cooperate."

Hurn also wanted Bryson to feel as if he were in control,

and to a large extent Bryson was. But Bryson still wasn't confident.

"Is he going to be able to walk on the rest of this shit?" Bryson asked Hurn, wondering if the whole story would ever emerge.

"No, man," Hurn said. "The defense hasn't thought this through. You're going to give Berdella and the defense attorney a false sense of security. If we get a nibble, we're going to be able to prop the door open for further admissions by Berdella."

Bryson paced anxiously in the small room.

"Fuck it, man," he said. "If I say no, this is dead in the water."

"You're right," Hurn replied. "We need you. Right now, the defense is just viewing things in the short term. We're looking at this as a way to get all the information out of him."

"Would you sue the motherfucker?" Bryson asked.

Hurn dodged the question. "If we make a mistake here, the parents will never know," he said.

Referring to the waiver, Bryson wondered, "Is there any way of getting out?"

Hurn figured there was a way, but replied, "Frankly, I don't know."

The next morning, Hurn took Bryson to Holtslaw's office before the plea began. Bryson wasn't required to be present for Berdella's actual plea, but Hurn wanted him to go. Bryson resisted. He wasn't sure how he'd react to seeing Berdella again, and wasn't sure he was ready yet. Hurn felt strongly that Bryson would be mired in a psychological swamp for a very long time if he didn't face Berdella now.

"Look, Chris," Hurn said. "If you don't look into this guy's eyes, you'll never get over this. You've got control. You've got him bent over and this time you're slammin' it to him. Show this son of a bitch that you're not afraid of him."

Bryson looked up at Hurn but didn't answer. Holtsclaw stood up to go to the courtroom. "I'll see you down there," he told Hurn and Bryson.

"I'll stay here," Bryson said. "Just send word back when it's over."

Hurn kept trying. "You sure? If you're not there, you won't be there for the moment of truth."

Bryson moved behind Holtsclaw's desk and slumped down in the prosecutor's chair. He was thinking about it.

Hurn said, "I'll stay."

"No, go," Bryson said. "You've earned it."

"You've earned it too," Hurn said. "Get your bag of bones up. We'll get this room with a window into the courtroom, we'll clear it and you can hear the testimony."

"Well," Bryson said, "I'll go over, but I won't go in."

"You need to do this," Hurn urged him. "This is for you, man. This is major. The press is here, but you don't have to talk to them. You need to show him he can't fuck you over anymore."

That hit Bryson.

"All right, man," he said. He smiled, stood up and gave Hurn a high five. The two went running out the door and caught up with Holtsclaw at the elevator, like a charged-up cavalry rallying behind a lone horseman.

Hurn led Bryson out of the courthouse to the Criminal Justice Building, to the same courtroom where Berdella was punched by Paul Howell several months before. A listening booth with a one-way window at the back of the courtroom had several people in it, and Hurn asked a sheriff's deputy to clear the room. The deputy seemed uncertain about this, and Hurn immediately assumed his most authoritative voice: "You will clear this room."

After the spectators were removed from the booth,

Hurn and Bryson walked in. Hurn fiddled with the volume knob on the speaker system as the proceeding began, but the sound wasn't coming through. Hurn opened the door slightly, so Berdella's voice could be heard. Bryson pressed up against the glass and stared at Berdella. He heard Berdella, in response to a question from Berrigan, say: "I kept him bound to a bed with ropes tying his hands and feet." His eyes never moved from Berdella. Bryson moved closer to the door.

While Berdella was on the stand, Parker realized that Bryson had never actually signed the lawsuit waiver. She discreetly got up from the prosecutors' table and walked back to Bryson and asked him to sign it. "Well, I'm here now," Bryson said resignedly, and he signed the document. Parker quietly breathed a sigh of relief and returned to the proceeding.

When Holtsclaw rose to ask Berdella some routine questions, Bryson tentatively pushed the booth door open and stepped outside. He found an open space and leaned against the wall near the door to the courtroom, still focused on Berdella. Finally, Bryson had come face-to-face with his tormentor. He could see for himself that Berdella was receiving another life sentence, that "the motherfucker" would never touch him again. No more fear, no more self-doubt about how he'd been drawn into such a lurid drama. Life could resume, maybe. Hurn stood behind Bryson, and placed his hand on Bryson's shoulder, proud that Bryson had overcome his anxiety about this final confrontation. Holtsclaw happened to glance toward the back of the courtroom and saw Bryson and Hurn standing there. He smiled knowingly. For the three of them, it was a brief, triumphant moment.

Chapter Eleven

Though not an especially enviable one, the mission of Pat Berrigan and Barbara Schenkenberg was to save Bob Berdella's life. One hurdle had been cleared, but at least one more remained, and the defenders didn't know how many murder charges the prosecutors ultimately would file. Berrigan and Schenkenberg also worked deep into the night, as Pat Hall was doing in the courthouse, searching for routes through or around the death penalty. Schenkenberg grew more repulsed by Berdella's crimes as he revealed more about them, but she concealed her emotions. Outside the courthouse, others let their feelings be known to her. Longtime acquaintances of Schenkenberg suddenly became distant. People who met her for the first time were indignant when they recognized her name. "Even other lawyers," Schenkenberg would later say in a magazine profile, "other *lawyers* for God's sake, said things that implied I was doing something really unsavory and wrong. They'd ask me how I could represent such a monster. The whole idea of due process and proper representation suddenly seemed to elude them."

It was clear to Berdella's attorneys that the prosecutors soon would present the Robert Sheldon case to a grand jury for a murder indictment and another attempt at the death penalty. So in late August, Berrigan called Hall and set up a meeting. The prosecutors entered the meeting warily, though they suspected the reason Berrigan called. Hall and Riederer felt the public defenders had connived to outfox them in the first murder plea. No one ever pleads guilty to Murder One without at least notifying the prosecutors first, they thought. What sneaky maneuver would Berrigan try this time?

Berrigan was cautious but confident. He was a veteran of these meetings with Hall, as well as a survivor of Hall's courtroom onslaughts. He knew Hall had to be treated carefully, especially now.

"Our client is prepared to plead guilty to all the remaining murders he committed," Berrigan said, "in exchange for an agreement from you not to seek the death penalty."

"How many murders?" Hall asked.

"Well, we have several conditions we'd like to discuss," Berrigan said.

Of course, thought Hall. Nothing's ever easy. It wasn't much of a deal so far. Berdella already had life without parole. Why agree not to seek the death penalty, when that was the only other penalty left? Hall was immediately skeptical.

Berrigan couldn't discuss how many murders Berdella might admit. If no agreement was reached, and he revealed a number, Berrigan would be violating the attorney-client privilege. Instead of specifics, he directed the discussion to the topic of the transcript of a proposed confession. If Berdella were to confess, there would be only one copy of the transcript, and it would be kept in the public defender's office, Berrigan said. Hall practically laughed out loud at that one. Is this going to be their trick? Have Berdella plead guilty to dozens of murders, then attack the confession on appeal, while the prosecutors had no access to the transcript? And what about the marketing potential of such a confession? Surely there were all sorts of sleazy types willing to pay big money to get their hands on the seamy details of Berdella's crimes. And the public defender would control all this? Hall had no problem rejecting that condition unconditionally.

Tempers rose. Hall started to feel that this meeting was a waste of his time. This condition about the transcript was obviously another of Berdella's ploys, he thought. It was also a ridiculous condition. Hall was ready to present the Sheldon case to the grand jury, and he'd fry Berdella on that one. Before Berrigan could even reach the next condition on his list, the meeting was over.

The following Friday, September 2, Hall returned to the grand jury with several witnesses and more police reports and lab findings. In Jackson County, a grand jury meets almost every Friday and is impaneled for about six months. Hall had the same group of jurors he faced for the Pearson indictment, and didn't have to review much of the circumstantial murder case against Berdella (as if anyone in Jackson County weren't intimately familiar with the case already). Again, Hall didn't have a definitive cause of death for Sheldon, but he had Dr. Long's testimony that the log kept by Berdella indicated Sheldon had received a toxic dose of animal tranquilizers. There was also the possibility, now that Berdella had admitted one suffocation, that Berdella killed all his victims by placing bags over their heads. That same morning, with little hesitation, the grand jury charged Berdella with first-degree murder.

Riederer wouldn't say whether he would seek the death penalty against Berdella. But Sheldon's father in California wasn't so equivocal. "That animal needs to be put to death," he told a reporter. "He had my son's skull in his house and his teeth in a sack. He's killed other people . . . I'll sit in front of that prosecutor's office and make sure he gets him the death penalty." Sheldon said he was going to raise the money to fly to Kansas City for the trial.

At Berdella's arraignment, on September 13, there was no surprise plea. Standing before Circuit Judge Robert A. Meyers, Berdella pleaded not guilty. Once again, Hall and Berrigan exchanged paperwork, Hall handing over the indictment, Berrigan providing his request for discovery. When Berrigan looked through the papers Hall planned to file, he found Hall had already prepared his list of evidence and witnesses for the trial. Included in that was the prosecution's declaration that they would seek to have Berdella executed.

By mid-September, articles about Berdella had appeared in the *New York Times,* the *Chicago Tribune, Time* magazine and numerous other publications. Now the case was about to hit the big time. Geraldo Rivera was coming to town. Rivera was producing the second of his prime-time documentaries for NBC, this one on satanic cults. Rivera's researchers located several people willing to speculate that Berdella was a devil worshiper, including Carol Coe, a detective from Kansas City, Kansas, and a woman who claimed she had seen a young man sacrificed to Berdella during a satanic ritual. Bryson also agreed to be interviewed, under the conditions that his name not be used and his face would be hidden.

When Rivera himself arrived in Kansas City, he interviewed Coe, the Kansas detective, the anonymous woman, Bryson, Paul Howell, Bonnie Ferris, Harriet Sanders and Riederer. Then Rivera, joined by Coe, went for the home run. He took his cameras to the Jackson County jail to interview Berdella. Rivera and his photographers were allowed inside the jail, and as Berdella looked up from his cell that morning, he noticed the cameras being set up not far away. Berdella was stunned that Rivera had been allowed inside the jail, and eased back away from the cameras' view. He refused to be interviewed.

"Devil Worship: Exposing Satan's Underground" aired October 25, and Rivera devoted ten minutes of the show to claims that the police and prosecutors were blatantly ignoring the satanic aspects of Berdella's crimes. "One reason we think you haven't heard more about this is that many satanic crimes are simply not recognized as such," Rivera began. Standing in front of Berdella's house, he warned his nationwide audience: "These ritualistic crimes are everywhere, yet in most communities they are either overlooked or underreported. There's an example going on right now here in Kansas City that tells us why. In this house in a quiet residential neighborhood, a series of brutally violent, horrible crimes have been committed, and yet the police and prosecutor in this town seem either unable or unwilling to draw the *obvious* connection between what happened here . . . and Satanism."

Then Bryson appeared on the screen, his face plainly visible. "Call him 'Jay,' " Rivera said, but he may as well have called him Chris. When Bryson saw the show, he felt tricked. On camera, he told Rivera, "He [Berdella] took the transformer and hooked it to my genitals and stepped back and took pictures while I'm flopping around."

"What a sick dog," Rivera commented dryly.

"It seemed to never end," Bryson added.

The rest of the segment featured incorrect information sandwiched between Rivera's impassioned rhetoric. Rivera said a meaningless design above Berdella's front porch was a satanic symbol, that the remains of three people were found in the backyard, and a retired detective said that a jar with bird feathers and burnt wood was found with Pearson's skull.

But the inaccuracies were minor compared to the sensational interviews. Coe declared that other people must be involved since Berdella was in some of the photographs by

227

himself. "They're at large in the city, and you're going to be reading about it again in the next twelve to sixteen months," Coe said assuredly, although none of Berdella's torture photos were of him or appeared to be taken by someone else. The detective from Kansas City, Kansas, Lee Orr, said he was "sure" of a satanic aspect to Berdella's crimes, according to his "people." Cole called the detective the next day and asked him to provide his counterparts in Kansas City, Missouri, with any leads linking Berdella to satanism, but the detective could give none.

The most intriguing interview was conducted with a woman who said her ex-husband was a high priest of Satanism. She said she attended a meeting at which Berdella was seated on a throne, and a sixteen-year-old boy was killed as a sacrifice to Berdella. Rivera didn't ask for details of the murder or how the woman knew who Berdella was. He asked instead why she didn't report the incident to police. "No one wants to believe this happens," the woman replied. Detective Cunningham had interviewed the woman months earlier, and came away unsure whether to believe her or not. But Cunningham could find nothing to corroborate the woman's claims.

Despite a lack of corroborated evidence to back up his allegations, Rivera concluded with a brief, righteous sermon: "Now whether these cases are not being treated as ritual crimes because of embarrassment to the community or because it's easier for cops just to prosecute them as simple homicides, we don't know." The show's next segment featured a woman who claimed she gave birth to children who were used for satanic sacrifices.

The program attracted a huge national audience, and reignited Berdella discussions around office water coolers and neighborhood bars. Cole didn't know whether to laugh or kick in his television after watching Rivera. To be safe, he called Orr, the Kansas detective, then shrugged the whole thing off. He was convinced that Berdella had nothing to do with Satanism, and his commanders were happy to share that view. Riederer, who had only the police to rely upon, agreed with that conclusion. Berdella didn't get to see the program, though Berrigan and Schenkenberg later showed him a tape of the segment. He said he was amused.

The morning after the show, Detective Albert DeValkenaere was working in the Homicide unit when his phone rang. From somewhere in Massachusetts, it was Rachel DeKalb, Todd Stoops's wife.

"I saw that Geraldo show last night," she said. "Did Bob kill Todd?"

"We don't really know, ma'am," DeValkenaere told her. "We've got pictures of Todd taken by Berdella, and nobody's been able to find him, but that doesn't mean he's dead. Why, do you think Bob killed Todd?"

"Well, me and Todd used to live with Bob, from about '85 to about last summer. Then I left," DeKalb said. "I know he used to pick up guys downtown and take them back to his house and shoot them up with shit and do shit to them, I know he did that."

"Did you ever see him kill anybody?" DeValkenaere asked hopefully.

"No, I never did," DeKalb said. "But I always thought he was. That's why I got the hell out of there. I tried to get Todd to come with me, but he wouldn't."

"He was still there when you left?" DeValkenaere said.

"Yep. See, we was both hooked on shit and sometimes we were getting it from Berdella," DeKalb said. "Todd had an easy connection there and he didn't wanna give it up, you know?"

"Well, Todd's folks and brothers have ID'd Todd in some

229

of these photos we found in Mr. Berdella's house," DeValkenaere told her. "And it looks like Todd's being tortured in some of these shots, although it's hard to tell exactly what's going on."

"I bet he's dead," Dekalb said bluntly.

"Why?" DeValkenaere responded. "Why do you keep saying that? What else did you see going on in that house?"

"I can't talk anymore," DeKalb said. "I'm at work. I'll call back tonight at 6:00 when I get off work."

"OK," DeValkenaere said. "Where are you?"

"I'm in Massachusetts," DeKalb said. "I cleaned up out here, I'm off the shit completely."

"Where in Massachusetts?"

"Gotta go. I'll call you," DeKalb said, and she hung up.

DeValkenaere began thinking about how to handle this potential witness when she called back. Should he have her flown back to Kansas City? If she and Stoops lived with Berdella for two years, she could be an invaluable source of information. She might know about Howell or Ferris, or some other victims the police didn't know about. DeValkenaere reported the conversation to Cole. The sergeant told him to try, as delicately as possible, to find out where DeKalb was. If she wouldn't agree to return to Kansas City, possibly DeValkenaere could fly to Massachusetts and interview her.

DeValkenaere stayed past the end of his shift at 4 P.M. to await DeKalb's call. It never came. She was not heard from again.

The Rivera program, even the new murder indictment, both were mere distractions for Berdella by late October. Having regained his house and all his property in the Bryson plea bargain, Berdella was preparing a huge auction of all his merchandise, his artwork, his furniture, anything anyone would buy. His lawyer, Pender, hired an auctioneer and an appraiser, a catalogue was compiled and mailed to collectors across the country, and a warehouse rented in the city's West Bottoms for the actual sale. The news media were intrigued by the prospect of a massive garage sale by a convicted murderer, and the appraiser, R. Bond Blackman, was glad to oblige the reporters with his salesman's hyperbole.

"This is the largest collection of its kind I have ever seen," Blackman told a reporter. Berdella had excellent supply connections to Africa, Asia, South America and Pacific Rim countries, Blackman said. Pieces of thin Roman glass were up to two thousand years old. Rare beads, Greco-Roman pottery, Tibetan bronzes, Middle Eastern prayer boxes and pre-Columbian art: all were expected to bring serious collectors willing to bid competitively. Berdella had done a "superb job" of amassing his collection, Blackman said. "He bought slow and from reputable sources." Trying to dispense of any evil overtones, Blackman declared: "One thing he was not is a Satan worshiper. Nothing in this collection refers to Satanism or is used in Satan worship." To dispose of the more than two thousand items, the auction would be held over two weekends in mid-November.

Berdella was utterly preoccupied with every detail of the auction: the display of the items, the descriptions in the catalogues, the appraisals, everything. He demanded the auction be videotaped so he wouldn't be swindled. He fired Pender when Pender wouldn't accede to his every whim. He hired other lawyers to ensure the auctions were held the way he wanted, and also to sue Pender. He met with Blackman and the auctioneer, Gary Ryther, in the jail to discuss his concerns. Berdella had spent the last twenty years gathering these items, and now he was frustrated that he couldn't be personally involved in their sale.

The first auction session opened on November 12, without the hordes of curiosity-seekers that the auctioneers feared. About two hundred folding chairs were filled with demure collectors, some making notes in their catalogues. The first item, a statue from New Guinea, brought two hundred dollars. But the bidding was more subdued than the auctioneers, or Berdella, had expected. "You're really stealing some of this stuff," Blackman told the crowd at one point. A Roman-Syrian glass vase that he thought would go for two thousand dollars was sold for five hundred-fifty dollars. But by the end of the day, the auction had raised more than sixty thousand dollars.

The next day, another large crowd turned out and began bidding on the remainder of the antiquities and then Berdella's furniture and household goods. At the back of the room, local millionaire businessman Delbert Dunmire began outbidding the audience on every item that interested him, including a bed and several ceremonial robes. Within two hours, he had spent about $15,000. The performance was typical Dunmire. A convicted bank robber, Dunmire had started an airplane parts company just south of Kansas City and built it into a highly profitable corporation. He donated money generously, and flamboyantly, to civic and political causes. Dunmire told the *Kansas City Star* he thought the Berdella items might make a good exhibit for a local museum. "We need more reasons for people to come to Kansas City," he said.

Next, Dunmire began negotiations to buy Berdella's house. "I'm looking to see what asset of value it could be to young people," Dunmire told the newspaper. When the auction resumed on November 19, Dunmire wasn't present as items from Bob's Bazaar Bizarre were sold, including a T-shirt promoting Berdella's neighborhood: "South Hyde Park: Making yesterday's neighborhoods safe for today."

The fourth and final day of the auction of Berdella's personal belongings was canceled when Dunmire agreed to buy all of them. The next month, Dunmire also bought the house at 4315 Charlotte Street for an undisclosed amount.

From the jail, Berdella used the proceeds from the sale of his house and collection to pay the auction staff and various lawyers. When that was done, about sixty thousand dollars remained. Berdella told the Reverend Coleman he wanted to set up a trust fund for the families of his victims and his mother, with a second, smaller fund set aside for himself. Coleman hired a lawyer to draw up the paperwork, and Coleman also agreed to administer the trust, handing out funds periodically. Berdella hadn't told him yet how many families there would be, or who they were. But he had advanced to the stage where he now was facing up to what he had done. Emotions such as guilt and remorse, not witnessed by Dr. O'Connor, were starting to surface in the weekly conversations with Coleman. Berdella knew he couldn't repress the memories of his acts forever. The evidence was clustered in front of him in his small cell, including copies of his logs. He was nearly ready to unburden himself, to tell all, but first he wanted the trust funds in place.

Before that could be completed, Chris Bryson sprung a surprise. He filed suit against Berdella for $1.5 million, seeking damages for the mental and physical injuries Berdella inflicted. Bryson's attorney claimed in the lawsuit that when Bryson signed the waiver agreeing not to sue Berdella, he didn't understand what it meant. Where once it had appeared to Hurn and Holtsclaw that Bryson just wanted to get Berdella out of his life, now Berdella was becoming a lasting presence. Bryson also signed a contract

233

with a local free-lance writer to do a book on his experience, reportedly receiving half the book's proceeds. He gave two more television interviews, to the nationally syndicated tabloid news shows *Inside Edition* and *Inside Story*. Local news media had been withholding Bryson's name from their reports on Berdella, as is standard practice with the victims of sex crimes. But after the lawsuit, and Bryson's appearances on national television, the newspapers and TV stations began referring to "the man wearing nothing but a dog collar" by name. Berdella's civil attorneys gave Berdella a handwritten motion to dismiss the suit, based on Bryson's waiver, and Berdella signed and filed it with the court in early December. The judge rejected Berdella's motion.

Elsewhere in the courthouse, Berrigan and Hall resumed their negotiations over a possible confession. Berrigan still wouldn't be specific about how many murders there were. "It's more than you know," he told the prosecutors once, "but it's less than seven." The subject of the confession's transcript was still a sticking point. Berdella didn't want it to become public. Berrigan understood the prosecutors had to have a copy, but he wanted assurances it wouldn't go straight to the news media after the confession ended. That was fine by Hall. He just didn't want anyone profiting from the thing. He wouldn't release it, except to the families of the victims, if they wanted it. Both the prosecutors and the defenders would get one copy.

The conversations between Hall and Berrigan were informal, but laced with mutual distrust. Hall was suspicious of every offer, every idea Berrigan had. Berrigan was never sure when the prosecutors were totally straight with him, and always wondered if they'd turned over everything the police investigation had uncovered. The distrust slowed the process considerably, and resulted in more negotiation sessions.

Hall wanted to ensure that the question-and-answer session would be definitive, airtight, unchallengeable. Though Berrigan could make objections during the questioning, Hall wanted no restrictions on the types of questions he could ask. He didn't want Berdella filing motions some time later claiming he didn't really admit to something. Berrigan agreed. On the other hand, Berrigan noted, when the actual guilty plea was held in court, there was no need for a lot of questions about details of the crimes. Only enough to establish how the death occurred, and whether Berdella was aware of what he was doing. Hall agreed. The media would be there in droves. No need to put on a big show for the vultures.

The lawyers talked about Bryson and his lawsuit. That whole episode had already been resolved in court, at least the criminal aspect. Having Berdella discuss his capture and torture of Bryson might just draw all of them into the civil litigation, and certainly anything Berdella said about Bryson would become a central part of the case. Hall and Berrigan decided to exclude the Bryson case completely from the confession.

Berdella had another condition. He wanted the families of all of his victims to sign a waiver saying they wouldn't sue him. Hall and Riederer rejected that one almost immediately. They were beginning to regret ever getting involved with a waiver on Bryson, and they didn't want to have to convince more families to sign such an agreement. Besides, the Bryson waiver hadn't kept Bryson from suing anyway. No deal there, Hall said.

In another meeting, Hall asked Berrigan about the Pearson murder. Although Berdella had already admitted it, would he discuss that one in detail too? That should be part of the record, Hall said. Pearson had no wife or children, and his family in Wichita didn't appear likely to sue. Berrigan took the request back to Berdella, and Berdella said he would discuss Pearson.

The negotiations began to wind down in early December. Small details were discussed and agreed upon in writing. There would be no video or audiotaping of the sessions, only a stenographer and her coded notes. The confessions would be held in the county jail, in absolute secrecy. Berrigan estimated it would take three days to cover everything.

Who would be present for the questioning? Hall asked. Two people from all sides, he and Berrigan decided. Two defense attorneys, two prosecutors, and two policemen. Berdella had a specific demand: Ashley Hurn could not be one of the policemen. Hall was puzzled by that request, but shrugged and agreed. Hurn theorized that Berdella was trying to gain a small measure of revenge for the photo session Hurn had conducted in the jail back in April. The defense attorneys would be Berrigan and Charlie Rogers. Rogers replaced Schenkenberg, who now was gone from the public defender's office. The prosecutors would be Hall and Riederer. Parker had left the prosecutor's office for private practice, and Holtsclaw also was preparing to depart. Holtsclaw had much more firsthand knowledge of the case than Riederer and was disappointed that he wouldn't be allowed to attend, but Riederer was the boss, and it was his call.

Only one person would be allowed to ask questions: Hall. The others could take notes or pass questions to Hall, but Berrigan didn't want Berdella facing a firing squad of inquisitors. Hall agreed. Who would be the stenographer? The lawyers decided not to use one of the many court reporters in the courthouse, but to hire a private stenographer, Theresa M. Taylor.

The deal was nearly concluded. All that was needed was the agreement of the victims' families, meaning the Howells and the Ferrises. Riederer wasn't looking forward

236

to this task. He knew Paul Howell and Harriet Sanders, James Ferris's mother, wanted Berdella's blood. A deal in which Berdella's life would be spared wouldn't go down well with them. But it would give them the answers they wanted, a certain peace of mind. A combative, circumstantial trial almost definitely wouldn't do that. And without a skull, the Howell case was never going to trial.

Riederer called Paul Howell and Bonnie Ferris to his office several days later. Harriet Sanders and her husband Gary Sanders were not invited. The prosecutor told Howell and Ferris that he had the opportunity to make a deal. Berdella would tell them whom he had killed, and what he had done with the bodies. All the murders. In exchange, he would get life without parole. If the prosecutors took the Sheldon case to trial, seeking the death penalty, they would probably never find out if Berdella killed Jerry Howell or James Ferris. This would solve everything, Riederer said. A trial could leave countless questions unanswered. It was up to the families.

Bonnie Ferris nodded in assent. If that's what it takes, she thought, I'll do it. She had waited more than three years to find out what had happened to her husband. She wanted to know. She told Riederer yes.

Paul Howell also said yes. Though Riederer hadn't said it explicitly, he thought the plea bargain meant he could finally recover his son's remains, and give Jerry a decent burial. Such a thing might finally put the ordeal to rest. But after he left the prosecutor's office, Howell realized that Riederer hadn't told him anything about locating Jerry's body. He figured Berdella would just say he'd cut up the bodies and disposed of them where they could never be found. Howell didn't want to hear that. He called Riederer back. Fuck it, he said. He wanted the death penalty.

Though Howell backed out, the prosecutors proceeded anyway. All they had to do now was make sure they were doing the right thing. Hall and Riederer talked about the deal at length. They meditated on it separately. Riederer was torn: Parts of the public would howl long and loudly if Berdella were allowed to live. What if the laws were changed some day, and "life without parole" was somehow shortened? What if Berdella found some way to appeal his guilty plea? What if he escaped? Riederer would be the scapegoat for not obtaining the death penalty in the first place.

Then Riederer thought about the families. Wouldn't they want to know what really happened, more than anything? Not just the Howells and the Ferrises, but families like Todd Stoops's folks. They had seen pictures of their son being tortured. Maybe Berdella hadn't killed him and knew where he was. For Paul Howell, the nightmare had to be the worst. Suspecting for four years that his son was murdered, yet not really knowing. Riederer thought about his own children. If one of them disappeared for a long period, wouldn't he rather know definitely what happened to them, rather than stagger on under a cloud of uncertainty? A full confession could banish that cloud for a number of families. It could also remove the case from the city's constant consciousness. A trial would undoubtedly prove the largest media circus in Kansas City history, and simply revive ugly memories and images for months or years to come.

The only remaining fear was, how many murders are there? Berrigan had said less than seven, which alleviated any concern that there were dozens of bodies somewhere. But even if there were more than seven murders, the deal was that Berdella could confess to all of them and not get the death penalty. Riederer was ready. He told Hall to sign the deal. A room was arranged in the county jail, and dates were set for the following week, December 13, 14 and 15. Several days before the confessions were to begin,

Hall met with Charlie Rogers to find out what exactly would be discussed. Rogers gave him a list of six names: Jerry Howell, Robert Sheldon, Mark Wallace, Walter James Ferris, Todd Stoops and Larry Pearson. Six murders. No new names, none the police hadn't heard before.

Hall called Cole and told him about the plea agreement, and that Hurn would not be allowed in the confession session. If the police had any questions they wanted to ask, Hall said, they should collect them and pass them on to him immediately. Cole, and whichever detective he appointed, should expect to spend three days in the jail next week, listening to Berdella describe six homicides, Hall told him.

Hurn had heard of the negotiations for a confession, and was preparing to participate when Cole told him he was out. Hurn was disappointed but understanding, and met with Hall in the days before the confession to review the case files and the available knowledge about Berdella. Cole selected Detective DeValkenaere to join him in the confession, a pick which surprised and flattered DeValkenaere, who'd been in Homicide less than a year. DeValkenaere and Hurn both solicited questions for Berdella from the other members of the squad. Most of the inquiries were basic: Where are the bodies? Why did you do it? Are there more? Some of the detectives were surprised to learn that Berdella would confess to six murders. They had thought the number would be higher. Most were pleased that Berdella hadn't revealed any unknown victims. All the squad members, and the squad typist Jennifer Cullen, received commendations from the police department for conducting the most extensive investigation in the city's history.

Hall prepared for the confession as he would a crucial cross-examination in a trial. Surrounded in his office by the evidence, he made notes about what areas he wanted to cover. Sometimes, Hall would jot down a specific question, but mostly he wrote reminders to himself about certain things. He wanted to delve into Berdella's background, his upbringing, his life in Kansas City before the flea market. He wanted to ask about witnesses or accomplices; could he really have done this alone? He wanted to ask about Satanism, and the various indicators that Berdella had more than a passing interest in strange rituals. He wanted to know where the bodies were. And he wanted to know why. Why did Bob Berdella go from shopkeeper to the worst serial killer the city had ever known?

Chapter Twelve

A small, tan cinder block classroom, with a blackboard and bright fluorescent lights, was selected by jail director Charles Megerman as the setting for Berdella's confession. Three large glass windows along the wall separated the sixth floor room from the hallway, but Megerman ordered the windows covered with sheets of brown paper. Stackable plastic chairs were arranged around three brown, vinyl-topped tables which were pushed together. A jail guard was stationed just outside the door.

Berdella sat calmly in the room, with Berrigan and Rogers seated on either side of him, awaiting the arrival of the prosecutors and police. Whether he realized it or not, what Berdella was about to embark upon was a rare journey for serial killers: besides describing the explicit details of each murder, he would attempt to explore his thought processes as he inflicted sadistic torture and fatal injury on his captives. Serial murders are rarely able to articulate their innermost feelings concerning the crimes they committed. If he was open and honest, Berdella was ready to provide new insights into the thoughts and actions of a multiple murderer.

Shortly before 9:30 A.M., the morning of December 13, Hall, Riederer, Cole, DeValkenaere and the stenographer, Theresa Taylor, walked in and took their places. Hall nodded to Berrigan, but did not acknowledge Berdella. There were no handshakes. Hall was carrying not only his own notebooks but a stack of exhibits, such as Berdella's logs and photographs, which he planned to ask Berdella about. He arranged his things in front of him on the table while Berdella watched silently. Hall positioned himself across the table from Berdella; Riederer sat to his right, and then Cole. DeValkenaere sat at the far end of the table. At the near end of the table, between the two sides, Taylor pulled up her chair. Riederer and Cole brought out pens and notepads. Taylor set up her stenographer's machine, and placed two miniature tape recorders on the table, with the understanding she would erase the tapes after she had completed the transcript. When Taylor was ready, Hall told Berdella to stand and raise his right hand. Taylor asked Berdella if he swore to tell the truth and nothing but the truth. Berdella said he did. The deposition began.

"Mr. Berdella," Hall began, "you discussed this with your attorneys. And I think the appropriate way to start out the interview is for you to give an opening statement. What we would like the opening statement to consist of is a chronology, or an order, of occurrences of all homicides that you have committed here in Jackson County or any crimes that started in Jackson County and ended in a homicide in another county. We would like to know the names of the individuals, the dates of the homicides, where they occurred, how they occurred and the disposition of the bodies, if you would like to begin."

Hall's tone of voice set the mood and pace from the start. He was direct, unwavering, professional. He looked Berdella in the eye, and Berdella mostly returned the gaze, sometimes glancing down at his papers. Hall wanted to wring as much information as he could from Berdella without being respectful or deferential. His initial query seemed to work.

"OK," Berdella said. "At this time do you just want a brief outline?"

"Yes," Hall answered.

"The first victim was Jerry Howell," Berdella said. "I believe he died on July the second of '84," he said incorrectly. "His death happened in my house, as did all the deaths."

Rogers asked, "What's the address?"

"4315 Charlotte, Kansas City, Missouri," Berdella said, naming what is now perhaps the single best-known address in the city. He continued with a brief description of how he killed Jerry Howell. "After being drugged, the second day he was at my house, in the process of changing and tightening his gag, along with redrugging him for the evening, he apparently asphyxiated from body fluids that he may have brought up or he was not being able to get enough air."

Berdella responded to Hall's impersonality with his own. His voice was level and detached, especially when reading from his notes, as he was now. He began to describe his second murder.

"Robert Sheldon was at my house. Robert—"

"What happened to the body of Jerry Howell?" Rogers asked, making sure Berdella satisfied all the elements Hall had asked for.

"In all the bodies, they were disposed of," Berdella said. "They were cut up and wrapped, put into trash bags and put into dog food bags and then re-bagged in plastic, sat out on the curb for the trashmen to pick up on Monday morning."

The *trash*. Hall had learned this in a meeting with Rogers and Berrigan, but Cole and DeValkenaere were hearing it for the first time. The *trash*. The detectives had always felt Berdella either buried the bodies somewhere, or fed them to his dogs. No one had ever considered the city's garbage pickup as a method of evidence disposal. Cole and DeValkenaere dared not show any emotion at this revelation, but both stared straight ahead and waited for the next surprise.

"Sheldon first showed up at my house on April the tenth and died on April the fourteenth," Berdella explained, "basically in the same manner and cause that Jerry Howell died." Then he stopped. "No, I'm sorry. On that one, Sheldon died when I put a trash bag over his head, tied it and allowed him to suffocate."

He moved on to Mark Wallace. "Mark was in there mid-summer to early fall, approximately. On the night of a rain-storm—"

"What year?" Rogers asked.

"Oh, '85," Berdella replied. "I found him out in my back toolshed hiding from the rain. Brought him into my house with, at first, his desire. I drugged him and then further drugged him to make him captive. He, on the second day that he was in my house, basically died the same way as Howell. When I had put a new gag in and redrugged him, he apparently asphyxiated."

Next was James Ferris, whom Berdella called by his given first name, Walter. "Walter Ferris was in the fall of '85, somewhere between August and October," Berdella esti-mated. "He came into my house upon his own. Was at the time very drunk. Took some Valiums on top of that. And then I drugged him in the food I gave him for supper. He passed out. I bound him. And the next day, again, asphyxi-ated basically in the same manner as Howell and Wallace."

Cole presumed that when Berdella said Howell, Wallace and Ferris had "asphyxiated," he meant they had drowned in their own vomit, drugged, gagged and bound. But there was no way to know for sure. Berdella wasn't a doctor, and ap-parently there were no bodies on which to perform autop-sies. Hall didn't ask Berdella to clarify what he meant, though he subsequently questioned Berdella about how he knew the men had died.

The fifth victim was Todd Stoops. "I had known Todd previously," Berdella said. "Picked him up at Volker, or at Liberty [Memorial] Park that evening, that afternoon. Brought him home. He had on the way stopped and got some Ritalin and Talwin for him."

Hall asked, "The approximate date on Todd Stoops that we're talking about?"

"June of '86, approximately the seventeenth to the thirtieth," Berdella said. "Todd died because at one point I fist-fucked him, rupturing the anal wall. And between the loss of blood and infections that set in, he died of not getting proper treatment."

Larry Pearson was the final victim. "Pearson, Larry Pearson, had been staying at my house the summer of '87. And after a couple weeks I then drugged his food one night. Tied him up. Kept him in the basement for a week. And then with his cooperation moved him up to the second floor where he stayed with me and was fully cooperative up until the evening of August the fifth of '87. While performing oral sex on me he tried to bite my penis. And I killed him by putting a trash bag over his head and securing it so he would suffocate."

"The six individuals that you named," Hall said, "Jerry Howell, Robert Sheldon, Mark Wallace, Walter Ferris, Todd Stoops and Larry Pearson, are those the only individuals that you have murdered in Jackson County?"

"Not only in Jackson County but anywhere else," Berdella responded.

Berdella's manner was deliberate, as if he were slowly discussing a series of rational events. His mouth sometimes dried up as a result of one of the medications he was taking, so he regularly drank from a small glass of water. But the process didn't appear to bother him.

Hall launched into a series of biographical questions for Berdella: Where was he born? Where was his hometown? Who were his parents? Where did he go to school? The inquiries didn't delve deeply, just basic information. Hall thought that he might be able to get at the root of Berdella's sickness, or his motivation, if only to provide some answers for the victims' parents. But Berdella limited his responses to the facts, and Hall recognized that Berdella wasn't going to volunteer the information he wanted. Even though Berdella's answers were scarcely revealing, Berrigan upbraided Hall during a break that morning, saying he was surprised

Hall would "do something like that."

"You never find out why," Hall said later. "It's the hardest thing to explain to them [the families], you never find out why. After all these years, I still tried to do it. I was stupid. You just come as close as you can."

Berdella described the numerous restaurants he worked for around the Kansas City area, and how he got started at the Flea Market and eventually opened the Bazaar Bizarre. Hall asked about Berdella's business card, the "Dragon Nagari," with its multitailed dragon and seemingly evil verse about death. Berdella said it had no meaning to him, that it was "amusing and interesting, curious," pulled from a book on the history of magic. Hall asked what types of religions Berdella studied in the late sixties and early seventies, and Berdella listed Taoism, Buddhism and witchcraft.

"Other than reading," Hall said, "did you meet with any individuals and discuss witchcraft with them?"

"No," Berdella said.

"Did you at any time attend any meetings of any people who participated in witchcraft?"

"No."

"Did you in the late sixties or early seventies study Satanism?"

"I studied," Berdella said, "or I examined a couple of books." He went on to say that several devout religious homes had sprung up in his neighborhood, which piqued his interest in the exact opposite of what his new neighbors were preaching. But, he added, "At no point in my reading of witchcraft, the occult, or the supernatural did any of these beliefs appeal to me enough to start studying any further or to adopt them as belief or practice. Period."

"So you never at any time practiced any form of witchcraft or Satanism?" Hall asked.

"Basically, yes," Berdella said, irritatingly evasive.

"Did you at any time, in any way, practice any form of witchcraft or Satanism?" Hall repeated.

246

"Never any kind of Satanism," Berdella said. Witchcraft took many forms, he informed the prosecutor, and things such as drinking herbal tea or wearing a birthstone could be considered witchcraft. Other than that, nothing, Berdella said.

Referring to the Geraldo Rivera program, Hall asked, "Did you at any time have any involvement in any Satanic coven, group, whatever you want to call it?"

"None whatsoever," Berdella said.

"What about the bird feathers in the backyard?" Hall asked.

"I'm going to have to see pictures of those," Berdella replied. "I have no idea. I've racked my brain. But if you can show me a picture or the actual item, I would like to find out what those bird feathers are."

"There are bird feathers buried in jars that were recovered in several places in the backyard," Hall told him. "Are you telling us that you don't have any recollection of that?"

"I've only lived in the house since '69," Berdella said. "I have no idea what may have happened in that backyard prior to that date. I have never buried, to the best of my recollection, any kind of feathers in my backyard."

Berrigan suggested it was time for a break. When the questioning resumed, Hall returned to more inquiries about witchcraft and Satanism. Berdella remained steadfast in his denials. "And to defend myself against some of the accusations that people like Rivera are making," Berdella said, "I would simply have to turn around, that if I was involved in any group as powerful as people like Rivera are pointing to, how come I had no kind of escape plan?"

"What do you mean?" Hall asked.

"Well, on Saturday morning I got a call at my shop saying that the police were all over the house. I left my shop and drove to the house, knowing that there was probably only one reason for the police to be there in that number. Walked over to the one police car that was still in front of my house and turned myself in. This does not indicate that you are associated with people that can get you out of the country."

The prosecutors and police were taken aback by this statement. They had always assumed that Berdella just happened to return home that morning. He had turned himself in? That was news.

"Who gave you that call?" Hall asked. "Who placed the call to your shop?"

Berdella gave the name of one of his neighbors.

"And that's what caused you to come from your shop to your house on, I believe it was a Saturday, April 2nd, in the afternoon?"

"Yes."

"And you're telling us that when you came to your house that Saturday afternoon you knew good and well why the police were there?"

"That's correct."

"And you still came?"

"That's correct."

Berdella returned to his list of restaurant employers, and described his limited financial resources. Then Hall directed Berdella to start from the beginning of the crimes, with Jerry Howell. Berdella told of meeting Jerry through his father at the Flea Market, of seeing him hustling at 10th and McGee, of trying to help him when he had some trouble with the law. Berdella occasionally supplied Howell with Valium or marijuana, saying he got the Valium through a prescription he had with his doctor. Hall then asked, "Were you also procuring drugs from a veterinarian for your dogs?"

"Yes," Berdella said. In addition to vitamins, vaccines and calcium pills, Berdella also obtained the animal tranquilizers acepromazine and chlorpromazine, and the anesthetic ketamine. Hall wondered if Berdella got the tranquilizers from a veterinarian too. No, Berdella said, a veterinarian supply shop. He said no prescription was required for any of the drugs, including chlorpromazine, a form of Thorazine that is a very strong tranquilizer.

"But you're telling us," Hall said, "that you never at any time up until July injected any of these chemicals into Jerry Howell?"

"That's correct."

Hall and Berdella agreed that Berdella met with Jerry Howell on July 5, 1984. Berdella said he was already angry with Freddie Kellogg and Foster Simmons because he had helped them out repeatedly, and they made no effort to repay him. Berdella mentioned the Camaro he repossessed from Kellogg, and that it was stashed in Parkville, Missouri, northwest of Kansas City. The car wasn't running, and Berdella said Howell had agreed to go with him to Parkville that evening to look it over.

"When I picked him up, he announced that he didn't have time to go to look at the car, that he wanted to get to this dance contest at about 7:00," Berdella said. "But he wanted to party between that before I took him to the dance. And he started asking for drugs. And at that point I just started giving them to him. I had some Valium in the car and some acepromazine tablets. We got a six-pack of Coors. And then we got over to my house, and he still wanted to get more drugged. At that point, I misrepresented what a couple of pills were and gave him enough medication for him to pass out."

Berdella felt that Howell owed him for the favors Berdella had done. "This was not the first time that Jerry would agree to do something to start repaying this and then just blow it off," Berdella commented.

Hall said, "So when he made this announcement that he didn't want to go up to Parkville what did you do?"

"Externally I kept my cool," Berdella recalled. "Internally, I lost it. I became very upset. And I think, from the time we got to the house on, that I wasn't working in a particularly rational state of mind."

Hall handed Berdella two sheets of paper with handwrit-

249

ing on them and asked him to identify the papers.

"These are the notes that I took with, of Jerry Howell on the date 7-5-84. And it continues until 7-6-84."

"The notes consist of dates and times and certain activity on those dates and times?" Hall asked.

"That's correct," Berdella said. "And it shows here that Jerry Howell passed out at 6:40."

"OK," Hall said. "What was your purpose in making this, and we'll call it a diary from this point on, the Howell diary?"

"Kind of, I guess, compulsive behavior," Berdella answered. "I've always been a note taker. An example is when my dogs had pups. I would weigh them at birth and keep a record of the sexes, colors, growth development over the first week or two."

"Other than your pups," Hall said, "prior to July fifth of '84, had you ever made a diary regarding your activity with another human being?"

"Yes," Berdella said. He said that he had kept notes on several people, whom he also photographed, to record the effects of the drugs they had injected and whether he had sex with them after that. The people he named were all alive, and Berdella said he hadn't sodomized any of them.

Hall brought Berdella back to the Howell diary. Howell passed out in Berdella's bed after ingesting one tablet after another. Looking at a photocopy of the diary, Hall asked Berdella about the entry at 7:00, "1 cc PH arm." Berdella said "PH" stood for a tranquilizer one of Howell's friends had given him, "a heavy tranquilizer that he and his friends didn't like because it was too strong."

"Had you ever shot anybody up with it before?" Hall wondered.

"No."

"One cc, I take it, indicates that you did inject it into him," Hall said.

"That's right."

250

"And into his arm?"

"Right."

"And prior to that," Hall said, "you had never injected any drugs into Mr. Howell?"

"That's correct."

"And Mr. Howell told you that he did not take drugs intravenously?"

"That's correct."

"At 7:00 when you injected the drug into him was he unconscious at the time?" Hall asked.

"Yes."

"What was your purpose then in injecting him again, injecting him at 7:00?" Hall asked.

"Initially, I think I just wanted to tranquilize him enough to have sex," Berdella said. "Somewhere along between, I would say, 7:00 and 8:00 is where I started doing things for motives at the time that I don't think were clear to me. I just wanted to initially have him helpless and from helpless to, I guess, under my control."

Berdella and Howell had had consensual sex before. Hall was puzzled. "Why did you feel it necessary at this time to inject him so you could have sex?"

"I don't think it was injecting so I could have sex," Berdella reasoned. "At this point I think I was functioning on a level of, 'He's backed out again. I'm really mad at him. I'm going to be in control of him.' And I drugged him and then tied him up so I could control him. This is the first time I had done anything like this."

"To anyone?" Hall asked.

"To anyone."

"And when you did it on this particular occasion," Hall said, "you were mad at Howell?"

"Among other people," Berdella said. "He became the culmination of a long frustration."

"And I take it that you found it to be pleasurable to bind him and then inject him?" Hall asked.

251

"Perhaps not pleasurable, but satisfied a need or an emotion that I had at that time."

Going down the first page of the diary, Berdella said that he injected Howell again at 7:25, then with 2 cc of chlorpromazine at 7:30, 3 cc of chlorpromazine at 7:55, and then 11 more cubic centimeters of chlorpromazine, this time injected into the buttocks, at 8:00. Each injection was noted in the diary.

"Up to this point had you attempted to have sex with him?" Hall asked.

"I think sex was one of the goals," Berdella said. "But I was functioning more on a level of 'I don't care anymore.' And I just wanted to have control over the situation."

Hall asked: "And was that, I'm trying to understand what was going on in your mind at that time, was that in order to dominate him or in order to hurt him, to kill him, or a combination?"

"There was no intent to hurt him," Berdella said, "i.e. torture or anything like that. My motivation was mainly to have control over the situation and to have sex in a situation where I'd be in complete control."

At the 8:40 entry, after another 11 cc of injections, the number 29 was circled. Berdella explained that this was the cumulative total of cubic centimeters he'd injected into Howell so far. At 8:45, Berdella wrote "Tied." That meant Howell's hands and legs were tied to the bed. Where before he had at least been moving involuntarily, now Howell was completely unconscious.

"9:00 and 10:00, both have the entry 'F,' " Hall said.

"Which would be the abbreviation that I used for fuck," Berdella said calmly.

"Would that have been anal intercourse then?" Hall inquired.

"Yes."

Hall moved down to the notation at 11:30 that indicated Howell was vomiting. "At that point in time," Hall said, "did you realize that Mr. Howell was having difficulties and that in fact by vomiting he could die?"

"Probably, yes," Berdella said. "I don't remember a clear recollection of that. But at this point I guess I was functioning on automatic pilot. I was just going through events as they came."

Hall said, "And you certainly knew what the events were because you were recording them at the time?"

"That's correct."

"You also have a notation, 'Eyes blank,' " Hall said. "What does that mean?"

"I checked his eyes, and the pupils would have been in a pinpoint state with no response to light movement."

"11:45, 'BF?' " Hall said, continuing down the page.

"Which would be butt fuck."

"Another anal sodomy?"

"Right."

"Is that 'Snoring'?" Hall asked, pointing to the next word in the 11:45 entry.

"Yes."

"What do you mean by that?"

"He was snoring," Berdella said. "After the sex he started snoring."

"Still tied at this time?" Hall asked.

"He was kept tied the entire time."

"12:30, 'BF' again," Hall noted. "Anal sodomy?"

"Right."

Berdella continued making notations through the night, noting Howell's appearance, his reactions, and also the amounts of the injections, which continued as well. As did the sodomization. According to Berdella's log, he sodomized Howell at 1:30 A.M., 2:30, 4:30 and 6:30, writing "BF" each time. Berdella pointed out that he would wash Howell's eyes and mouth periodically, then replace the gag he had tied around his captive's head. Between the sexual assaults, Berdella lay next to Howell, either sleeping or resting.

253

About 8:15 A.M. the morning of July 6, Berdella noticed that Howell seemed to be rousing from his temporary coma. Berdella remedied that promptly. He injected 6 cc of chlorpromazine and 10 cc of acepromazine, but Howell was still "active," according to the diary. So at 8:30, Berdella administered two more shots of 5 cc apiece. That calmed Howell down. He apparently was unaware of what happened to him next.

" '8:40 CF.' What's that, what does that mean?" Hall asked, dreading what he suspected would be the answer.

"I believe at that time that was a carrot fuck," Berdella said.

"Can you tell us what you mean by a carrot fuck?" Hall asked. Though he had absolutely no desire to hear the explanation, he wanted everything explained, and this was one of the more sickening acts depicted in Berdella's photo collection.

"I used a carrot to sodomize the anus."

"Had you ever done that on any individual before that day?"

"No."

"Where did you get the idea of doing that?"

"I have no direct source," Berdella said. "I guess what I had in the house that would fulfill the job."

"It is something that came upon you at 8:40 to stick a carrot up his anus?" Hall asked incredulously.

"Apparently, yes, sir." Berdella said.

Berdella injected Howell once more that morning, at 11 A.M., and then left for his shop with Howell tied to the bed. When he returned at 3 P.M. that Friday afternoon, he gave Howell another shot of a mixture of the tranquilizers.

Hall raised a point. "Why did you have these needles and syringes in your house?"

"Well, initially it was to take care of my dogs," Berdella said. "I was vaccinating my own puppies, doing my own shots to the bitches when they had a litter, doing a lot of home veterinary work. It got to, I found I could get tranquilizers through the veterinarian supply. And I did. That's I guess when I started using drugs to attract young men."

Hall asked, "So you could have these when young men came to the house to inject them?"

"Yes."

"And up to this point had it always been voluntary on the young men's part?"

"That's correct."

Hall theorized to Berdella that being at his shop for four hours must have given him some time to cool off a little bit, and Berdella agreed. "And yet," Hall said, "when you got back to the house you started up again?"

"That's correct."

"What was your reason for doing that?"

"I can't give you a defined reason," Berdella said. "I think from the point that I tied him up on, I was viewing the situation as irreversible."

"What do you mean by that?"

"What was I to do?" Berdella asked. "Untie him? Let him get up?"

"Let him escape?" Hall added.

"Yes," Berdella said. "Either let him go willingly or have him escape. At this point I guess I just figured that I had burned my bridges and this is what was going on. And I stayed involved with the situation."

"At this point," Hall said, demonstrating that Berdella fully knew what he was doing, "you knew that there were only two alternatives: one, that he escape and report what you had been doing and the consequences that would automatically follow from that. You were aware of that result?"

"I believe so, yes."

"The other consequence was to never let him leave?" Hall asked.

"I guess that would be a correct way of putting it," Berdella said. "I at that point did not intend or have a desire to kill him. But I was probably under the functioning recollection that there were only two options; he stayed here or he leaves."

"And you picked the option that he would never leave?" Hall said.

"That's correct."

"That he would never leave?"

"Well, basically, yes."

At 5:15, Berdella had made the notation "RP," short for "rape," because Howell was conscious and resisting. "I think at that point he made some kind of response such as, 'Why are you doing this to me?' or 'Let me go' or something," Berdella said. Instead, Berdella prepared two huge injections totaling 21 cubic centimeters of tranquilizers. But at 5:40, by Berdella's notes, Howell was "Still fighting restraints, eyes fixed/some mov in lips." Berdella also wrote "Still fighting" at 6:00, after the notation "Cuc R." Hall asked what that meant.

"Cucumber rape," Berdella said. He said he had never done it before, and again Hall asked where he got the idea for such a revolting act. Berdella replied it was just something that was available "that could be used in a sexual manner or an assault manner."

"For the purpose of having sex with him," Hall asked, "or for the purpose of assaulting him?"

"I guess assaulting him."

"To cause him pain?"

"I don't think it caused him any pain," Berdella said coldly. "I think he was medicated to the point that he really didn't notice that much."

"But your purpose was," Hall reminded, "I'm not asking if it did, was your purpose to cause him pain?"

"Probably, yes, sir."

At 8:45, Berdella hit Howell in the buttocks with a metal ruler. Hall took this opportunity to reexamine Berdella's motive for killing Jerry Howell. His friend, his sex partner, seemingly a harmless kid.

"Mr. Berdella," Hall asked, "was this caused by the fact that he had refused to pay back what you had given him?"

"I think that triggered the events of the fifth and sixth," Berdella said. "But the frustration that built up, the anger that built up inside of me prior to that, I guess, is what allowed this to happen."

"Not just anger towards Mr. Howell certainly?"

"That's correct."

"But anger towards all of these young men?"

"That's correct."

"You thought these young men were using you?"

"Yes."

"And this was your way of getting back at them?"

"Or being able to recast myself," Berdella said, "in a role that would allow me to deal with the reality that I was going through. Possibly the way I handled situations prior to this, I saw myself in a weak state. This was a way where I was no longer weak and helpless."

"But predominant?"

"Yes."

At 9:45, Berdella said, the notation "Front F" was short for " 'front fuck,' which would not have been sodomy."

"What is a front fuck?" Hall asked.

"Just using the leg area as a friction spot," Berdella said. He changed Howell's gag and washed his mouth. Howell fought him weakly. "And the notation at 10:00 that he was no longer living," Berdella said. "Dead."

Hall looked at the log and said, "10:00 the entry is two letters, DD?"

"Yes, dead."

"Is that all that meant, dead?" Hall asked.

"Yes."

"So he would have died on Friday, July the sixth?"

"At 10:00 P.M."

"And what did he die of?" Hall asked.

257

"The best I could tell, either because of the gag and/or the medications, that he either asphyxiated on vomit or the combination of the gag and the medicines were too strong for him to be able to catch breath, or breathe," Berdella said.

"Your intent throughout this, I guess it would be approximately twenty-eight hours of torture," Hall said, "would have been to torture him?"

"I don't think at this point, with Jerry, torture didn't really step into the picture," Berdella said. "It may have started with Robert Sheldon, who is next, and slightly involved with Mark Wallace. But it wasn't until I got to James Ferris that I intentionally tortured anyone."

"But it was to cause Mr. Howell pain?" Hall observed.

"Yes."

"And to assault him?"

"Yes."

"In the course of that assault you used narcotics," Hall said.

"Restraints," Berdella added.

"And sex," Hall said.

"Right."

"And he died from those?" Hall said.

"Yes."

Hall looked up at the clock over the blackboard. It was nearly 1 P.M. The lawyers decided to break for lunch.

To this point, Hall was satisfied. He was surprised at how candid Berdella was, how willing he was to answer every question. Hall had expected Berrigan to jump in with numerous objections, but Berrigan had said almost nothing in the first three and a half hours. Though he had read and re-read the case file, Hall still hadn't been sure how Berdella would react under these circumstances, and Hall was intrigued by Berdella's cooperation. Riederer was surprised somewhat by Berdella's candor, but he was also sickened. As they left the room for lunch, Riederer turned to Cole and said, "I could reach over and cut this son of a bitch's throat."

The session started again at 1:25 P.M. Hall asked Berdella how he had known Jerry Howell was dead. Berdella said that Howell hadn't been breathing, and when Berdella had tried mouth-to-mouth resuscitation and pressing on his chest, nothing happened. "At that time," Hall said, "then what did you do?"

"After thinking a while how to handle the situation, I first moved him down to the basement," Berdella said.

"And how did you move him to the basement?"

"I just drug him down."

"You say you thought a while on how to handle the situation," Hall said. "What alternatives did you come up with while you were thinking up there in the bedroom?"

"The only one in my mind that would work was to dismember the body," Berdella said, pausing briefly as he recalled more. "First I was going to dismember the body and wrap it and put it in pieces, and it just occurred to me to just set the stuff out Monday morning for the trash to pick up."

Hall for the first time asked about accomplices. "From that time that you knew he was dead to the time that you drug his body down and you came back up, had you called anyone?" Hall asked.

"No."

"During the two days of July fifth and July sixth, 1984," Hall said, "was there anyone else living in your house?"

"No."

"During the time July fifth and July sixth while Jerry Howell was alive and bound upstairs, had anyone come to your house?"

"No."

Hall figured he knew what was coming next in Berdella's macabre chronology. "What did you do then after you got downstairs?" Hall asked.

"I secured one of the old antique pulleys that I had to a

259

beam and hung him," Berdella said, "drug him feet first so that I could drain the blood from his body."

"I take it you also took a photograph of him hanging upside down?" Hall asked.

"Several photographs, yes."

"What was your purpose in doing this?"

"I guess forming some kind of trophy or record of the event," Berdella said, "I think my feelings were somewhere along those lines."

"You had, in fact, photographed several of the events that occurred while Jerry Howell was alive in your house," Hall said.

"That's correct."

"And your purpose in doing these photographs was what?"

"To keep a record of the events."

"And why did you want a record of the events?" Hall wondered.

"Initially, I don't know."

"Did you later, after this, go back and go through those photographs on occasions?" Hall asked.

"Yes."

"And what was your reason for going back and going through those photographs?"

"I was using them for stimulation for masturbation," Berdella said.

Next, Berdella detailed how he placed a large cooking pot beneath Jerry Howell's head, and made incisions with a knife on the inside of Howell's elbows and on the jugular vein in his neck to drain his blood. At this, Cole's mouth fell open. He had been working hard not to show any emotion, but this was too much. How can any human being do this? he thought to himself. Not only that, but Berdella didn't seem particularly ashamed or upset as he related the grisly details.

Berdella left Howell's body suspended overnight and then

through most of the next day, Saturday, as he went to work at his shop. While he puttered around the Flea Market, he pondered ways to dispose of the body. When he got home that evening, he put on a cook's apron and gathered several sharp cooking and boning knives as well as the electric chain saw. He poured out the blood, then laid a sheet of black plastic on the floor and began the dismemberment. For cuts through joints, he used the knives. When he had to cut through bone (for example when he separated Jerry Howell's head from his body) he used the chain saw. Using newspaper, he wrapped all the body parts and placed them into several plastic trash bags. The trash bags were then stuffed into several empty dog-food bags, and the paper dog-food bags were all placed into one large trash bag.

Hall could wait no longer to ask the question that had gone begging all morning. For the first time, his tone rose above a deadpan level. "Did you have any remorse at this time for what had happened?" he demanded of Berdella.

"I wouldn't know if at that stage I was able to feel remorse," Berdella said defensively. "That is something that, in trying to reconstruct all these events, to find out the point where I stopped having feelings such as remorse."

"What were your feelings?" Hall responded.

"First ones were disposing of the crime, I guess," Berdella said. "Not just of the body but of the crime. By Sunday evening when I got home, Paul Howell Sr. called looking for Jerry. And from that point on I had to deal with a lot of pressure and then eventually threats from Paul Howell. And I believe that trying to deal with those threats and that pressure probably deviated me away from the chance to start having feelings, emotions, dealing with it on a personal level, as opposed to trying to survive Paul Howell."

"So you're saying," Hall said, "that your main thoughts starting on Sunday evening were how to survive Howell or how to survive the authorities, and you had no feelings basically for what you had done to Mr. Howell?"

"That's correct."

Berdella worked in his shop again on Sunday. That night, he finished bagging Howell's remains, as well as Howell's clothes, the needles and drugs he'd injected Howell with, the pulley he suspended Howell with; all were readied for pickup the next morning. Between 6 A.M. and 6:30 A.M. on Monday, Berdella took four or five trash bags out to the curb, then stood by a window at the front of the house to wait for the garbage truck. He estimated the truck came by between 8 and 9 A.M.

"Did you go out there when he picked up the trash bags?" Hall asked.

"No."

"You just watched them from your house?"

"Yes."

"Did you save any parts of Howell's body?"

"None."

"Other than the actual dismembering or cutting up, did you skin Mr. Howell?"

"No."

"Did you perform any sexual acts on Mr. Howell after he was dead?"

"No."

"Other than the pictures showing Mr. Howell hanging upside down, did you take any pictures of the dismembering process?"

"No."

"Any pictures of the body packed up?"

"No."

That was it. Jerry Howell's body was somewhere in a Kansas City landfill, where the city-run trash trucks empty their loads daily. Berdella was so chillingly precise in his detail, in his description of cutting and bagging the body, that he seemed almost certainly to be telling the truth. Hall moved next to Berdella's photographs, all enlarged to eight by ten inches, with a set given to Berdella. The first set of pictures were shots the police had figured were of Jerry Howell. One by one, from the upside-down picture through the carrot and cucumber assaults, Berdella unhesitatingly identified each one. One showed a syringe sticking out of Howell's thigh muscle. The prosecutors and police refrained from shaking their heads in disgust. In the previous eight months, they'd had that reaction dozens of times. Now, as the actual suspect was describing the actual acts, there was no way to react.

After a short recess, Hall shifted the discussion to Robert Sheldon. Berdella related meeting Sheldon through Kellogg and Simmons at Quincy Research Center. After an experimental program ended at Quincy, Kellogg and Simmons invited many of the graduates, including Sheldon, to a party at Berdella's house. Kellogg told people they could get shots of Thorazine from Berdella, and Berdella said he agreed to give them. "It was, I guess, my connection with the group," Berdella said. "Prior to probably '81 or '82 I was pretty staunchly antidrug. I found that that was not a way to get involved with people in the Westport area, specifically gays or the bisexual crowd. For having a little drugs or a little booze around, you're a lot more popular."

From time to time, Sheldon roomed with Berdella, paying some rent, drinking heavily, having no physical contact with Berdella. Sometimes, Berdella said, Sheldon would drink whatever income he had, fail to pay the rent, and Berdella would ask him to leave. One of these times was in the winter of 1984, Berdella said, and again in early 1985, months after Jerry Howell had been killed. Berdella was having trouble remembering exact dates, but then Hall handed him a calendar for 1985, on which Berdella had written extensively. In January, he wrote, "RS on binge," meaning Sheldon was drinking extensively. But Sheldon normally would "at least acknowledge the debt" he owed Berdella, and occasionally show up with a check. Hall asked, "We have a different situation than we had with Mr. Howell in the fact that he really hadn't let you down?"

Berdella replied, "Other than the annoyance of his behavioral pattern when he was drinking, that is probably a correct statement." In his penchant for being intellectual and precise, Berdella sometimes used a lot of words to say, "Yes."

Looking at his calendar, Berdella said that Sheldon appeared on his doorstep again on April 10, 1985, asking to stay for a couple of days. Hall then handed Berdella four sheets of paper, the first of which had "4/10" on the top. Berdella said they were his notes on Sheldon's capture and torture. The first entry was "9:30 Asleep." Sheldon had fallen asleep on Berdella's first-floor couch. Hall asked, "What is your purpose in starting a diary or notations at 9:30?"

"At about 9:30," Berdella said, "I had the intentions of trying to drug him and keep him."

Berdella gave Sheldon several injections into his arm and shoulder, some of which Sheldon absentmindedly brushed away, as if a bug were biting him. Hall asked why Berdella wanted to capture Sheldon. "His behavior was becoming annoying," Berdella said, adding that when Sheldon kept showing up unannounced, expecting accommodations, "it becomes an inconvenience."

Was Sheldon sexually attractive, then? Hall asked. No, Berdella said. "I don't think anything made him physically attractive to me," Berdella added, then expounded further: "The best I can interpret what happened was, the impulsive behavior that started with Jerry Howell became a reality for me. You're looking at what would be some of my darkest fantasies becoming my reality, where I was capturing people, controlling them. You don't necessarily need sexual attractiveness to do that." Again, Berdella was venturing into uncharted territory for serial killers, attempting to dispassionately analyze his actions. Hall moved away from that for now, but he would return.

Berdella gave Sheldon another shot at 12:30 A.M. but left him on the couch. Ten minutes later, while Berdella was upstairs, Sheldon was up and walking around. He told Berdella he felt like he'd been poked in the back. When he went toward the kitchen, he stumbled and fell down. Sheldon returned to the couch, and Berdella gave up trying to capture Sheldon that night.

The next day, Sheldon told Berdella he had soreness in his muscles, which Berdella figured was from the injections. Berdella took Sheldon to the University of Kansas Medical Center, where Sheldon already had a record from his injuries in a bar fight several months before. "At that point I had basically written off trying to capture him," Berdella said. Sheldon was examined, given some antibiotics and released, and spent the night at Berdella's. The next day, Friday, April 12, Berdella went to work. When he returned home, Sheldon was drunk. Berdella pulled out his previous page of notes on Sheldon and started making entries again. Hall asked, "Had you reformulated the idea of capturing him and dominating him?"

"Yes," Berdella said.

When Sheldon asked him for a Valium that evening, Berdella suggested he take one of his antibiotics instead. Then, while Sheldon remained on the couch, Berdella emptied the powder from an antibiotic capsule and poured in the powder from five crushed sedative tablets. Sheldon conked out, and Berdella began injecting him with a mixture of tranquilizers. By 9 P.M. Sheldon was completely unconscious. Berdella rolled Sheldon on to the floor, took his pants off, and tied his legs together at the ankles. Berdella then carried the limp young man up the stairs, setting Sheldon down on the landing between the second and third floors. There, he gave Sheldon a mixed shot of tranquilizers, though he was learning through trial-and-error that one small shot of ketamine was just as powerful and effective for his purposes. He moved Sheldon up to a third floor bedroom at 10 P.M.

Berdella was now warming to the task, and Hall hardly had to ask questions. Berdella began a sort of narration, based on his notes, with Hall interrupting only to clarify something. "11:15 is a notation that I butt-fucked him," Berdella declared. "Then 11:25 a notation of 'DC,' which is drain cleaner, to the left ear — no, left eye, I'm sorry. That he had pinpoint pupils at that time. And after the drain cleaner to the eye he was screaming, although a muffled scream, for about one or two minutes."

"Now when you say drain cleaner," Hall said, "are you referring to something like Drano?"

"Basically, yes."

"And what type of a mixture did you use?"

"This was just a cotton swab of the drain cleaner," Berdella said.

"Placed in his eye?"

"In his left eye, yes."

"What was your purpose in doing that?"

"Obviously to damage his eye and cause some pain," Berdella said, as if the question were an unnecessary one. "Perhaps getting into being able to permanently damage his eyes, which would have then made it easier to keep him and to control him."

"And again," Hall asked, "other than his lackadaisical attitude, Mr. Sheldon really had not done anything against you?"

"In retrospect," Berdella replied, "people like Sheldon and the next individual, Mark Wallace, I expressed some of the anger and frustration that I had toward other people on these individuals."

"So you had nothing against him [Sheldon]," Hall said. "You just found him someone to use to take your frustrations out on?"

"Basically."

"And I take it when you placed the drain cleaner to his left eye that you had no intentions of ever letting him leave your house?"

"Correct."

"And you formed the intent to kill him at that point?" Hall asked.

"No," Berdella said. "The killing of him took place because of coming home and finding Phillip Bukovic up on my roof doing some tree work that he was supposed to do two or three months prior to that. And I knew that Bukovic would come into the house to use the bathroom etcetera. And I could see I didn't know what to do with Sheldon other than to suffocate him."

Hall pointed Berdella back to the early part of the capture. Berdella said he attempted to put a tattoo on Sheldon, but Sheldon was resisting him. Berdella then gave Sheldon a shot of ketamine, knocking Sheldon out. Using a hot needle, Berdella then tattooed the word "Hot" on Sheldon's back left shoulder. "I think the act was putting my mark on him," Berdella explained. "But what I put on him wasn't significant."

"Putting your mark on him to stay forever?" Hall asked.

"Yes."

Sheldon tried, intermittently, to plead for mercy, Berdella said, but that didn't stop the torture. Berdella deciphered "S and W" to mean a soap-and-water enema he performed on Sheldon before another sodomy with a carrot. The vegetables remained incomprehensible to Hall. "To you, this was a way to dominate by sexual pleasure, or what?" Hall asked.

"I didn't receive sexual gratification," Berdella clarified. "This was a gratification on the level of dominance, control, earning back."

Sheldon was tied to a bed and heavily drugged, so Berdella left him at 2:45 A.M., but returned at 6:10 A.M., according to his notes. After checking Sheldon's restraints, Berdella gave him some more injections and had anal intercourse again. Below that entry were the words "Plugged ears". Berdella told Hall, "I had a caulking gun and just filled his ears with caulking to reduce the amount that he was able to hear."

This was a new, detestable detail. Hall tried to keep the edge out of his voice as he asked, "Caulking like you would use on your house?"

"On windows, yes," Berdella replied.

"You placed that into his—"

"Just pumped a little of that into each ear, more to block his hearing than anything else," Berdella said. "It didn't cause any pain or problems, etcetera."

"That you know of," Hall said.

"Correct. But the following night I was able to pull them out," Berdella said. "They apparently did not adhere to the sides of the ear."

Hall followed up. "You didn't want him to hear what was going on? Or—"

"Basically another way of depriving him of some of his senses," Berdella said.

"OK," Hall said. "Again then, this would have been not to prevent escape but just to dominate him?"

"Pretty much so, yes."

Berdella's experiments in torture continued that morning with what he described as "acupuncture with needles. I tried to see what kind of response, using regular hypodermic needles, of pain spots, or where spots that he would react to . . . along the lines of like, bamboo under the fingertips."

"And that's where you placed them, under the fingertips?"

"Yes." Berdella couldn't recall Sheldon's reaction to this treatment, but theorized that "he was probably sedated enough that he couldn't vocalize that."

Berdella went to work that day, and Hall wondered about Berdella's thoughts while he had a man tied up in his house. "Probably a combination of being concerned," Berdella said, "having some fear that he may get loose, but I think probably stimulated by that fear."

"The concern would not have been for him," Hall observed.

"The concern, if he got loose, you could be in trouble?"

"I've thought about that for the last eight months," Berdella said, embarking on another self-examination. "And I am in no way trying to defend my actions. I'm still trying, myself, to understand some of them. These were not people that I thought of, once I had them bound and was using them, that I thought of them as being people. They became something other than people to me." He paused, still speaking deliberately, then continued. "And the responsibility for my actions, the way I thought about my own actions, the way I thought about myself, I did not see them as people in my mind or the punishment. I didn't concentrate on the punishment. I didn't really concentrate on the possibility of getting caught."

Berdella kept going. "I think if you look at any of the pictures, starting with Jerry Howell and the haphazard way he was tied, that I was just responding to the situation, that I didn't have a long-term game plan. I had not, never thought it out to the level of, 'What if one of these bodies gets loose?' "

Hall pounced. "You didn't think of them as people. You call them bodies. What were they to you? When you were there at work from 1:00 till 5:00, you were apparently getting some pleasure with the thought that you were dominating him."

"That's correct."

"He could not control his surroundings. You controlled them?"

"That's correct."

"What was he at that point besides a source of pleasure?" Hall asked.

"Reduced to the level of, say, a blow-up doll or a clay figure you would make as a kid and moving around, having complete control of," Berdella said.

"Something that you had created?"

"At least had control of."

"For your enjoyment?" Hall said.

"I don't know if enjoyment is the word I'd want to use," Berdella said. "Physical and mental satisfaction possibly."

After Berdella returned home that afternoon, he began sodomizing Sheldon again, and Sheldon protested. "You have to let me loose," and "You can't do this to me," Berdella recalled his captive saying. Berdella said he responded by hitting Sheldon in the back of the head with a rubber mallet. The injections were continued and duly noted, including a shot of sugar and water, "thinking it might have some nutrient value to it," Berdella said.

Later that night, at 3 A.M., Berdella wrote "EK," "which is one of my abbreviations for using the transformer." He said he also used "EKG."

"Is this the first time you ever used that?" Hall inquired.

"Yes."

"And this is the first individual you ever used that on?"

"That's correct."

"And the EK to shoulder and back, would that be the placement?"

"Yes," Berdella said. "I think with Sheldon I had two hypodermic needles where I could tie the wire coming from the transformer to, so I could actually anchor them into the skin." Berdella would then snap on the transformer and shock Sheldon for several seconds.

Berdella said he bought the transformer sometime after Jerry Howell died, he wasn't sure just when. "I take it then," Hall said, "that after you finished with Howell you had the intent in your mind of torturing other people?"

"No," Berdella said. "The first several months, three to five months, I was repulsed by what had happened to Howell. I couldn't stand to look at the pictures nor the written material. I kept them in a very secure place where no one would find them or be able to get to them. It wasn't until four or five months after that that I started developing an urge to see the photographs, to use them for excitement or masturbation purposes."

"This would have been eight to ten months after you had killed Howell?" Hall asked.

"Probably around that time frame, yes," Berdella said. "And at that point, I think I was starting to build up a desire to catch somebody else."

"So we're talking about February or March of '85," Hall calculated, "when you started going back over what you had done to Howell finding enjoyment from that."

"Yes."

"And thinking in your own mind, 'It's time to do it again'?"

"I was developing it into a conflict," Berdella said, "between wanting to do it again and never wanting to know about it, see about it, think about it again. But as the desire to do it grew, I started accumulating drugs again. And Sheldon came along at a point where I guess my ability to resist this compulsive behavior no longer controlled my actions or my thoughts."

Berdella toyed with the electrical shocks on Sheldon for only a few minutes, then went to sleep. In the morning, after sodomizing Sheldon, he went to his shop from 10 A.M. to 5 P.M. When he came home, he sodomized Sheldon again. He noted that he was binding Sheldon's wrists with piano wire "to cause nerve damage to the hands, so that if I ever did untie him, he wouldn't have control or be able to use his hands."

The next morning, Monday, April 15, Berdella went downtown to a trade show, and returned to find Bukovic working on his roof, the job Bukovic had agreed to perform weeks earlier. Looking down at his notes, Berdella recalled, "I had come home, saw Phillip on the roof. Didn't know what to do with Sheldon. Went up. Put a plastic bag over his head and suffocated him." Berdella said he spoke briefly with Bukovic before going inside, telling him he had to "take care of something." Once in the house, Berdella said, "I took a quick inventory of the drugs that I had available as to

271

whether they would knock Sheldon out quick enough and deep enough that I wouldn't have any problems if Bukovic came into the house. Determining that that wasn't possible, I then suffocated him."

Berdella had a roll of plastic trash bags on the third floor. He pulled one out, "put it over his [Sheldon's] head and secured it around the neck with a sash, or a piece of rope."

Hall asked, "When you put the trash bag over his head, do you stand there and watch?"

"I watched long enough to take the one photograph," Berdella said, referring to his one shot of the dying man. "I took care of a couple of other things on the third floor until I was sure that he was dead."

"When did you take the photograph showing him there with the—"

"When I first put the bag on," Berdella answered abruptly.

"While he was still alive?"

"That's correct."

"As you stood there watching his lungs grasping for air," Hall said, "what thoughts came into your mind at that point?"

"Just concerned with dealing about Bukovic," Berdella said.

"You say you paid no attention to what was happening?" Hall asked.

"Don't remember," Berdella replied. "Just things that, I know I didn't stand over Sheldon the whole time. And I just stayed up on the third floor until he was dead so that I would be there if he had started making any noises etcetera."

Bukovic stayed around Berdella's house for about ninety minutes while Sheldon lay dead on the third floor. When Bukovic left, Berdella dragged Sheldon's body to a bathtub in the third floor bathroom, took a razor blade and made cuts in Sheldon's joints to drain the blood. He waited four or five hours, then used a boning knife, some razor blades

272

and a bow saw to dismember Sheldon's body. The legs and arms were amputated that night, but Berdella left the rest of the body in the tub until the following night, when he completed the cutting and wrapping of the parts.

"Now the head," Hall pointed out, "you had different plans for Mr. Sheldon's head than you had with Mr. Howell's body, didn't you?"

"Apparently, yes," Berdella said quietly.

"What did you do with the head on Monday night after you had cut it off?" Hall asked reluctantly.

"I think I stuck it in the freezer for a couple of days," Berdella told him. "One evening I took it out in the backyard and buried it." The head was wrapped in a trash bag before being placed in an upright freezer on Berdella's back porch, and then before burying it, Berdella removed the skin and hair.

"What was your reason for doing this?" Hall asked.

"I don't even understand what my reason for keeping the skull was," Berdella said. "So I really don't understand what drove me to remove the skin."

"No idea why you did that?" Hall asked skeptically.

"Not really."

"How long did you leave the skull buried?"

"Until I buried Pearson's skull back there," Berdella said, "which would have been August of, well, it would be earlier than August of '87. It may have been a month or two before I got around to exchanging the skulls."

"Did you retrieve the Sheldon skull before you buried the head of Larry Pearson?"

"I recovered it at the same time I dug the hole to put Pearson's in," Berdella said.

Berdella said he put the rest of Sheldon's wrapped body parts in the basement, where the cool temperature would keep them from decomposing rapidly and spreading the odor of death through the house. The following Monday, he set the bags out on the curb and again, the bags were taken away uneventfully.

"Did you have any remorse?" Hall pressed him.

"I know that's always going to be a question on your part," Berdella said, his voice starting to show signs of emotion for the first time. "And it will always be a question of mine. I think at this point I was insulating myself — I was insulating myself enough from my own emotions and old feelings that I just didn't deal with it. It's like it didn't happen. It wasn't until I was arrested and brought over here that I ever confronted what I was doing."

Berdella stopped, seemingly upset, and Berrigan asked for a short pause. Wiping an apparent tear from his eye, Berdella composed himself, and added: "If I've been able to sit here and somewhat objectively discuss the matter, it has been after a very intensive eight months spent here working with the psychiatrist, the caseworker, Pat, etcetera, that have allowed me to objectively discuss what's going on. . . . It has taken me eight months to bring myself to the point that I can sit here at the table and discuss this with you." Cole and DeValkenaere glanced at each other, both immediately skeptical of Berdella's emotional display. Cole thought it was for show, a cheap ploy for sympathy. As is her practice, Taylor kept her eyes focused on Berdella, and she felt his distress was genuine.

Hall plunged ahead, picking up a sheaf of nineteen photos identified as being of Sheldon. One of the photos was taken while the 7,700 volts of electricity were coursing through Sheldon's rigid body. Others showed Sheldon being injected, or sodomized.

Hall then asked Berdella if he ever told anyone, prior to his arrest, about torturing and killing Sheldon. Berdella said he hadn't. Hall asked whether any Kansas City policemen knew of or had assisted him in torturing his victims, a recurrent rumor. Berdella repeatedly said no. Finally, Hall asked, "Do you have any idea of why it was you buried Sheldon's head in the backyard?"

"I think I just filed it away for future reference," Berdella answered crudely. "I can't come up with a direct reason as to why I kept his skull." Berdella paused, then added: "Since you have to deal with the families, let me make the statement that it was not kept as any kind of religious, occult or any-kind-of-belief reason for keeping the skull. Its significance that it was buried, as best as I can tell, is giving it no more importance than any of the skulls that I had discarded in the trash."

Hall decided not to pursue it any further, at least not that day. "It's 5:00," he said. "Why don't we break for the day." Everyone nodded and began folding up their papers. Berrigan and Rogers leaned over to Berdella and gave him some final advice before leaving. Hall, Riederer, Taylor, DeValkenaere and Cole rose and left the room silently, accompanied by the jail guard.

They rode the elevator to the ground floor with almost no discussion. Hall was content with what he'd accomplished, still surprised that the session had gone so smoothly. Riederer was angry at Berdella, with an animosity he didn't usually feel toward the thousands of criminals his office had prosecuted in the last eight years. He had read all the police reports too, but hearing it in person was far more powerful to him. Cole and DeValkenaere were less overpowered, but both were mulling the new things they'd learned, especially the disposal of the bodies. They'd spent so much time looking for the burial sites in the spring and early summer. And the torture. God, Cole thought, caulk? Piano wire? Enemas? What could be next? That thought entered all four men's minds as they emerged from the jail and walked wordlessly to their cars in the chill December darkness.

Chapter Thirteen

By prearrangement, Day Two began earlier than Day One. All sides arrived by 8:30 A.M. and Hall's questioning began several minutes later. Hall barely revised his notes after the first session ended, staying with what he'd prepared over the weekend. But he didn't have the sense of anticipation that accompanied him into the jail on Day One. Day Two was more of an obligation, though Hall reminded himself to be as thorough as possible. He informed Berdella that he was still under oath, and then asked him to relate the story of the murder of Mark Wallace.

"It would have been midsummer of '85," Berdella began. He explained that he met Wallace through another man who had been cutting Berdella's lawn. Wallace had been inside Berdella's house once or twice with his friend, but had said almost nothing. Hall handed Berdella three sheets of paper, which Berdella instantly identified as his torture logs for Wallace.

"When you saw that," Hall said, "you immediately thought this related to Mr. Wallace. What was it about it that makes you think it was Mr. Wallace?"

"Well," Berdella said, "the first notation, 'Toolshed.'"

Berdella recalled that a severe thunderstorm swept through the city the night of June 22, 1985, and when his dogs wouldn't stop barking, he found Wallace huddled inside the backyard toolshed. "I invited him in the house to dry out and get warm," Berdella said. "We talked for about an hour. For the most part, he talked. He was very drunk and very depressed."

Looking down at his notes, Berdella continued. "I gave him at 12:45 an injection of 1½ cc of chlorpromazine in his vein, with his cooperation."

Hall stopped him, and asked how much he knew of Wallace's background. Berdella thought Wallace was gay, lived near 43rd and Oak Streets, and wasn't sure whether Wallace used drugs. Hall asked, "Did you have any idea about his family members or—"

"That's one of the things that we covered in the conversation for that first hour," Berdella said.

"What did he tell you about that?" Hall asked.

"That his mother was out of the country," Berdella said. "That he really didn't know where she was at. He had a couple of sisters in town, but they didn't like him to hang around because he was so depressed and depressing."

"Now the 12:45 injection," Hall said, returning to Berdella's log. "You said that was with his consent?"

"Yes."

"Could you explain then to us what happened?"

"He was very uptight, tense, depressed," Berdella said. "Even with the alcohol that he had in him he didn't appear that he would be able to get to sleep that evening. I volunteered to give him a shot of chlorpromazine, telling him that it maybe would calm him down and relax him. And he readily accepted. So that made me believe that he had shot drugs previously."

Hall asked, "But it was not at that time that you formed any intent to capture him?"

"That's correct."

But thirty minutes later, with Wallace asleep on Berdella's couch, something in Berdella's mind changed.

"Now when you went down there at 1:15," Hall said,

277

"at that time had you formed the intent to capture him?"

"I was," Berdella started, paused, then resumed, "either had formed it or was in the process of finalizing the decision."

"What led you to make the decision on Mark Wallace?"

"Aside from any emotional decisions that would have affected me," Berdella answered, "angry from some other situation or under duress, it was just that he was here. There was nothing to really link him to my house that night and that he didn't have family that would come around looking for him."

Hall asked what other elements might have affected Berdella. Berdella said he had taken Freddie Kellogg to small claims court earlier that month, and he was trying to track down Foster Simmons for some money Simmons owed him. He looked at a calendar from 1985, on which he had jotted what was going on, and remembered the tension he felt trying to wring his money out of Kellogg and Simmons.

Moving his attention back to the Wallace log, Berdella recalled pricking Wallace's arm with a needle to see if Wallace would notice. He did. Thirty minutes later, Berdella tried again. This time, Wallace was sleeping soundly. Berdella injected 5 cc of chlorpromazine, and made a note of it in his log. He snapped a photo of Wallace, and made a note of that, too. Several minutes later, he gave Wallace two more injections, including one of ketamine.

"Now the ketamine," Hall asked, "you found in your experience was extremely effective in knocking people out?"

"Yes," Berdella said, adding, "I may not have had that experience by the time I did this, but this would probably be part of the learning process."

Berdella continued injecting Wallace, and keeping a running total of the amount of drugs he'd used. He began shooting Wallace in the neck, and Wallace would sometimes rouse incoherently, then fall back into a stupor. When Berdella felt Wallace was sufficiently incapacitated, he undressed him and tied him up, writing down, "Out like a light." He then sodomized him twice, once with a carrot.

At 4 A.M. Berdella carried Wallace up to a third-floor bedroom. Wallace's hands were tied behind his back, his ankles bound together. Wallace occasionally tried to speak, but he wasn't making any sense, Berdella said. Berdella sodomized him at 4:30, 5:30 and 6 A.M., according to his notes, as Hall followed along and the others listened in sickened silence.

"I want to ask on these," Hall interrupted, "and I think it appears in the other diaries, when you have the 'BF' for the anal sodomy and 'FF' for the front F, you have those in a box. Was there any reason why you have them in a box?"

"Just to be able to notice them or separate them from the rest of the copy," Berdella said, as if he had been highlighting class notes before an exam.

"When you were making the notes," Hall asked, "did they also have some use for you during the occurrence to have these notes?"

"Yes," Berdella replied, "to keep a kind of record of the responses, what reaction each one would have to what drugs. This wasn't a sat-down-and-planned scientific experiment by any means, but just to have some record or reference to it in the future or at that time."

Moving down the page, Berdella read, "Between 6:45 and 7:05 there was front fucking, a notation about alligator clips. No drugs at this point. He was fighting and resisting."

"Okay," Hall said, "what are the alligator clips?"

"These are just the little clips I guess you could find at most hardware stores," Berdella said.

"What would you do with the alligator clips?"

"I attached them to his nipples."

"Why would you have been doing that?"

"At this point," Berdella said, "I would have to say that I was beginning to get into sadomasochistic sex."

Hall was slightly confused. "Prior to this, with the other individuals," Hall said, "you did not consider yourself to be getting into sadomasochistic sex?"

"I know it would look and sound contradictory," Berdella

279

replied. "But up until this point there was a pretty clear separation between inflicting pain and then at another time having sex. It was only, I think, at this point where I first got into inflicting pain during the period where I was having sex."

The injections, and the sex, continued through the morning. Intermittently, Berdella would also club Wallace in the back of the head with a rubber mallet, "to cause a little disorientation." As the time approached for Berdella to open his shop on Sunday morning, he administered two large injections to Wallace, in the neck and buttocks, then headed out.

Berdella returned home at 5 P.M. and found Wallace sitting up, trying to free himself. Berdella gave him two more stiff doses of the drugs. Consulting his notes, Berdella said he sodomized Wallace from 5:30 to 6:10 P.M., then began "playing around with the needles."

"I'm sorry," Hall said. "I didn't understand."

"Playing around with the needles," Berdella repeated, "the hypodermic tips, to see what kind of response the body or muscles would give."

"Where would you be doing that?"

"It says back," Berdella said, referring to his log.

"So you would have just been putting the needles, puncturing the back with the needles?"

"Yes."

"And to do what?"

"Kind of a bizarre acupuncture," Berdella said, "trying to see if there were spots or areas that the body would still respond to."

By 6:30, Wallace was completely unconscious again, so Berdella turned to his electrical transformer and hooked up the wires to alligator clips. Hall pulled out the photos police had figured were of Wallace and handed them to Berdella. Berdella explained when and where he took each one, and what he was doing to Wallace when the photo was taken.

"Third photo is an illustration of a syringe in his anus with soap coming out," Berdella typically explained, as if he were an art museum tour guide. "This is when I gave him the enema." When he finished going through the pictures, Berdella observed coolly: "I should note that there is one photo, at least one photo, that is missing, and that was the second photo of the attempted fist fuck." He even recalled photos he had taken that weren't included. Hall just said, "OK," and continued on.

"Next notation is 7:00," Berdella said. "And at that point I came up and checked on him, and he was no longer breathing."

"Did you check for any other vital signs?" Hall asked.

"Well, at that point I turned him over," Berdella said, "checked his eyes to see if there was any response on that. Checked for any kind of sign of life at all. And there was none."

"Perhaps it's an unfair question to ask," Hall said, "but do you have any opinion as to what caused his death, what he died from?"

"I think mainly just a combination of the drugs, the gag, the lack of oxygen," Berdella replied.

"How about striking the back of the head with the mallet," Hall said, "were you striking him hard? Or how would you describe the blows that you administered to him?"

"Firm but not overly hard," Berdella said, "I guess what you'd call a mild concussion."

"But these — the drugs, the gag, the striking — were administered by you to him in the course of restraining him against his will?" Hall inquired.

"Yes."

"And his death would have been at approximately 7:00 on Sunday evening, June the twenty-third, 1985?"

"That would be correct."

Berdella untied Wallace, dragged him into the bathtub in the third-floor bathroom, and made cuts in his "arms and groin and leg areas to allow the blood to flow out." Berdella said he had dismembered four of his victims in this bathtub,

281

and dismembered only Jerry Howell and Larry Pearson in the basement. Since the trash collectors were coming the next morning, Berdella had to slice up Wallace's body that night, but "he was a small individual, so it was nowhere near as awkward nor bulky as Howell and Sheldon were." None of Wallace's body parts were kept, and Berdella stuffed Wallace's clothes into the trash bags as well.

"Was any part of his body sold to anyone?" Hall asked.

"Nor his nor anybody else's body in any way, shape or form," Berdella answered emphatically. "Let me state at this time that I understand that the police had investigated the possibility as to whether I was cutting these bones up and selling them as beads and jewelry. No."

Hall asked if anyone else was involved in the killing, if there were any other photos or notes. Berdella said no. Hall was working up to something.

"Did you record the events through a tape recorder?"

"No."

"Or make any notes on a tape recorder?"

"I never used a tape recorder on any of these events," Berdella said directly.

"Never?"

"Never. If I can," Berdella added, "I believe I know the tape that you were thinking about, the one that's three pages [of notes] that were initially determined to be the types of sounds that a person is clubbed, drug across the room, etcetera."

Hall pulled out the transcript that Detective Hurn had prepared of the audiotape pulled from under Berdella's bed, the tape that had been sent to the FBI for possible enhancement. Berdella also had that transcript handy.

"If you want to look at it," Berdella said, "that is a tape of Phillip Bukovic masturbating on the third floor."

This sounded like complete bull to the police and prosecutors. Hall looked down at the transcript and read aloud, "There are several entries of 'Bitch.' 'I'm going to have to kill you motherfucker, I'll kill you!' Movement back and forth on the bed, or what appears to be moving back and forth on the bed . . . You're saying that this is just a recording of someone masturbating?" Hall asked incredulously.

"Yes," Berdella said, "this is Phillip Bukovic talking to his penis."

The others in the room said nothing, and Berdella sensed they didn't believe him.

"I'm serious," Berdella said. "I'm not trying to make this up."

"Are you present while he's doing this?" Hall asked.

"No," Berdella answered. "He did not know that I had a microphone in his room, up in the front room on the third floor, that I just ran the cord down the heating duct to the gallery area on the second floor and could attach a tape recorder to it."

"How do you know that he was masturbating?" Hall followed up. "Did you confront him with that, you had the tape, or what?"

"I think if you listen to the tape," Berdella said, lapsing into his condescending tone, "and you start hearing some of this stuff along with the bed movements etcetera, it was pretty clear that he was masturbating."

"Are you saying that the only voice on that tape is Phillip Bukovic's?"

"I believe so, yes."

"And that this has nothing to do with any type of torture activity?"

"That's correct."

Hall let it drop.

"Back to Mr. Wallace," Hall said. "I'm just, if it's possible, trying to find out why. Do you have any idea why Mr. Wallace, who you didn't really know that well, why him?"

Berdella inhaled deeply, then began. "I think at this point it just came down to, he was there. I think my attitude, the events of '85, I responded to the Jerry Howell incident initially with disgust, fear. As I went into '85 and running into the frustrations of these individuals that I lived with and dealt with in the past, my attitude became, 'If they're there, if they make themselves available, fuck it.' I just gave up caring anymore. I became calloused."

"When you first started with Mr. Wallace," Hall said, "at that time what was your intent to do? What did you intend to have happen?"

"I don't think objectively I ever consciously had an intent," Berdella said. "It became, 'They didn't catch me the first time. They're not going to catch me now. Who gives a shit?' "

"To do what?" Hall queried.

Berdella waited for a moment, trying to think of an example of the many influences that started him down such a degraded path. "A film that I saw as a teenager," Berdella said, "that, I guess, left a lasting fantasy, a dark fantasy, in my mind was a film called *The Collector,* * about a man who lived the fantasy of kidnapping this one woman and then kept her as a captive in a small shed, trying at that point to build up a relationship with her while she was captive.

"And I think that's probably the first clear event that became a mental fantasy of myself that relates to any of this.

*The Collector, based on a John Fowles novel, was released in 1965, when Berdella was sixteen. The film starred Terence Stamp and Samantha Eggar, who won Best Actor and Best Actress awards at the Cannes Film Festival that year. Eggar played the role of the captive. After seeing Stamp's huge butterfly collection, Eggar tells him: "Now you've collected me. . . . This is death, nothing but death. I'm dead. You're dead. Is that what you love—death?" Stamp doesn't understand why Eggar isn't more appreciative. "You think a madman would have gone to this trouble?" he asks her. Finally, Eggar's character catches pneumonia and dies. Stamp wrestles briefly with this problem, then declares, "It was her fault. She asked for everything she got. . . . I ought to have got someone who would respect me more. Someone ordinary. Someone I could teach." The film fades to black as he pursues his next victim.

There were incidents, thoughts, prior to that movie. The movie just gave me the framework to be able to fantasize it. And in '84 I started allowing my dark fantasies to come true."

"I think the next one in line is Walter Ferris," Hall said, after a brief recess. Berdella recounted how he met Ferris through Gene Shaw at the Flea Market, how he once sold them a bottle of chlorpromazine and later traded it for marijuana, how he sold them some more marijuana even though a stranger accompanied them. In early 1985, when Berdella was questioned by Independence police about a drug sale, he immediately figured that Ferris and Shaw had set him up. He didn't see Ferris or Shaw again until September 1985, after he'd already killed Howell, Sheldon and Wallace. He picked up Ferris hitchhiking on September 24, beginning a two-day odyssey of meetings with Ferris and Shaw that led to Ferris's capture.

Berdella grew increasingly annoyed by the stoned pair's late-night phone calls, unexpected visits and rooting around in his belongings while he was gone. On September 26, after Ferris and Shaw had broken into Berdella's house and kept him up until daylight, Ferris called and asked Berdella to meet him at the Midnight Sun, a gay bar in midtown Kansas City. Berdella, still trying to find Kellogg or Simmons, had errands to run, but ended up joining Ferris at 7:30 P.M. He knew this because his log started with the entry, "7:30 Bar," and "Ferris" was written just below that.

Ferris asked if he could stay at Berdella's house, but first he wanted to pick up some clothes and personal items from his house.

"At that point in time," Hall said, "when you're at the Midnight Sun and you offer to let him crash at your house for a couple of days again, had you formed an intent to capture him?"

"Yes."

"What was it that caused you to form that intent on capturing Ferris?"

"At that point," Berdella said, "specific anger towards Ferris, both for getting me involved with the situation on this drug agent and his behavior over the last couple of days. He presented himself basically as somebody that nobody would really miss or look for, with the exception possibly of Gene Shaw."

"With this knowledge," Hall stated, "and with what you believe he had done to you and the nuisance he had been, you had formed the intent to go ahead and capture him?"

"That's correct."

"Other than capturing him, did you form the intent also to torture him?"

"I don't — no," Berdella said, "I don't think I captured him with the intent of the electrodes etcetera. I had captured him with the intent of anger and probably hurting him."

"Killing him?"

"No. At that point I didn't capture any of these individuals with the intent of and purpose being to kill them. I was capturing them first, and then what developed developed."

Berdella and Ferris picked up some of Ferris's belongings, then drove to Charlotte Street, where they arrived about 8:30 P.M. "Between 8:30 and 9:00 I prepared something to eat," Berdella said, "which were some microwaved burritos and chili. And in the chili that I gave to him I had crushed up some of these tranquilizer pills."

In addition to two Valiums that Ferris had requested, Berdella had added several powdered tranquilizers and sedatives to Ferris's dinner. Ferris ate the chili on Berdella's bed in the second floor bedroom, and then passed out about 9 P.M. Within minutes, Ferris was snoring, so Berdella pulled Ferris's clothes off and then tested his reactions with a needle. Ferris didn't move. The cycle of injections, photographs and sodomy began anew.

Over the next several hours, Berdella sodomized Ferris

with his finger, his penis, a carrot and a cucumber. Ferris was tied to the bed and gagged, occasionally reacting slightly to the repeated assaults. At midnight, Berdella noted that Ferris was fighting, so he restarted his program of 7,700-volt electric shocks. He ran the electric current through kitchen spatulas this time, and "I used the electricity on his buttocks, his shoulder, testicles."

"So," Hall asked, "these are similar to the paddles we see when they're trying to revive someone's heart; are you talking about that type of situation?"

"In an obviously much more amateur operation, yes," Berdella said.

"And what caused you to develop this system?"

"I guess because the ways that I had used the electricity before were kind of short and minimal. I probably, in my mind when doing this, gave me an opportunity to move around where the pain would be without having to connect and disconnect."

"And leave the machine on and just go from one place to the other?"

"Yes."

"Was he conscious at any time?" Hall asked about Ferris.

"He was conscious enough to — I think he asked questions like, 'What the fuck do you think you're doing?' But they were not connected sentences. One sentence didn't relate to the prior sentence."

"Well, what would some of his comments be?" Hall asked.

"It would be the equivalent of him yelling at me," Berdella said, "as far as, 'Why are you doing this?'-type comments. I don't have any specific notes."

"How long would you have performed this 'EKG' on the different parts of his body at that particular time?" Hall inquired.

"Probably no more than two to four minutes, two to five minutes, at one time."

Berdella's torture was becoming more viciously painful,

287

and his "bizarre acupuncture" with hypodermic needles was tested on Ferris in the most painful areas imaginable. The sodomies followed through the night.

"Five o'clock the patient started moving, and I gave him two to three shots of the electricity," Berdella said, using the term "patient" as if clinically discussing a surgical procedure. "No notation as to what part of the body." Berdella also kept injecting his "patient" with heavy doses of tranquilizers. Daylight approached, but Berdella continued his sadistic practices with unceasing diligence. The torture didn't relent until Berdella left for work at 10:45 A.M.

Berdella's medical tendencies really started to flower about 4:45 P.M. when he had the idea to take Ferris's temperature. It was 99 degrees. Berdella injected 3 cubic centimeters of penicillin into Ferris's buttocks to fight the slight fever.

"You knew that he needed medical attention?" Hall said.

"That's correct."

"You were trying to give that medical attention?"

"Give what help I could at the time, yes."

"And your reason or purpose for trying to give medical attention to him?" Hall asked, his contempt now noticeable.

"To keep him from getting worse or possibly dying," Berdella said.

"Would this have been for his sake or just to keep him available to you?" Hall asked pointedly, punctuating the question with his most sarcastic glare.

"Well, to help him recover from whatever problems he was having at that time. The only problem that he was giving a direct sign of was running a fever."

Berdella continued to take copious notes, even checking Ferris's eyes to see if his pupils were dilated. By now, Ferris was delirious, barely resisting as Berdella kept up his nonstop sexual assaults. Through the evening, Berdella maintained a steady stream of injections and sodomies, including three more sexual assaults between 11:15 and 11:30 P.M. Ferris was objecting, but just barely, Berdella recalled. He wrote in his log, "Unable to sit up more than 10-15 sec." The other, concluding entries:

> *11:30 2¹/₂ cc ket nk + shoulder*
> *Gag loose, no resit in retie*
> *11:45 Very delayed breathing, snoring*
> *12:00 86*

"What do you mean by 'delayed breathing'?" Hall asked.

"Instead of being a regular process, you could hear that there was delays in the breathing, in-suck or exhaling the breath; it wasn't a continuous regular pattern," Berdella said.

"Did that indicate to you at that time that he was having some problems?" Hall wondered.

"In retrospect, yes. But at the time it didn't," Berdella said. "Delayed breathing was a fairly common side effect or symptom of these tranquilizations."

"So you didn't think that there was anything out of the ordinary," Hall said, "other than a normal reaction to the drugs you had been injecting?"

"That's correct."

Berdella moved to the last line on the page. "When I checked on him at 12:00, however, he was then dead."

"Why did you put '86' for dead?" Hall asked.

"Basic terminology in the restaurant business," Berdella said, "which I had been in, was 86. It meant anything from 'Throw it out' to 'Stop the project'—just things brought to an end and/or discarded."

"Does 86 also," Hall asked, "or the expression 86 similarly mean, 'To kill' or that 'He's dead'?"

"That would be the terminology that could also be used when 86 went into the general public's use of the term."

"So by what we have here," Hall concluded, "Mr. Ferris would have died in the late night hours of Friday, September the twenty-seventh?"

"Yes."

"Because you know he was dead by midnight?"

"That's correct."

"Was his death then caused by the constant injections of the drugs acepromazine and chlorpromazine and ketamine?" Hall asked.

"Obviously I'm not in a medical position to make that determination," Berdella said defensively. "It was either the drugs in connection with his physical response and also on the basis that his gag had just been retied and in response to that."

"So by overdose or asphyxiation or a combination of the two?"

"That's correct."

As with his previous two victims, Berdella dragged Ferris to the bathroom on the third floor, made cuts in his arteries and let the blood drain out of his body. The following evening, he dismembered the body, wrapped it in various paper and plastic bags, filled several large garbage bags, and set them out on his curb Monday morning, watching the bags from his house until they were picked up.

"And what was your purpose in keeping his driver's license identification?" Hall asked.

"Really no reason other than to keep it."

"Some sort of memento?"

"Probably at most," Berdella said.

Hall leaned down and picked up the photo enlargements which had been sorted into one group, all thought to be James Ferris. Berdella flipped through each one and described what was happening, when the picture was taken, and what Berdella was doing. In some of the photos, Berdella's arms or legs were visible as he held the camera over Ferris, sodomizing or torturing him. Berdella pointed out one photo that depicted Larry Pearson, not Ferris, and said that one of the Ferris pictures had been placed with the Jerry Howell group. Although the victims' faces weren't always visible in the pictures, Berdella knew right away who was being photographed and at what stage in the torture process.

Hall suggested the group break for lunch, but Berdella raised his hand slightly and said, "Let me make one brief notation while we're still on the Ferris case." Hall looked at Berdella but didn't object, so Berdella continued. "Ferris had, apparently at one point, been in an auto accident, which I believe by his statements had broken his nose again. He had a very deep, raspy voice. That was one of the things that controlled the volume of his vocal; he couldn't yell loud or — he had a voice that wouldn't allow him to yell rather loudly, even if he had a gag out of his mouth. That was something that I observed and which led to the injection of the Drano into some other people's throats to try to destroy or damage some of their vocal cords."

Hall struggled not to betray his thoughts, again. He asked, "You mean that because of Ferris's condition that he just naturally could not call for help or scream out?"

"Yes, loudly."

"And that was nothing you did by injection?"

"That's correct."

"But after you saw the advantage of that, you started doing it?"

"Right."

"And what did you use to do this?"

"Either liquid Drano or one of the generic things that would be comparable," Berdella said.

"And what did you believe that that product would do to the throat?"

"It would damage," Berdella said, "well, I didn't use the throat. I just concentrated right on the voice box."

"By injection?"

"By injection. Usually trying to make sure I didn't go all the way through the throat to where it would be going down, but just in on the outside area directly around into the throat box, trying not to go all the way through."

"And what did you think that would do?"

291

"Damage the voice box enough so that he would have a raspy voice and not be able to yell for help loudly," Berdella explained.

"Did you think that would be permanent?" Hall asked.

"Well, this started with Todd Stoops," Berdella said. "After he had been there about a week I injected his throat initially rather cautiously, because I didn't know whether it would cause problems like poisoning etcetera, whether the Drano would stay basically in the throat area and concentrate its damage on the throat." Berdella stopped momentarily, then another thought occurred to him. "May I also point out that, as I have read some of the police reports, that I've never injected any kind of drain cleaner, battery acid etcetera into anybody's veins or into any muscle or part of their body for any kind of discomfort. And any time I used it, it was strictly on the voice box area."

Hall felt that about covered that aspect completely. "OK," he said, rising to his feet and turning to the door without another word.

Berdella sat alone in the small classroom during the lunch break, eating off a tray of food brought to him by the jail guards. Taylor was the first one to return to the room, since she had eaten in the jail cafeteria on the same floor. Though she was amazed by what she was hearing, she also felt some sympathy for Berdella. He was baring his soul, confessing completely, for the record. Taylor's maternal instinct persuaded her that Berdella was, in a way, vulnerable. He was humiliating himself even as he described how he humiliated others. Sitting in the same room with someone who had already described four horrific murders, she thought about this man who had once been a chef at some of the city's classiest restaurants and private clubs. Now he was picking at paltry jail food. She made small talk about the food, which Berdella gladly joined. It would be so easy to make those potatoes more palatable, and she mentioned a recipe she often used. Berdella suggested adding another spice or two to make it even better. In no way did this man seem threatening, Taylor thought. One by one, the lawyers and policemen returned to the room, and the conversation ended.

"OK," Hall said, "I think in the chronology the next individual we need to talk about is a man by the name of Todd Stoops. And you told us in your opening statement that you believe that his capture began in June of '86, is that correct?"

"I believe so, yes."

"And apparently it started at the Liberty [Memorial] Park?"

"That's correct."

"It is my understanding," Hall said, "that you had known Mr. Stoops for some time prior to that?"

"I had not seen him for about a year prior to seeing him at Liberty Park," Berdella said. "But I had previously; he had stayed over at my house previously."

Berdella started to recount how he met Stoops at 10th and McGee in the spring of 1984. Hall asked if 10th and McGee was "a common place for chicken hawks to sell their wares?"

Berdella answered, as if confused, that "chicken hawk is not along with my understanding of the terminology. I grew up believing that the chicken hawks were the persons that were young men or women before they had any signs of puberty. It would be untrue to categorize the kids, the young men, down on 10th and McGee as being children."

"Would you agree," Hall posited, "that the people down at 10th and McGee were men who sold themselves as prostitutes to other men?"

"Another man and/or other women."

The term "chicken hawk" means different things to different people. In some cities, a chicken hawk is the person who pays for the prostitute, who presumably preys on the young "chickens." In Kansas City, police call the male prostitutes chicken hawks because they often turn their customers into victims, robbing, conning or beating them rather than performing sexually. In Berdella's twist on this, the downtown male prostitutes didn't qualify as chicken hawks because they weren't young enough, though they were often savvy enough to earn the nickname. In a way, it was surprising that Todd Stoops would get into a car with Berdella in 1986, when many of his street colleagues stayed as far away as possible from Berdella, because of his perceived links to Jerry Howell's disappearance.

But in 1984, Stoops was just another junkie looking for some quick cash for a fix. Berdella went downtown that night intending to meet up with Lamar Rich, but Rich didn't show at the agreed-upon time. Instead, Stoops wandered over and got into Berdella's car. Berdella took Stoops to a dope house to pick up some Ritalin and Talwin, and Stoops and his wife moved in several days later, even though Kellogg and Simmons were also living in Berdella's house. Berdella thought he was helping Stoops and his wife kick the street life, "get themselves straightened out." Neither did, and the young couple moved out for good in late July. Berdella said he saw Stoops occasionally around 10th and McGee, whenever Berdella was "window shopping" as he put it, not necessarily buying.

Nearly two years later, on June 17, 1986, Berdella drove to Liberty Memorial Park, still looking for Kellogg or anyone who knew where he was. Cruising around the traffic loop in front of the park's huge monument, Berdella saw Stoops and pulled over. "He first approached the car like he didn't recognize me," Berdella recalled clearly. "And then when he did recognize me, he got right in." The two men chatted like old buddies, and Berdella commented he hadn't seen Stoops in a while. Stoops said he'd been in jail in Oklahoma, and that he and his wife had split up. Stoops asked Berdella to take him to a drug house to buy some "1 & 1s," and after they did that, the two men headed to Charlotte Street.

"Was he going to spend the night with you at your house?" Hall asked.

"At that point we didn't get into any discussions," Berdella said. "After about an hour or so, I made the decision to try to capture him."

"And where did you make that decision?"

"Either in the car or over at my house," Berdella said. "When we got to my house, as he was preparing his shot, I gave him some milk that had Advils crushed up in it; they dissolved easily."

"You had crushed up some Advils in some milk?" Hall asked, wondering how aspirin would knock out Stoops. Berdella said that these weren't over-the-counter pills, and Advil may not have been the right name of the drug, but they were "rather potent, and they dissolved in liquid and were nontastable in food."

Between sips of milk, Stoops prepared his shot of Ritalin and Talwin. Berdella left the room and crushed some tranquilizers. Stoops said he was hungry, and "the only thing I had to give him to eat was a peanut butter sandwich," Berdella said. "So I just put it [the tranquilizer] in the peanut butter that was on the sandwich and his milk that he drank with the sandwich."

Number Five was about to go down. Hall wondered what it was about this one, this particular person of all the people Berdella met or knew or entertained. "What was it that formed your intent to capture Todd Stoops?" Hall asked.

"I was very sexually attracted to him," Berdella said. "When he had stayed at my house before, especially when he started getting into head trips about the sexual aspects of it, this became a cause for stress and anxiety for me."

Berdella had already told Hall that Stoops agreed to provide his "services" in exchange for room and board during his first stay in 1984, but he was preoccupied with what his wife would think. "And the whole time he would be with me, obviously he was very concerned about Rachel and wanted to be

295

with her."

"And this caused you a great deal of frustration and anxiety?" Hall asked.

"That's correct."

"So the sexual frustration and anxiety that he had caused you in the past was a part of the reason for your deciding to capture him?"

"That's correct."

"What else?"

"Again, he was very attractive, well built," Berdella said. "And that from what he was telling me, with Rachel gone he wasn't really associating with anybody in Kansas City on any kind of regular basis."

"And you found that attractive for what reason?"

"That no one would come looking for him."

"Any other reason why you decided to capture him?"

"Not any logical reasons, no."

"Any other reasons?" Hall repeated.

"Just to deal with a way of," Berdella said, "I guess, handling other stresses that would be in my life; it became a stress release. And to have a sexual say with a sexual toy."

Stoops ate his peanut butter sandwich and milk and never left Berdella's house again. He was alive for about two more weeks, Berdella said. Hall pulled out Deposition Exhibit 14, four sheets of lined paper from a stenographer's notebook. Berdella identified them as the first part of his Stoops torture log. Exhibit 14A was eight more pages of lined notebook-sized paper, which detailed the Stoops captivity to its conclusion. Before Hall could start his next line of questioning, Berrigan asked for a break, and Hall agreed.

DeValkenaere, numbed almost into senselessness, stood up to stretch and decided to use the break to go to the bathroom. One of the guards directed him down the hall to a door on the left. As DeValkenaere stood at the urinal, he heard the door open behind him and thought, Geez, what if it's Berdella? Naw, they've got separate facilities for the inmates. But the man who waddled in next to him was wearing the jail-house greens; sure enough, it was Bob Berdella. DeValkenaere whipped his head around to the bathroom door and saw the jail guard standing there, laughing heartily. DeValkenaere was less than amused. On his way out, he put his finger in the guard's face and advised him, "Don't pull that shit again."

When the session resumed, Berdella and Hall looked at the first page of the log and saw that Berdella had written "6/17" and below that, "11:30 Park." Stoops apparently took his shot of Ritalin and Talwin at 2:30 that afternoon, then later went upstairs to Berdella's bed and passed out. At 5:20 P.M., Berdella began the first of a series of injections of ketamine, and at 5:50 the first of many sodomies was committed. At 7:00, Berdella, ever the clinician, held one of Stoops's eyes open and snapped a photo of it, to show that the pupils were "fixed." Stoops wasn't tied to the bed until 7:40, after which Berdella administered "the electricity," as he sometimes called it. This was followed by more sexual assaults, and then another jolt of electricity at 9:45 P.M. Though he hadn't written it down, Berdella remembered that he was using spatulas as his conductor between the electric wires and the skin, and in this particular session one of the spatulas was placed near Stoops's eyes.

"When you say to the eyes —" Hall started, but Berdella cut in.

"This was with the eyes closed," Berdella said, "but using them as one of the areas that the electricity would enter."

"So the eyelid?"

"Yes."

"Through the eye?"

"At this point I was trying to blind him," Berdella remarked unemotionally.

"And why were you trying to permanently blind him?" Hall asked.

"To disable him as far as any long-term captivity."

The routine continued through the evening. A cucumber was used for the first time on Stoops at 11 P.M., followed by more electric shocks. Stoops would revive at times, struggle briefly with his restraints, then fall back into unconsciousness. The sexual assaults kept up into the morning hours, along with more injections. Berdella recounted sodomies at 1:40, 2:00, 4:00 and 4:40, always in a straightforward manner. "2:00 was buttocks, a butt fuck," Berdella said, basically translating his notes. "Turned to front down," he read, explaining Stoops's position in the bed. "Quiet. 4:00, again, butt fuck. No other notations made . . . 4:30, 'four acepromazine hot' would have meant that I used the crushed tablets as opposed to a liquid injectable. Injection to the arms. Some reaction. 4:40, carrot/cucumber fuck. Grunts. No movement."

Hall stopped him for a clarification. "Would these have been used separately or together, the carrot and cucumber?"

"Separately," Berdella said without additional comment.

"OK," Hall said. No need for further information.

"5:30, he was making some whimpering sounds," Berdella said, looking again at the log. "Three cc of ketamine to the arms. 6:30, front overhead fuck. No reaction. Again, that I tied him down on his back."

The torment continued all the way to 11 A.M., when Berdella finally left for the Flea Market. Stoops had just endured nearly seventeen hours of continuous hell. When Berdella got home at 3 P.M., he started back in with the sodomies and the injections. Sometimes, Stoops would respond to the pain Berdella inflicted as he bit Stoops or bent his fingers backward, but Berdella didn't know if those were conscious reactions or just involuntary reflexes. If Stoops was conscious, he wasn't saying anything, Berdella observed.

As Berdella detailed another night of torture, it occurred to Hall that Berdella must have incredible stamina, if he was telling the truth. "You're basically going all night," Hall said. "Does this exhaust you also?"

"Not on the first night or so," Berdella replied. "If I went in to work and was drowsy, I had some caffeine tablets that I would just take part of them, and they gave me enough stimulation to stay awake."

One of Berdella's notations was "anal bleed," and Berdella said that he noticed blood coming from Stoops's rectum. Berdella moved on down the page and then to the next one, and realized he had not mentioned a significant event. "Let me check this," Berdella said, glancing back through the papers he'd already turned over. "I'm looking, trying to find at which point that I fist-fucked him. We may have missed that. That happened one morning."

"We can come back to that later," Hall commented.

"At the time that I fist-fucked him," Berdella said, "he did not bleed, but then started to bleed rather heavily." The reason Berdella found this significant would be revealed several minutes later.

Moving on, Berdella said Stoops began fighting back when Berdella bit him, so Berdella whipped Stoops with a belt. Hall asked, "What's your purpose in whipping him when he's fighting?"

"At this point, I was trying to terrify him," Berdella said, graduating to the level of psychological torture. "Had I not ruptured his anal wall and caused him the severe blood loss that he had, he would have, by further indications, reached a point where he would be much more cooperative. At this point I wasn't even asking him for that cooperation. I was trying to terrorize him."

"You knew at that time," Hall said, "that you had broken his anal wall from the fist fuck?"

"That's correct."

Still, the sexual assaults continued on Stoops. At 2:50 A.M., Berdella tried his latest experiment, "an injection of drain cleaner into the neck, or voice box, area."

"This was something that you learned just from Walter Ferris's natural problems," Hall said, "that it would be advantageous to cause—to take away a person's voice?"

"Or at least restrict it some."

"And you were doing that by injecting—"

"Drain cleaner."

"—into the voice box?"

"Voice box area, yes."

Hall didn't linger on that point, and then noticed that the dates Berdella had written on the papers skipped over several days. Berdella said one page appeared to be missing, and there may have been one or two days when he didn't make notes. "There were probably periods," Berdella said, "where I didn't make notations or keep accurate notations either because of just being worn out, or I think at times I didn't think he was going to be able to make it much longer, that I may have just stopped making notes."

Hall wondered, "During his captivity, did you ever feed him?"

Berdella said he gave Stoops some liquids, and tried some ice cream and soup, but Stoops "wasn't able to keep anything down," and wasn't given any solid food. Berdella said he gave Stoops some antibiotics to fight his fever and infection, in both pill form and injection, all duly noted as if on a hospital chart.

Hall asked Berdella, "Were you trying to monitor these people's reactions as a doctor would monitor someone's reactions in the hospital?"

"In a twisted way, probably," Berdella said.

On the next page, Berdella related that Stoops asked for a soft drink and a sandwich. But in the sexual encounter minutes earlier, Stoops had resisted, so Berdella denied his request. Stoops began crying. Several hours later, Berdella said he had "a discussion on the facts of life" with Stoops, talking about "what he would have to do, to cooperate and not have any more whipping or electricity."

Hall observed, "You had basically by this time reduced him to a child."

"Basically."

"And he didn't cooperate. You were asking the child, so he had to start crying—"

"Yes."

"—which was your intent to do?"

"Yes."

The next day, Berdella gave Stoops some chicken soup and soda pop, which Stoops was able to hold down. Hall asked, "As he became more cooperative, you would reward him again?"

"Yes."

On Stoops's thirteenth day of captivity, Monday, June 30, Berdella moved him from his bedroom on the second floor up to another room on the third floor.

"Was there a reason why you were moving him up to the third floor now?" Hall asked.

"Basically at this point he was physically pretty deteriorated," Berdella said.

"You knew that the end was near?"

"Not really," Berdella said. "It was just that he—because of his fever, drug withdrawals, whatever—was having problems as far as sleeping, being quiet. It wasn't worth the continued discipline on him to try to make him do something that he couldn't do. I just moved him up to the bedroom on the third floor, and I just kept him up there."

Despite Stoops's obvious descent toward death, Berdella still sodomized him that night, though he emphasized there was no penetration, only friction. He also beat Stoops with a belt and administered some brief electric shocks. During what Berdella called a "front fuck," he laid out his photographs of Stoops from almost two weeks earlier, when Stoops "was in better physical condition," a strapping young man. Now Stoops's face was drawn and withered, his body shriveled to half its normal proportions. Berdella had even shaved off Stoops's curly hair, so that Stoops looked like an inmate at a concentration camp.

The next morning, July 1, Berdella carried Stoops into the bathroom and gave him a bath, both to clean him up and try to reduce his fever. At about 11 A.M., Berdella lifted Stoops out of the tub, dried him off, and helped him back to a chair in the bedroom. He tied a sash around Stoops's chest to secure him to the chair "so he could sit up, to see if that would help him."

Berdella paused, looking down at his notes. "I went back to check at 11:30, and he had expired. He was dead."

"The entry of '86'?" Hall asked.

"That's correct."

"After you gave him the bath," Hall inquired, "and sat him in the chair to see if that would help him, why did you think placing him in the chair would help him?"

"To give his lungs a chance to drain," Berdella said, "or give him a chance to breathe in a sitting position."

"All of this time with you," Hall continued, "under your captivity, when you were injecting him with the drugs, he had a continuous fever, I guess, from the bursting of his anal wall?"

"Yes."

"At the time when you had him sitting in the chair, did you have him gagged at that point anymore?"

"No," Berdella said. "I don't think I used a gag at all when he was up on the third floor."

"He was in such a state that he couldn't do anything?" Hall asked.

"Basically, yes."

"Do you have any idea what killed him?"

"I can only guess that he was so weak as to not be able to breathe in a sitting position," Berdella theorized.

"Do you think it was asphyxiation?"

"Yes. [Or] it could have been the fever," Berdella added.

"Fever caused by your fist-fucking?"

"That's correct."

Berrigan asked for a break, and everyone let out deep

302

breaths. Stoops had been held for nearly two weeks, by far the longest captivity, and his death was probably the most gruesome. As the police and prosecutors stretched their legs, they thought about how Berdella had progressed in his innovative repulsiveness from victim to victim. The final victim, Larry Pearson, would no doubt be extremely ugly.

The interview resumed shortly after 4 P.M. Berdella recounted taking Stoops's body back to the bathroom, propping him in a sitting position, making cuts in his elbow joints, lower legs and groin area, and allowing the blood to drain out of the tub. Berdella said he performed the dismemberment over two nights, leaving the body in the tub when he went to work or to run errands.

He used the same boning knife he had used to cut up previous victims, along with a bow saw and a safety razor. The garbage pickup wasn't for several days, so after wrapping the body parts in paper bags and separate plastic bags, Berdella took the separated corpse downstairs to his basement, where the cooler temperature would slow the decomposition. On Monday morning, July 7, Berdella set the large bags out by the curb, then watched the bags from his front window until the garbage collectors drove up, "just to make sure that they were picked up and that nobody bothered them."

Hall asked Berdella about the electric chain saw police had found, which had pubic hair, blood and human tissue in it. "Who did you use that on?" Hall asked.

"It would have just been Larry Pearson, because he was the only individual in the basement," Berdella said. "The other people I used the bow saw on."

"Back on Howell," Hall asked, "did you use an electric saw on him?"

"I used an electric chain saw that I threw out with everything else," Berdella said.

The obligatory review of Berdella's photo collection came next, with Berdella unemotionally describing each picture as if hosting a dull vacation slide show for reluctant friends.

303

"This is where he's been bound at the hands and then what would be his right leg was in the air, being held by one of the two vinyl dog leashes that I used to keep his feet tethered," Berdella narrated. The next picture: "This is of Todd at the period where he was bound faceup. And it shows on his torso a couple of marks as a result of the belt strap."

Berdella had recorded all of the gruesome highlights with Stoops, and DeValkenaere thought to himself that Berdella was enjoying this. He was proud that his memory was so sharp, so exact, each moment perfectly captured for future enjoyment. It was a sick performance. As usual, Berdella picked out the photos that were improperly grouped. Here was one of Larry Pearson, now came one of Mark Wallace. Who could be so dumb?

"How are you able to tell that this is Wallace?" Hall wondered.

"His hands," Berdella explained, "shape and size of his buttocks, and knowing that it was just a series, one of the other series," as if referring to a fashion shoot.

When Berdella finally finished with the large stack of photos, Hall asked if anyone else had been in the house during the two weeks Stoops was held there. Berdella said no. "And no one even came into the house or living room to visit or anything?" Hall asked.

"That's correct."

"All the pictures were taken by you, no one else?"

"That's correct."

"Did anyone else cooperate in the torture of Todd Stoops?"

"No."

"Other than attorneys hired by you, have you told anyone up till today the circumstances surrounding the two weeks of torture and death of Todd Stoops?"

"No."

At last, Day Two was finished. Berdella and Hall had covered three murders, and all the participants were exhausted as they headed toward the elevators. Hall, normally detached from feeling too much emotion toward his target, was outraged. Even he hadn't expected the gory details Berdella had provided. He wanted to reach over and punch Berdella, who could be so smarmy and unfeeling about torturing and killing these young men. Berdella's unaffected tone while reviewing the pictures particularly ticked off Hall. No one was particularly anxious to hear any more answers, but one more day of testimony remained.

Chapter Fourteen

The final day promised to be the hardest. There was only one murder left to cover—Larry Pearson—but Berdella's pain laboratory had progressed to such a gruesome level that everyone dreaded the latest discoveries Berdella might reveal. Also, under the agreement reached by both sides, if Berdella had any more killings to discuss, he could confess to them now and not face any stiffer penalty. The irregular intervals between the murders seemed to suggest that Berdella could be holding back, that he had killed some men and left no logs or photos laying around his house. Berdella had killed Howell in 1984, then three men in 1985, but only one in 1986 and Pearson in 1987, plus Bryson in 1988. Did he kill three in one year, then go back to one per year after that? Hall hoped so.

Pearson's case was the one with the most unanswered questions. So far, Berdella had kept logs up until the death of his victims. But his log for Pearson ended on July 9, and Pearson had bitten Berdella on August 5. Berdella testified in his first guilty plea that he killed Pearson on August 5. Was Pearson a captive all that time? There were also more photos of Pearson than any other victim. And, of course, Berdella had kept Pearson's head.

Berdella told Hall he had noticed Pearson walking around downtown in the spring of 1987, and that by

306

chance Pearson stepped into Berdella's shop several weeks later. The two became friends, with Berdella giving Pearson a ride whenever he spotted him walking on the streets. Pearson stayed in Berdella's house occasionally, but the two men had no physical involvement then, Berdella said. Looking at his notes, Hall told Berdella that Pearson was arrested for indecent exposure on June 5, 1987. Two days later, as Berdella was preparing to drive to Ohio to visit his family, Pearson called from jail and asked Berdella to post his bond. Berdella said he was pleased that Pearson was polite and amiable in his request, and he agreed, so long as Pearson would accompany him to Ohio.

When Pearson and Berdella returned to Kansas City several days later, Pearson moved in with Berdella, sleeping on the downstairs couch. Over the next two weeks, Berdella said Pearson showed little interest in getting a job or paying rent. This of course irritated Berdella, who said Pearson "really expected other people to do the responsible work for him." On June 23, Berdella and Pearson went to the movies together on Berdella's day off. They saw *Creepshow II*, a horror movie, and ate lunch together. "At one point while we were driving around," Berdella said, "he started telling me about how he used to roll queers down in Wichita. He was basically bragging about it, which was kind of an unusual situation." At that point, Berdella decided to capture Pearson.

"And your relationship with Pearson," Hall said, "had been, although he was irresponsible, friendly for the most part?"

"Yes."

"What was it that caused you to form this intent to capture him?"

"Probably the frustration of trying to deal with him not only sexually but on all other matters," Berdella said. "And then when he started doing his little lecture on rolling queers, I quickly formed the opinion, 'This is somebody that no one's going to end up missing; they aren't going to know where he's at, 'etcetera."

"If you thought back on it," Hall said, focusing on the critical moment, "if Mr. Pearson had not brought up this conversation about rolling queers back when he was in Wichita, do you think you would have formed the intent? Or did that just kind of trigger it?"

"I guess that was the trigger," Berdella said. "I hadn't been thinking about it for days before or anything."

Berdella's log on Pearson started that afternoon. Pearson said he wasn't feeling well, so Berdella crushed some tranquilizers and put them into capsules, telling Pearson they were antibiotics. Pearson swallowed the capsules and headed upstairs to watch television in Berdella's bedroom. A short time later, Pearson returned downstairs. "When I saw that the pills were just making him a little drowsy," Berdella said, "I challenged him to a shot contest, downing shots of alcohol."

Berdella described himself as a light social drinker, just some wine with friends periodically. But on this afternoon, "We went through everything," he said. "Every partial bottle. Peppermint schnapps to vodka etcetera. He and I at that point had probably consumed twelve to fifteen shots."

"Apiece?" Hall asked.

"Yes."

Pearson passed out at 6:25 P.M. Ten minutes later, Berdella gave him three injections of chlorpromazine, which Pearson barely noticed. After a fourth injection, Berdella clicked off the first photograph of his new captive. Then he went down to the basement and cleared away a spot to hold Pearson.

"You decided at that time to do this torture or captivity down in the basement?" Hall asked.

"He was not slight," Berdella said. "He would have pre-

308

sented a problem as far as trying to drag him up even to the second floor."

"Of the people that you had held in captivities, was he the biggest?"

"Oh yes."

At 7:50 P.M. Berdella wrapped Pearson in a blanket and dragged his limp body down the steps to the basement. Berdella tied Pearson's hands together over his head, then linked the rope to a chain that was wrapped around a brick column. With that completed, Berdella gave a small injection of drain cleaner to the neck, to immobilize Pearson's vocal cords. Then he brought his electric transformer to the basement and shocked Pearson several times, just "to see what his response would be."

Berdella's voice was becoming dry and hoarse. During the first two days, Berrigan and Rogers had brought him some hard candy to suck on during the interview, but today there was none. Berdella asked for a break, and a guard brought him a cup of water.

When he resumed, Berdella began going line-by-line through the log, which was inside the same spiral notebook that contained the notes on Bryson. Only with Pearson, the log was twenty-four pages. Hall tried to speed him up.

"Going through this a little bit more rapidly," Hall urged, "how long did you keep him down in the basement?"

"Larry was kept in the basement until the following Sunday evening," Berdella said.

"So it would have been from Tuesday the twenty-third until the evening of the twenty-eighth?"

"Yes, I believe that would be correct."

Berdella said Pearson occasionally regained consciousness in the basement, and sometimes was cooperative during sex. To ensure Pearson's continued submissiveness, Berdella conducted one of his "talks," where he told Pearson, "if he would cooperate, 'I won't hurt you as much.' "

"This young boy who you had been friendly with," Hall said, "what was his reaction when he woke up and discovered that he was chained down in the basement and you were doing this activity to him?"

"Well, first of all," Berdella said indignantly, "let's not call him a young boy. A young man, please." Pearson was twenty. "First, he made remarks like, 'Stop it,' " Berdella recalled. "At one point later on, I believe, he made some kind of comment about, 'What about Mom?', my mother."

"Did you talk to him about that?" Hall asked.

"The times that I talked," Berdella said calmly, "the attitude I was taking at that time and started taking with Todd Stoops is, I would tell him when I wanted to hear from him. Otherwise, he should keep his mouth shut."

"You explained the rules of the house to him?"

"Yes. Or at the point before I would explain the rules, I wouldn't respond to him at all."

Berdella brought a mattress down to the basement, where Pearson was lying naked on the cement floor, though Berdella noted, "not so much at that point for his comfort but for mine, as far as when I was laying with him or having sex." On Thursday, Berdella wrote in his log that Pearson said, "Can I ask you a question?" Berdella answered, "No." He explained to Hall, "At this point I wasn't really talking to him so much. I was just completely dominating him." That morning, Pearson yelled for help, and complained that his hands hurt because they were now bound with piano wire. "I told him that he wasn't supposed to make any noise," Berdella said, "and gave him five shots of the electricity and covered his head with a pillowcase."

"You would have then followed the normal routine that morning of gagging him, having sex with him and shooting him up with drugs before going to work?" Hall asked.

"Yes," Berdella said simply.

Besides the sodomies, Berdella was returning to his role

as nurse and doctor, and he determined on Thursday night that Pearson needed a shot of penicillin, "to ward off or help him fight any infections, especially in the throat." Berdella also was hitting Pearson intermittently with an iron bar, "to basically try to break some of his hand bones."

"And what was your purpose in trying to do that?" Hall inquired.

"To incapacitate him," Berdella said.

Hall was still trying to push Berdella to move along more quickly, not to explain every line, but Berdella would put his head down and just read line after line. For the first time, Hall started feeling the pangs of physical sickness. Cole and DeValkenaere were getting impatient, and felt that Berdella was doing this to torture them. They were Berdella's captive audience, and he was enjoying every second of it. Not only were the authorities forced to sit there and listen to him, but he was clearly reliving his memories in all their vivid gore. Cole thought Berdella was getting a sexual charge out of his detailed re-creations.

At one point in the first few days, Pearson asked Berdella why this was happening. "Is it because I didn't obey you?" Pearson asked meekly. Berdella responded by taunting Pearson for his childlike interest in wizards and witchcraft. "This is reality. All this stuff about wizards etcetera is fantasy," he told Pearson. "And you're going to have to deal with this as reality."

"What was his reaction to that?" Hall wondered.

"Cooperation."

That afternoon, after work, Berdella gave Pearson a haircut, much as he had done with Robert Sheldon and Todd Stoops, because their long hair was getting tangled in the bindings. Berdella also shaved Pearson's face, and gave him some soda pop and sugar water, all as rewards for Pearson's cooperative nature. Still, Berdella held another attitude class, telling Pearson that he would be completely

311

cooperative and submissive; that he wasn't supposed to talk unless I was there with him and told him OK and gave him permission. No screaming. As far as if I was up on the first floor, I would be down to check on him, and he would not call up to me to have me come down."

"And he apparently became very cooperative after the explanation?" Hall asked.

"That's correct."

"Of all the people that you held captive," Hall said, "was Pearson the most cooperative?"

"Yes," Berdella said, then added, "I think, as we discussed with Stoops yesterday, that had he not had a serious blood loss, he would have come around to be fully cooperative."

"And this goes on until August fifth I think you've testified in court," Hall said. "The fact that he lasted so long, over almost a month and a half, was that due to his cooperation with you?"

"Yes," Berdella said. He went on to explain that he had Pearson so completely under control that when he moved Pearson upstairs to his bed, "he had trained himself to sleep the entire night without moving," so as not to bother Berdella. One night, Pearson asked Berdella, "How long am I going to be your sex slave?" Berdella told him, "Don't ask." After that, Pearson began calling Berdella "Master Bob."

On Sunday, June 28, Berdella affixed a dog collar and leash to Pearson, and walked the naked hostage up to the second floor. Berdella said Pearson was "fully cooperative" in the move, and didn't attempt to escape, in part because his hands were badly swollen from the beatings and the piano wire that had been tied around his wrists. However, "I probably had a wood stick, a tree limb, in my hand in case he tried anything," Berdella said. From then on, any time Pearson wanted to leave the bedroom, even to use the bathroom, Berdella controlled him with the leash. When Berdella left the house, "the leash would have been tethered onto the bed, and his legs would have been spread and tied to the foot of the bed."

Hall asked about a notation in the log, "Kept disturbing." Berdella said, "One of the things I was teaching him was, if I was, you know, there with him and watching TV, I didn't want to be disturbed. I explained to him that if he created a problem . . . that I would just as soon move him back to the basement, that he would either behave himself or go back to the basement. He didn't want to go back to the basement." When Pearson "kept disturbing," Berdella said, "I informed him that he was going to get a couple of shots of electricity. Tied his legs. Put the gag in and not tying his arms in any fashion. He fully cooperated while I gave him the three shots of electricity."

"Do you recall where you gave those shots to him?" Hall asked.

"I think it was the shoulder to the leg," Berdella said, referring to the two locations where he attached the wires to Pearson's body. "There would be a photo of that somewhere," Berdella added.

During an anal sodomy at 2 A.M. that night, Pearson made the comment that he was "going to die," according to Berdella's log. Berdella explained that Pearson "was saying things like this not because he felt he was going to die or anything. He thought that the comments would add pleasure to me while he was having sex with me. He acknowledged basically that I was dominating him. . . . He was finding ways, I assume from some of his previous hustling or improvising, to try to find any way to please me. He knew that when he pleased me, especially without being told to, that I would reward him with something."

The next morning, Berdella rewarded Pearson with solid food for the first time, cooking him a breakfast of eggs, toast and sausage. But always he was returned to the bed, sodomized, and then tied down. "Did he really realize the reality of what was going on, what you were doing to him?" Hall asked.

"I think there was never any doubt after maybe the first or second day of what situation he was in," Berdella said. "He had been plainly informed that he was being kept as a love slave, a sex slave."

"And telling him the situation he was in," Hall asked, "did you give him any indication how long the situation was going to last or if there would be any relief from the situation?"

"That would have never been discussed," Berdella said flatly. "He would have taken it for granted that I would not allow him to escape or release him."

"Was there ever any discussion," Hall said, "about, 'Can I ever get out of this?' Or did he just assume this was it till death?"

"I don't know if he assumed to death," Berdella said. "I just figured he knew he was not going anywhere and cooperating made it a lot easier on himself. The example that I would have given to him, like when we were having sex at one time and his arms were hurting, I asked him to compare the pain in his arms to what the electricity felt like. And letting him compare, you know, 'You can either accept the pain in your arms, or you can get some electricity. Which level of pain do you want to deal with?' Obviously, he'd stick with just his arms."

Scanning his log slightly faster, Berdella noted that July 8 "was the first time I allowed him to perform oral sex on me. Cooperated. No hassle. Next notation is 7-9 A.M., again oral sex. No hassle. And I think my notation is that while this was going on, Ollie North was on television."

"While he was orally copulating you?" Hall asked.

"Yes," Berdella said. "This would have not been a

314

planned event. We just had the TV on, and apparently something about Ollie North came on."

Berdella's notetaking began to be less detailed, and on most days he didn't keep any notes at all. Several pages in the log tracked the amounts of antibiotics that Berdella had given Pearson, and one page noted the color of his urine and the quality of his voice.

"Did his voice get worse?" Hall asked. "Or did it get better?"

"After the swelling had gone down he had a coarse but understandable voice," Berdella said.

"Between July ninth and July twenty-sixth," Hall said, "was it just a daily routine?"

"Pretty much so."

"Did you have to use any type of torture to get him to submit to you?"

"Never."

"Were you using, for instance, the electrocution during that time period of July?"

"Not at all."

"So he had completely submitted to you?"

"That's correct."

"From July twenty-sixth until August fifth," Hall asked, "were you having to use any torture?"

"No."

"You would go to work?"

"The routine would be," Berdella began, "I'd wake up in the morning. Have sex with him. Prepare breakfast for the both of us. Feed him. Tie him down while I went to work or ran any errands that I might have ran. Gotten back from work. Came up. Untied him. Gave him a couple of cigarettes to smoke. And I would always bring a cold drink up from the kitchen when I first came up and allowed him to drink that while I prepared supper or made my phone calls or fed the dogs or whatever else I had to do. Then I would usually just go up and spend the rest of the evening with him, unless I had some meeting or errands that I had to run. He would be very cooperative. He'd allow me to tie him back down."

After five practice victims, Berdella had perfected his method for utter physical satisfaction. Total domination at all times, sex in any variation whenever he wanted it. A defeated, compliant captive. Pearson not only had no hope for escape, he had no desire. And to re-create the situation with another young man, Berdella needed only to consult his extensive case log, all neatly kept in one spiral notebook, along with his photographic documentation. Cole wondered how long Chris Bryson would have been kept if his spirit had been broken by Berdella. Bryson had maintained his will to escape, though. Otherwise, someone else might be tied to Berdella's bed right now.

"Let's go over what happened on August fifth," Hall said.

"When I had come up and untied Larry," Berdella recalled, "with the exception of the dog collar and leash, I gave him a Coke and cigarettes while I took care of phone calls etcetera. When I finally went in to spend some time with him — in the mail I had gotten an advertisement for men's clothing or something, basically I think it was from IM, or International Male. It would usually show a lot of beefcake and then a swimsuit or something that went with it."

Berdella paused, took a drink of water, then continued. "I had him perform oral sex on me while I was looking at this magazine. What ended up happening was, he then bit me on the penis severely. He was not tethered to anything. When he was doing the oral sex I usually would just hold the leash in my hand. He bit me. I finally got up off the bed. He was standing in front of me with some blood dripping out of his mouth. My penis was bleeding at that point

316

rather profusely. I grabbed a rag and held it to my penis while I talked to him. And after about five or ten minutes of explaining to him, 'This is not the way to handle this—' "

"After he bit your penis," Hall interrupted, "did he say anything to you?"

"He was yelling something basically about, I really don't have a coherent memory of it, discussing something about how he wasn't going to be treated this way. Probably at that time I thought that he was talking about being held captive because he made no effort to escape, he allowed me to tie him back down. I think this is the first time I had used anything like a magazine for that and wasn't giving the direct attention to him. I think more than anything else he bit me because he wanted attention."

Hall and Cole were astonished by that bit of reasoning, but Hall allowed Berdella to continue. Berdella went to Menorah Medical Center, to the emergency room. "The first doctor that came in and looked at me gave me, I think, Demerol or something for pain. And then a little later another internist or somebody came in and talked to me and explained that they were going to have to keep me for a couple of days. At that point, I explained that I had a dog at home, a female dog, with pups, and I was going to have to find some way of getting home to let her in."

Berdella stopped, realizing he'd forgotten part of his narrative. "I guess I'm leaving out one part," he said. He remembered that after tying Pearson to the bed, and injecting him with 10 cubic centimeters of acepromazine, he went to the bathroom to wash up. When he returned, he picked up a stick and told Pearson, "Now you're going to feel what it's like," and started hitting him with the stick. One of the blows hit Pearson on the back of the head, and "that blow just knocked him out," Berdella said. "That was basically the condition that I had left him in when I went to the hospital. . . . When I found out that I was going to have to spend a couple of days there, I did have to get home to bring the dog in. When I got home, I brought the dog in to her pups, made sure she had plenty of food and water to last a couple of days. Went upstairs to check on Pearson. He was completely passed out, either because of the events or the blow to the head or both."

"But still alive?" Hall asked.

"Still alive," Berdella confirmed. "Trying to decide what to do with him, looking at my own condition, and saw that between the blows to the ribs, which were now very heavy red marks, and his jaw and face, that I put a plastic bag over his head and killed him."

"You got up to the bedroom," Hall said, "and looked at his body but determined that he was now useless to you?"

"I guess the quick evaluation that I did was," Berdella said, "the condition that I was in, not knowing how long it would take to heal, etcetera."

"How long you might be in the hospital?"

"Being in the hospital and how long it would take for my penis to heal," Berdella said. "Period. And seeing that I had probably hurt him as far as the ribs and skull and chin, possibly severely, that it would—coming back from the hospital and being able to take care of myself and try to heal him just wouldn't be a possibility, that it was better for both of us. And I just put him to sleep."

"Realizing that you were killing him?"

"Yes."

"You then went back down and got a trash bag?" Hall asked. "Or was a trash bag up there?"

"I'm not sure," Berdella said. "Just got a trash bag. Put it over his head. And secured it with a sash. Did the other things I had to do."

"What were the other things?"

"Basically I fed the dog and etcetera, making sure she had water and food and that the doors downstairs, the rest

318

of the house would be shut so that she couldn't get in there. And went up, checked on him. And he was, at that point, dead."

"And what did you check to see that he was dead?"

"To see whether he was still breathing," Berdella said. "At this point the plastic bag, which had been kind of bubbly, was now sucked out of all air and was very tight around his face. Locked up the house, and the way Menorah had sent me to my house was in a taxicab. They didn't want me to drive myself. And I just got back in the cab. Went into the hospital, and they operated on me."

Hall backed up. "When you went back to Menorah, I take it the cab was there. Was all this activity within minutes?"

"Well, the cab was outside waiting."

Riederer was revulsed. Berdella had killed Pearson because he didn't want to keep the cab waiting? Even at this stage, Berdella could still shock.

"And when you went back to Menorah," Hall said, "you just left his body lying there?"

"Yes," Berdella said. "I left the air conditioner on, closed the other doors so that room would stay cool enough to — so that he wouldn't rot, etcetera."

"There is a picture of, I believe, Mr. Pearson with a sack over his face," Hall said.

"I believe two or possibly three pictures," Berdella corrected.

"Were those all taken before you left to go back to Menorah?"

"That's correct."

"You then went back to Menorah and were operated on?"

"That's correct."

"And then how long did you remain at Menorah?"

"I got home Friday afternoon around 2:30 or 3:00."

319

"You apparently killed him on Wednesday, August the fifth?"

"That's correct."

Berdella returned home two days later, wearing a catheter. He dragged Pearson's body to the basement, and started the dismemberment the next day. But this time, "instead of working on a long-term basis, because I was too weak and painful to do that, I would go down and do one process at a time, like opening the stomach and pulling out all the internal parts. Then go down later and start cutting him up. And I'd go down and start packing. This was done over the course of about two days."

Hall turned pale. Too much, he thought. He began to feel sick. Cole leaned over and asked Hall, "Are you OK?" Hall waved him off and gamely continued.

"There was never any hoisting him up onto the beam?" Hall asked.

"No."

"What tools did you use for that process?" Hall inquired.

"Basically the same safety razor, boning knife," Berdella said. "Because of my condition I relied on the chain saw a lot more. I would cut down to the bone, and the meat, the muscle and skin would fall apart. And just used the chain saw to get it cut apart as opposed to the bow saw."

"At this point," Hall said, "you make a determination to save Mr. Pearson's head?"

"That's correct."

"And, I take it, the dismembering process took Saturday into Sunday, and then you put the rest of his body out for the trash on Monday?"

"That's correct."

"All the same process, except for the head of—"

"Pearson," Berdella said, finishing the sentence. "Initially I just put it in a plastic trash bag, and set it in the freezer."

320

"That freezer on your back porch?" Hall asked.

"Right."

"Before doing that or at any time before burying the head did you take the skin off of the skull?"

"No."

"You did leave the vertebrae attached to the skull?"

"I didn't make any attempt to remove it, no."

"And how long did the head remain then in the freezer?" Hall asked.

"Probably for a week or so until I was in better condition," Berdella answered.

"You would have buried it then probably the following weekend, you think?"

"Something like that, yes," Berdella said. "I didn't want to keep something like that in the house where somebody might stumble upon it."

That pushed Hall over the edge. "Can we take just a two-minute break, please?" he said. He stood up, walked quickly to the bathroom, and began to cry.

"We are back on the record now, after a short break," Hall announced after he returned and everyone took their seats. "Mr. Berdella, I think you were discussing with us that you had placed the head of Larry Pearson, with the vertebrae still attached, apparently in a bag in the freezer on the back porch and left it there for a week?"

"Or so, probably," Berdella said.

"Did you have a purpose in saving Mr. Pearson's skull?"

"Not a logical one," Berdella said. "And not one that I can even recognize or put into words myself. I don't understand myself why I kept the two skulls."

"You did desire though to keep the skulls, apparently?"

"Yes."

"And a week or approximately later," Hall said, "you

321

took the skull into the backyard to bury it?"

"Right."

"Now I think when we discussed Sheldon," Hall recalled, "you told us that you didn't take the Sheldon skull out until after you put the Pearson skull—simultaneously?"

"Yes," Berdella said, nodding.

"Was it buried in the same place as the Sheldon skull?"

"That's correct."

Hall pulled out a photo, handed it to Berdella, and asked him to identify it.

"This is a section of my yard," Berdella said, "boarded off around the edges and usually used as a vegetable patch for something like beans etcetera that I hadn't used this year. And what would be the corner closest to me is the corner where I kept the skulls buried, one at a time."

"Were those boards up there prior to burying of the Sheldon skull back in '85?" Hall asked.

"For several years, yes," Berdella said, adding that he put the boards there to keep weeds from growing into the patch.

"Then when you buried the Pearson skull and took out the Sheldon skull," Hall said, "would that have been at nighttime?"

"Probably late afternoon or early evening," Berdella said, "just as it had started to cool and darken."

"It didn't create any security problem," Hall asked, "as far as somebody being able to see that you were doing it?"

"That's correct."

"And you certainly would have made every effort to make sure that no one—"

"That's correct."

"I think that officers found—" Hall said, then glancing at Cole, "correct me if I'm wrong—some type of a rag or cloth material?"

"Yes," Berdella said. "That would have been when I bur-

322

ied the Pearson skull, the gag, and that was still around his mouth and neck."

Berdella said he took Sheldon's skull inside, along with the loose vertebrae, and soaked them in a bucket of water. After the skull was washed and cleaned, he removed the teeth with a pair of pliers, and placed them in two separate envelopes, one for the upper jaw and one for the lower jaw. He then put the skull and teeth in a closet in "my gallery area," where it stayed until police found it eight months later.

For the final time, Hall turned to a stack of pictures of a Berdella victim, and asked him to identify them. This stack was the largest. Berdella asked, "If I may, if it meets with your approval, for the expediency of identifying here — there were a lot of pictures — if we could break it down as far as photographs before capture; and when first moved to the basement; second floor while still being disciplined; and second floor while he cooperated."

"Fine. Fine," Hall said exasperatedly, not really caring how Berdella categorized his torture tenure. Berdella then proceeded to footnote many of the photos, such as: "The next picture is him sitting up as he was smoking. It would have been the second floor when he was fully cooperative. The next picture shows him sitting on the side of the bed, tethered with a leash and dog collar. This was when he first came up to the second floor. . . . The next picture shows Larry Pearson, second floor, during the period he is still being disciplined, as he receives the electricity shock."

The photos took nearly half an hour to dig through. When Berdella was done, Hall remembered he had something else to ask about the sequence of events: the police report Berdella made at the hospital after being bitten.

"Was it your intention to make the report?" Hall asked. "Did you ask the officer to make the report?"

"Yes I did."

"What was your purpose for doing that?"

"I, unlike the police report said, did try to file a charge against Larry Pearson," Berdella said, "therefore, diverting any—giving me at least an alibi why Larry wasn't hanging around anymore. The officer that took that report, I believe, was out there first to handle a gunshot wound. When he came into the room and he found the nature of my condition and the nature of the complaint, he tried to handle it as quickly as possible, behaving like he really didn't want to make this report in the first place."

"So you were at that point," Hall said, "trying to establish an alibi, knowing that what you had done or were doing was wrong and against the law?"

"That's correct."

Hall asked Berdella about the large trash containers in which police had found traces of blood when they were sprayed with Luminol. Berdella asked, "Does that just respond to human blood or blood of any kind?"

"Any kind," Cole offered.

"Then there was a lot of blood in various places in my house," Berdella said, noting that he purchased cheap meats in bulk, from veal to tenderloin, either for his own use or to distribute to neighbors and friends. He said he used the containers to store the raw meat, and hadn't stored any human blood there.

A photo of the robe over Berdella's bed was handed to Berdella, who quickly described it as "a common native or coat shirt from the Afghanistan area."

"Did that robe in any way have anything to do with the occult or Satanism?" Hall asked.

"No," Berdella said. "Strictly used as decoration or ornamentation."

"Okay," Hall said. "Other than the six individuals that we've gone over, from Howell through Pearson, were there any other individuals that you murdered in your house?"

324

"No," Berdella said unhesitatingly.

"Are there any other individuals where the crime started in Jackson County and they were murdered in another county?" Hall asked.

"No."

"Prior to March of 1988," Hall continued, "were there any other individuals that you held captive but lived, made it out of your house?"

"No."

Hall handed Berdella what appeared to be the last, unexplained torture log. "Do you recognize that, sir?" Hall asked.

Berdella looked at it for several seconds, then realized what it was. "This is when I first started getting some of the acepromazine, particularly the Thorazine was the first one I got my hands on. I don't remember what year. I didn't know what dosage to use on my dogs. I found a stray running loose one day, a large black dog. Took it down to the basement and ran an experiment with the chlorpromazine on it to see how much it really took to do a dog."

"So Exhibit 19 has nothing to do with injections into a human being?" Hall asked.

"That's correct."

Looking at the log, Hall asked, "And your 10:48 entry, what are those words?"

"Slowing and drowsy."

"Referring to the dog?"

"Yes. Then at 10:45 with the notation 'Down,' which meant he probably would have laid down." Berdella then read line-by-line down the log, explaining in the same matter-of-fact style as he did with his human victims how he injected and experimented on a stray dog.

Next, Hall handed Berdella his photos of men who were still alive. One by one, he identified each of the men. Some of them had been injected with various tranquilizers, and

325

in some cases Berdella admitted that he had "used for sexual relief," meaning he had rubbed himself against the man after he was passed out. But he hadn't tried to capture any of these people, for various reasons. For one of the men, Berdella said he started to keep a log, which was never found. The photos of the man were taken in 1986, Berdella said, and Hall asked him: "In '86, this would have been after most of the individuals we've discussed, the six individuals. If he was totally immobilized, why did you not choose to capture him?"

"At that point I had no desire to or need to," Berdella said, adding that many people would "come to my house, use drugs and leave."

Hall pulled out individual police photographs of Berdella's house. Hall asked him about a pair of antlers found on the stairwell, and Berdella said he usually kept them in the second floor bathroom, holding a roll of toilet paper.

"There is nothing of any occult or Satanic significance about the antlers?" Hall asked.

"No."

Hall asked about the *Black Mass* album that was found on the turntable on the third floor. Berdella said he once knew a young woman who ran the record department at a Main Street drugstore, and she provided him with stacks of promotional copies of albums. "These would not have been albums that, on occasion, I would have bought," Berdella said, pointing to the *Black Mass* LP.

Turning from the photos to some of the rumors and reports police had turned up, Hall asked Berdella if he had ever performed an exorcism of a devil from a child. Berdella was amused, smiled slightly and said, "No, I have never exorcised anybody. I don't even like aerobics." The attempted pun did not draw a laugh.

"Did you ever invite anyone to join a coven?"

"No," Berdella said, shaking his head.

"Did you see the Geraldo Rivera show?" Hall asked.

Berdella said his attorneys had brought a tape of the show to him and showed him the segment on his alleged cult involvement. Hall asked about the woman who claimed Berdella was a high priest, and who witnessed a human sacrifice to Berdella.

"I have no idea who that person was or why they would be saying this," Berdella said.

"What she said," Hall asked, "is it in any way true?"

"No," Berdella said.

Hall brought out some more photos, this time of items that possibly had Satanic significance. Berdella explained the origins of each one, and emphatically denied that any of them were part of a ritual process.

Hall moved to the rumors of Berdella's burial of bodies at the farms south of the city. "Did you ever dispose of any bodies at the farms?" Hall asked.

"None."

"Did you ever commit any murders on the farms?"

"Neither on the farms or any farms in Jackson County, Cass County or anywhere in the United States," Berdella said.

Hall asked about the report that Berdella had taken heavy trash bags to one of the farms. Berdella said the one time he did that, the bags contained "a lot of day lilies along with, I think, some raspberry bushes that had grown wild in my backyard," and that he took them to one of the farm owners to replant.

Hall touched on numerous other, more outlandish rumors and speculations. Berdella refuted all of them. Hall asked if, in Berdella's contributions to the flea market's pot-luck lunches, he used any human meat. "None whatsoever," Berdella said. "Nor did I use bones from human bodies to cut into bone meats."

"Did you ever feed the dogs," Hall asked, "the Chow

327

puppies or the Chow dogs, parts of human bodies?"

"No," Berdella said directly.

"Prior to March of 1988," Hall asked, "was there anyone that you tried to capture or intended to capture but were unable to do so?"

"I made an attempt on Lamar Rich," Berdella said, "in regards to giving him some crystal [methamphetamine] that I told him was speed. It was, in fact, dried-out ketamine. And while what I gave him was enough to kind of knock him to his knees for a minute, it wasn't anywhere near enough, apparently, to knock him out."

Hall asked for a short break, and then resumed with a final set of formalities, questions to ascertain Berdella's awareness of what he was doing when he committed the crimes. With each victim, Hall asked: "Were you able to conform your conduct to the requirements of law? Were you able to say, no; you were able to not do it, but chose, made a conscious choice to do it?"

"That's correct," Berdella responded each time.

Hall followed with a series of questions about whether Berdella understood what he was doing by pleading guilty and waiving a trial. Berdella said he did. Finally, Hall asked if "there is anything that you wish to clarify, any answers you wish to change or any other statement that you wish to make before we stop this questioning?"

"Not at this time, no," Berdella said.

Hall looked up at the clock and declared, "The time is now 3:58 on Thursday afternoon, December the fifteenth. And this completes the statement."

It was over. Everyone exhaled. The cumulative feeling of being punched in the stomach gripped most of the people in the room, but at least now there was no more to hear. The police and prosecutors stood, gathered their papers and photos, and started toward the door. Taylor folded up her stenographer's machine, turned off her tape recorder, then reached over and shook Berdella's hand. Berdella grasped it weakly, preoccupied with his lawyers and the next step in the process.

Hall, Riederer, Taylor, Cole and DeValkenaere made their final trip to the elevator, and again rode the six floors to the ground in silence. To Hall, the whole experience seemed like a sick dream. The confession was simply one more disgusting sequence, though maybe more vivid than the rest. Hall thought he was prepared for the questions, and the answers, by reading and rereading everything that had been compiled in the case files. But hearing it coming from Berdella's mouth, this man four feet away, looking him straight in the eye, had proved unsettling. He couldn't wait to put the last eight months out of his mind, to forget it all forever. Perhaps unwisely, he attended the public defender's office Christmas party that night, where he recalls being offered carrots and cucumbers several times by tasteless jokesters.

The next day, Friday, December 16, Hall and Berrigan asked Circuit Judge Robert A. Meyers to set a hearing date for the guilty pleas, preferably as soon as possible. Meyers said Monday morning was open on his calendar, and 9 A.M. the following Monday was decided upon.

Later Friday afternoon, reporters for the *Kansas City Times* learned that a guilty plea had been arranged, and that Berdella would admit to five more murders. For the most part, the secrecy surrounding the confession had been complete, and the public had no idea what Berdella was saying each day in the jail. At last, a total number of murders was made known, ending the months of speculation spurred by the intense news coverage. The Howell, Ferris and Sheldon families learned of the plea from the reporters. Bonnie Ferris immediately called Riederer and asked him if it was true, but Riederer would only say that he'd call her back over the weekend. Hall phoned Paul Howell the next day to inform him that he'd be hearing from Riederer on Sunday night. The prosecutors, still wary of the families' cooperation with reporters, didn't want any more information leaking out before the plea. Minutes after the 6 P.M. television news ended Sunday, Riederer called Bonnie Ferris and then Paul Howell, and told them both to be in his office at 8 A.M. Monday, where he would explain what Berdella had said about James Ferris and Jerry Howell. Robert Sheldon's family, in California, did not hear from the prosecutors until after the plea was over. Riederer also called the Stoops and Wallace families after the plea to confirm to them that Berdella had killed their sons too.

But the formality of putting Berdella on the witness stand one more time still remained. Hall and Riederer certainly weren't going to assume anything was completed until Berdella had formally admitted, before a judge, that he had brutally tortured and murdered a total of six young men.

Chapter Fifteen

In the carpeted waiting room outside Albert Riederer's office, Bonnie Ferris sat fidgeting constantly. She stared at the floor, hardly talking to her mother-in-law, Harriet Sanders, or Harriet's husband, Gary Sanders. Though the ordeal of James Ferris's disappearance had brought his wife and mother closer, there was still the tension between them that mothers harbor toward perceived intruders. They had cried together for months now, often in the fierce glare of television lights, but this muted climax, on a bleary, overcast Monday morning, somehow felt awkward.

A secretary appeared and invited them back to Riederer's office. Riederer motioned to them to sit down. Riederer moved to the chair behind his desk, sat forward with his hands clasped on the desk, took a short breath, and started.

"You know why you're here, so I won't waste any time," Riederer said. "We spent three days at the Jackson County jail last week listening to Bob Berdella confess to a total of six murders. One of those murders," he said, looking at Harriet Sanders, "was of your son, Walter James Ferris." Sanders could feel the tears starting to come again, even though she had tried to prepare herself for this moment. Her oldest son was dead.

331

"Mr. Berdella said he killed your son on September 27, 1985, apparently from an overdose of drugs and/or asphyxiation." Sanders began to sob. Bonnie Ferris's head started to spin, and she was too confused to cry.

"We asked Mr. Berdella what he did with James's body," Riederer continued, "and he said that he had dismembered the body and placed it with the trash at the curb for weekly pickup, and after that it was hauled to a landfill. Unfortunately, this means it will be impossible to recover James's remains."

"What?" Bonnie Ferris yelled. "What do you mean impossible? Why can't you dig it up?"

"Bonnie, it—" Riederer started.

"By God, you get some people out to the landfill and start digging," Ferris said angrily, her eyes watering.

"Bonnie, that's not feasible," Riederer said.

"That's right," Gary Sanders agreed. "That landfill—"

"You don't need to explain shit to me," Ferris said wickedly, turning to face her father-in-law. "James couldn't stand your ass, I don't know what the hell you're doing sitting in here."

"Bonnie—"

"I don't give a shit, you get some people out there and find those remains," Ferris raged, her temper overwhelming her.

Riederer tried to reason. "Do you realize the cost involved here?"

"I don't give a shit," Ferris repeated. "You guys should have stopped this shit a long time ago."

"Bonnie, calm down, we—" Harriet Sanders said.

"No, you calm down, I can't fucking believe this," Ferris said.

"Bonnie, shut your fucking mouth," Gary Sanders said loudly.

"All right, all right," Riederer said, rising to his feet, "let's all just calm down for a second."

Riederer succeeded in halting the bickering between Gary Sanders and Ferris, who was now crying. "Bonnie, if what Mr. Berdella is telling us is true, your husband's body was buried more than three years ago, and we don't even know what landfill it might be in," Riederer said. "There's no way we could ever find anything after that length of time. I'm sorry. But Berdella did provide us with a complete account of how he met James and what he did once he captured him, which provided us with a lot of answers. I won't go into the details here this morning, because they're simply too gruesome. But once the transcript of the confession is ready, I'll be glad to let you have a look at it. That goes for you two as well," he added, glancing at the Sanders. They nodded affirmatively, while Ferris kept her gaze on the floor.

"Mr. Riederer," Harriet Sanders said haltingly, "why did you make this deal in the first place? We didn't want this, we wanted a trial, we wanted the whole truth to come out."

"You would have never gotten the whole truth from a trial, I assure you," Riederer answered. "And in addition, we didn't have enough evidence on James's case to even file charges. That case would never have gone to trial, and you would never have known if Berdella had killed him or not. This way, we obtained all the details about all the murders, and I think he's telling us the truth."

"Right," Gary Sanders snorted. "Anything to avoid the death penalty. That son of a bitch deserves to die."

"Be that as it may," Riederer said, "without this plea agreement, you would never have known what happened to James. Instead, we have a full confession, and in a few minutes, he's going to plead guilty and be sentenced to

333

life in prison without the possibility for parole. We could have done a lot worse."

"Are there any other boys?" Harriet Sanders asked, referring to the number of victims beyond the six known.

"Mr. Berdella says there are no others, and I truly believe he is being candid when he says that," Riederer said. "The police didn't find any indication of any more victims, and we've accounted for everyone who was photographed or mentioned in all the evidence we removed from Berdella's house. As far as I'm concerned, the Berdella case is over."

The room was silent, save for Bonnie Ferris's sniffles. Riederer told them he would be available anytime to answer their questions, and then he ushered them out of his office so he could meet with Paul Howell. He stood outside his office doorway as Howell trudged toward him, his jaw set, his shoulders hunched with anxious tension. Howell was convinced that Riederer was part of a cover-up, that prosecutors and police had known about Berdella and refused to do anything about him. He thought it possible that Berdella had embarrassing information about some prosecutors, and had used that to avoid being caught.

Riederer gave Howell the same brief synopsis of what Berdella had said. Howell listened, nodded, but rarely made eye contact with Riederer. At one time, back when Howell was rooting through Berdella's trash for clues to his son's disappearance, he had considered the possibility that Berdella was placing the bodies there. But he figured Berdella was too smart for that. How could you set a body out by the curb and not have the trash bag torn apart by neighborhood dogs? Why didn't the police go into Berdella's house sooner, especially after James Ferris's disappearance? After Berdella gave this supposed

334

"confession," was he given a lie-detector test?

Howell paid attention to Riederer, sensing the prosecutor's uneasiness with his task. He asked few questions, knowing they would just be a waste of time. What about accomplices? There were none, Riederer said. What about devil worship? Berdella denied it, Riederer said. What was the next step in the investigation? The investigation was over. "He didn't any more want to talk to me than the man in the moon," Howell told a reporter after the meeting. "It was just something he had to do as a politician." The embittered parent stood up and stalked out of Riederer's office unsatisfied and walked the half-block to the Criminal Justice Center, where in April he had tried to pummel Berdella as he sat in the empty jury box.

Heavy security was in place at the Justice Center, first with the metal detectors at the front door, and then outside the closely guarded courtroom. Only family members of the victims, news reporters and courthouse employees were allowed inside. Courtroom sketch artists set up their boards along the front row. Riederer and Hall took their places at the prosecution table. Berrigan and Rogers were joined at the defense table by Barbara Schenkenberg, who had worked for months on the case and wanted to be present for the final scene. About 9:15 A.M., Berdella was led in by two jail guards, shuffling against the shackles attached to his ankles, his hands cuffed in front of him. Shortly after that, Judge Meyers took his seat on the bench. "This is state of Missouri versus Robert Berdella," Meyers intoned officially. "Are you ready to proceed, gentlemen?"

"Defense is ready, Your Honor," Berrigan said.

"State is ready, Your Honor," Hall said.

Berrigan stated he would waive the reading of the charges, and as Hall announced each murder count, Berrigan said that Berdella intended to plead guilty to each one. "All right," Meyers said. "Are you ready to proceed with the factual bases?" Berrigan nodded yes. "Swear the defendant," the judge instructed his clerk. Berdella arose and stepped to the witness stand for the final time.

Berrigan had Berdella state his name, age, his education, and his ability to read and write English. Berrigan then asked Berdella if he understood his rights to a trial by jury, to a change of venue, to be held innocent until proven guilty, to call witnesses, to refuse to testify, to appeal a guilty verdict. Berdella said he did. His answers were short and soft-spoken, his throat still sore from a minor infection. The audience, jammed into seven rows of benches, leaned forward intently to catch Berdella's every inflection.

"Is it your understanding," Berrigan said to Berdella, "that on your behalf, we, that is, myself, Mr. Rogers and Miss Schenkenberg, have negotiated a plea agreement that encompasses all of the five cases that are before the Court today?"

"Yes," Berdella said.

"All right," Berrigan continued. "Could you, to the best of your ability, state what you believe the plea agreement to be?"

"That the state is satisfied that admissions have been made in all the deaths," Berdella said. "That they are charging me with all those deaths, second degree with the exception of Robert Sheldon, and that I am to receive life imprisonment on each of the charges."

"Do you understand that in the case of Mr. Sheldon," Berrigan said, "if the Court accepts your guilty plea of murder in the first degree in CR 88-4273, that's life imprisonment without the possibility of parole; do you understand that?"

"Yes."

"That you will be in the penitentiary until you die; do you understand that?"

"Yes."

Berrigan moved to the factual facet of the plea, starting with the murder of Robert Sheldon. "Could you tell the Court first of all, prior to causing his death, did you deliberate about Mr. Sheldon's fate?"

"Yes."

"Do you understand what I mean by deliberate?"

"Yes."

"Tell me what you think that means," Berrigan instructed.

"I had decided action and was able to think about the cause, or the results of my actions," Berdella said.

"All right," Berrigan said. "And after deliberations, sir, what exactly did you do to Mr. Sheldon?"

"I put a plastic trash bag over his head and secured it with a rope and allowed him to suffocate," Berdella said. Again, he was utterly emotionless. He kept his eyes focused on Berrigan, avoiding the burning stares of the audience as well as Hall and Riederer.

"Did he in fact suffocate?" Berrigan asked.

"Yes."

"You, yourself, put the trash bag over Mr. Sheldon's head?"

"Yes."

"Anybody else participate in that offense?"

"No."

"Anybody else made aware of that offense prior to your incarceration?"

"No."

The reporters scribbled furiously, while the artists scratched away at the outlines of the judge's white-haired visage, Berdella's downtrodden, pudgy presence, the backs of the lawyers' heads. The high drama silenced even the most garrulous media representative.

Berrigan read from the filing on Jerry Howell, and eyes began to turn toward Paul Howell, who rocked nervously in his seat on the aisle. "What is it exactly that you did to Mr. Howell," Berrigan asked, "that causes you to believe that you committed that offense against him on July fifth and July sixth, 1984?"

"I had him bound with his hands behind his back," Berdella said matter-of-factly, "his feet bound, and they were tied then to the footboard of the bed."

"During the course of committing that offense," Berrigan asked, "did you do anything to Mr. Howell in the way of injecting him with substances and gagging him?"

"Yes, I did inject drugs into his body."

"Did you also gag Mr. Howell?"

"Yes."

"All right," Berrigan said. "As a result of gagging him and injecting him with the drugs you have spoken about, did some event occur on July sixth, 1984, leading to the death of Mr. Howell."

"Yes."

"What was that, sir?"

"Apparently," Berdella said, "the combination of the drugs and the gag made it impossible for him to breathe at that time, and he died."

Paul Howell cringed, his face reddening. He gave brief thought to grabbing a sheriff's deputy's gun and trying to kill Berdella right then, but he figured there were too many people in the way who might get hurt. Instead, he lowered his head and listened in silent agony.

Berrigan picked up another set of papers and read the charges pertaining to Todd Stoops. Berdella confirmed

338

that he had bound and gagged Stoops, and injected him with drugs. "Did you also," Berrigan asked, "insert your fist into Mr. Stoops's anus?"

"Yes." This was an unexpected shock to the audience.

"And that resulted in what physical injury to Mr. Stoops?"

"He had a blood loss," Berdella said. "The anal wall apparently ruptured."

"Did that also cause some infection, sir?"

"Yes."

"Is it true that Mr. Stoops died at your house at 4315 Charlotte on or about July first, 1986?"

"Yes."

"To the best of your ability," Berrigan queried, "could you tell us what the cause of death of Mr. Stoops was?"

"Combination of blood loss and infection," Berdella said curtly.

"That would be the blood loss and infection of his anus, is that correct?" Berrigan asked.

"Yes."

"And also the drugs that you injected into him during that time period, is that correct?"

"Yes."

Berdella was determined not to say more than he had to, and Berrigan knew from experience that his defendants were highly uncomfortable admitting to anything illegal. For the most part, he asked "yes or no" questions, seeking only to extract the bare minimum needed to establish that Berdella had full knowledge of the crimes, and understood what he had done. There would be no questions about the disposal of the bodies, or the motivations, or anything not directly related to the causes of death. To most of those in the audience, that was just fine. The disclosure about a ruptured anal wall was as

339

shocked as they needed to be six days before Christmas.

"Between the dates of June twenty-second, 1985, and June twenty-third, 1985," Berrigan continued, "did you have occasion to come in contact with Mr. Mark Wallace?"

"Yes."

"When you came in contact with Mr. Wallace, sir, where was he?"

"At 4315 Charlotte, Kansas City, Missouri, Jackson County." Berdella, again in a monotone, admitted tying up and injecting Wallace.

"To the best of your ability," Berrigan said, "could you tell us what event caused the death of Mr. Wallace on or about June twenty-third, 1985?"

"Again," Berdella said resignedly, "the combination of the gag and drugs that were in him made it impossible for him to breathe, and he died."

The last case was James Ferris. Berdella acknowledged injecting and gagging Ferris, then tying him to the bed. "At the time that you did that," Berrigan said, "did you know what you were doing?"

"Yes."

"All right. Did you do that purposely in order to effect the restraint or interference with Mr. Ferris's liberty?"

"Yes."

"And at the time that you did that, did you expose him to substantial risk of serious physical injury?"

"Yes."

"And again," Berrigan said, "he sustained serious physical injury. In fact, he died, is that correct?"

"Yes," Berdella said, taking a sip of water from a styrofoam cup.

"You knew at the time that that was against the law?"

"Yes."

340

"To the best of your ability, Mr. Berdella, could you tell us what caused the death of Mr. Ferris, on or about September twenty-seventh, 1985?"

"The combination of the gag and the drugs made it impossible for him to breathe, and he died," Berdella said again, as if very well-rehearsed. Tears coursed down the cheeks of Bonnie Ferris.

Berrigan cleared up another point. "Finally, Mr. Berdella, in all the cases that we've discussed, five homicides that are before the Court today, I'll ask you the following questions. During the commission of any of those offenses, did you have a mental disease or defect that rendered you incapable of knowing or appreciating the nature, quality, or wrongfulness of your conduct, or mental disease or defect that rendered you incapable of conforming your conduct to the requirements of the law?"

"No," Berdella replied plainly.

Berrigan tossed out a few more relevant questions. "Do any of the offenses involve any type of worship of Satan or any practice pertaining to the occult?"

"No."

"Have you ever engaged in any type of Satan worship or cult practices?"

"None," Berdella said.

"During the commission of these homicides," Berrigan said, "were any other persons present in your house participating in the offense or played, that is, that you imparted knowledge to any other persons about these offenses?"

"None."

"You're saying that you are the only person that is involved with these five homicides and any other offense that you have pled guilty to, is that correct?"

"That's correct."

341

Berrigan finished, and Hall stood up to review Berdella's rights, so that he would have no grounds for appeal by saying he didn't understand what he was doing. He also asked Berdella if he was satisfied by his legal representation. "Very much so," Berdella said. Hall asked Berdella if he was aware, as he was killing these men, that his actions were unlawful. Berdella said he was aware of that. For one last time, Hall asked Berdella if he was sure he wanted to waive his rights to trial. Berdella repeatedly answered yes.

Hall concluded, and the judge turned toward Berdella and said, "Mr. Berdella, there are a few questions I want to ask you." Berdella took another swallow of water and swiveled his chair toward the bench.

"I'm interested in your past, if there has been a past," Meyers said. "Have you been treated for mental illness at any time?"

"No," Berdella said.

"Ever been in a mental hospital like Western Missouri [Mental Health Center]?"

"No."

"Have you ever been seen by a psychiatrist at any time?"

"No."

"You yourself are convinced that you are mentally all right?"

"Yes."

"You have no mental disease or defect?"

"No."

Meyers looked at the defense table and asked, "What is each of your opinions as to competence to proceed here today?"

Berrigan rose and said, "Before they answer those questions, Judge, I want to clear up something Mr. Berdella just said. He is presently seeing, and has been since incarceration, a psychologist here at the Jackson County jail. However, whatever problems that he has been experiencing certainly do not rise to the level of mental disease of defect under [state law] Chapter 552, and he is certainly, without any doubt, at least in my opinion, capable of understanding the charges against him and assisting in his own defense."

Meyers asked, "You feel he's mentally competent to proceed here today?"

"Absolutely, yes, sir," Berrigan said.

"And Miss Schenkenberg," Meyers said, "what is your opinion about his mental competence to proceed here today?"

"Yes, I agree he is competent to proceed," Schenkenberg said.

"I also agree, Your Honor," Rogers added. "I have no question about his present competence to proceed whatsoever."

"All right," Meyers said, glancing down at the files in front of him. "Let me ask you directly, Mr. Berdella. In CR 88-4273, the charge of murder in the first degree, how do you plead to that charge?"

"Guilty," Berdella said, without looking up at the judge.

"And that's the charge involving Robert Sheldon?" Meyers asked.

"That's correct."

Meyers asked him the same question four more times, and Berdella answered him each time with just one word: "Guilty."

"Let the record show," Meyers said, "the Court finds the defendant is acting voluntarily, he fully understands his rights, he fully understands the consequences of his pleas, he is guilty in each of the five cases. . . . The Court will accept the pleas of guilty. Is there any legal cause to show why judgment and sentence should not be imposed at this time?"

"No," Berdella said.

"Do you have anything else you want to say about it?" Meyers asked him.

"No," Berdella replied.

"In CR 88-4273," Meyers declared, "on the plea of guilty, the defendant will be sentenced to life imprisonment without probation or parole." Meyers imposed four more life sentences, although those sentences did not have a "no parole" condition, since they were pleas to second-degree, rather than first-degree, murder. Those were moot points. Berdella now faced two life sentences without parole, plus five "conditional" life sentences. Meyer informed Berdella of his option to appeal the sentences if he felt his rights had been violated.

"Anything further?" Meyers said when finished.

"No, sir," Berrigan answered.

"All right," Meyers said. "Good luck to you, Mr. Berdella."

"Thank you," Berdella said.

The judge adjourned the proceedings, and the jail guards moved to Berdella's side and escorted him through a side door out of the courtroom. The audience filed out quickly, with the reporters clustering around the door waiting for the attorneys to emerge. After the initial, sensational shock waves that Berdella's case had sent through the city, this formal, lifeless ceremony was an anticlimactic finish.

Berrigan walked out of the courtroom carrying a stack of papers, and as reporters surrounded him, he gave each of them a two-page typed statement from Berdella. "Now that all charges have been satisfied, and all crimes allowed for," the statement opened, "I am free at last to present 'my side . . .' Firstly, to the families who have been affected by my actions, there is nothing I can say at this time that would reduce their grief and anger. This is a time to come to grips with feelings, and should be a private time, and I will not violate their privacy. There will be no discussions on my part until the end of the holiday season."

The reporters began shaking their heads and chuckling as they read. Paul Howell and Harriet Sanders walked over and picked up their own copies of the statement. It continued: "I will assure the families that I have taken steps to attempt compensation in such a way that money that should go to the families would not end up diverted into legal fees. You will be contacted directly shortly. These same steps will insure that I never profit from my crimes." The rest of the statement thanked Berdella's lawyers and individuals such as the Reverend Coleman, "who gave the personal support that enabled me to make it through some very difficult times."

"Shit," Howell spat, "I don't want any of this motherfucker's goddamn money." It was the first he had heard of the trust funds Berdella had created, using the remainder of his money from the sale of his shop contents and his house. The total was about $50,000, and set out rules for the gradual distribution of the money to the families of the six murder victims. Harriet Sanders said she'd probably take the money. As television cameras crowded around her and Howell, they both expressed their disappointment that Berdella wasn't going to get the death penalty.

A short time later, Riederer held a press conference back in the main courthouse. He explained for the first time what Berdella said he had done with the bodies. He

345

defended the decision not to seek the death penalty and strike a plea bargain. "It was a massive savings of resources," Riederer said. "It was unlikely that had we gone to trial, we would have found out the truth in each of these cases. And, if we got the death penalty, we don't know we could keep it," referring to the possibility of a successful appeal.

"But for me," Riederer added, "the most important consideration of all was the families of the victims. We were able to tell the families once and for all what had happened to their husbands, sons and brothers. I think, without exception, the families of those individuals supported that."

The reporters asked about the possibility of devil worship, of more victims, of official involvement. Riederer gave them Berdella's answers, as best he could remember. He said Berdella had "talked about the fact he had had certain dark fantasies. Those fantasies came to life and that's part of what went on." As the questions dwindled, Riederer came to a realization: the case, for him, was finally ending. He was glad he'd been a prosecutor for eight years before this case came along. He felt it gave him the necessary background and preparation to handle the legal twists that inevitably develop in a complicated case. Hall sat in the audience, watching silently. He couldn't wait to put Berdella out of his mind forever.

Across the street, at police headquarters, Riederer's feeling of relief was beginning to wash over Cole. Almost certainly the biggest case he would ever handle was over, and he had helped convict a cunning serial killer of six murders. So far as he could tell, he hadn't screwed anything up, either. For most policemen, the biggest concern isn't in doing something right but in not doing it wrong. Cole relaxed enough to give his first media interview since

346

the squad was formed, and told the reporter that the only thing about Berdella's confession that surprised him was the torture. "The types and the amounts of torture," Cole said. "He gave us some insight into that. It seemed to increase on the later victims." Talking about Larry Pearson, Cole revealed something that hadn't been made public before, that Pearson had been a captive for more than six weeks. "That poor guy was in hell," Cole said.

Cole ventured that Berdella showed little remorse throughout the three-day interview. "In my opinion, he was a cold-blooded serial killer. They're not going to sit over there and growl at you. He's sort of in our ballpark now, so to speak. But I'm sure if we could have seen him at the time this was going on, we would have formed a much different opinion" than that of the mild-mannered man who calmly confessed to five murders that morning. Though the families of the victims felt there were more killings, Cole concurred with Riederer that six was the proper total. "I feel like it's over," Cole declared.

Epilogue

In Bob Berdella's mind, the case was far from over. Berdella was determined to restore his image as a decent, sensitive citizen who just happened to make a few mistakes. His public relations campaign began after he read Cole's remarks in the *Kansas City Times*. The newspaper article crystallized, for Berdella, the two true culprits in all the suffering his crimes had caused: the police and the news media. After digesting the stacks of police reports, Berdella concluded that the police should have caught him sooner. But they were inept, insensitive to the lives of those who scratch and struggle for a living, such as those who work in the area of 10th and McGee Streets. If the police had stopped him after Howell, he could have argued that Howell's death was accidental, an unfortunate side effect of some overzealous sadomasochism. Then, five more young men would still be alive, and five families wouldn't be quite so miserable this Christmas.

And the media—especially the *Star* and *Times*. Mere pawns of the police and prosecutors, Berdella thought. The papers could do nothing but portray Berdella as evil. Evil, evil, evil, everywhere that word seemed to appear in the papers. One editorial column was headlined, "Is Bob Berdella evil incarnate?" Were there no reporters who cared to write the other side of the story, Berdella wondered. He often complained to Coleman about the lack of investigative journalism, the missing balance in these stories. Why weren't Berdella's friends and relatives quoted? What about all the positive things Berdella had done? All ignored, while the police and prosecutors stoked the city's hysteria to new levels of hatred.

Two days after Cole's seemingly innocuous remarks appeared in the *Times*, followed by an interview with DeValkenaere in the *Star*, Berdella called Coleman at 9:30 P.M. In a rage, Berdella instructed Coleman to take down Berdella's response and call the television stations immediately. Coleman balked. He was willing to be a friend, confidant and sounding board, but not a spokesman. Berdella insisted, finally saying he was almost suicidal over the police statements. Coleman relented, and copied down Berdella's declaration. "Their [the police] statements have been so venomous and without any regard to the feelings of the victims' families that they demand a response now," Berdella stated. "Many of their statements are intentional, vicious lies." Coleman called one of the stations shortly before it began its 10 P.M. newscast, and the station opened its news with Berdella's statement.

The next day, in an even more uncomfortable position, Coleman held a press conference in front of the county jail to explain Berdella's opinions. Berdella was particularly peeved that Cole had claimed Pearson was held captive for forty-three days. "The record will show that is not what he said," Coleman said, taking Berdella's word for it. He said Berdella told him Pearson was only a captive for five days. "That's what Bob said; that's what Bob did," Coleman told the reporters. "And he would like reported the actualities, rather than the exaggerations. . . . His feeling is he has been 100 percent honest with the prosecuting attorney's office. He has given all the information and evidence he has. . . . He wants to be seen as an honest person who did some terrible things, but one who's trying to face the future in a way that will be responsible to the families of the victims." Coleman tried to defend Berdella as best he could. "The way the paper looked at Bob is they've portrayed him, and even the detectives have, as something of a cold-blooded killer with no remorse. Bob does not see it that way. He is a person with a great deal of remorse. The reason he shows no emotion at this point is he's been through so much and he simply can't handle it."

Berdella's contention that he had been wronged by the police was absurd to a city which had long since made up its mind about Berdella. Although the gruesome details of Berdella's torture sessions and sexual practices were never made known through the papers or television stations, the hints and obscure references made by reporters conveyed the impression of events which would not merit sympathy. Six painfully tortured men, six deaths. Get this guy out of the spotlight.

Still, Berdella was dogged in his desire to fire one last salvo at the police and media. He asked Coleman to contact Channel 19, the public television affiliate in Kansas City. He would grant them his first, exclusive interview. The producers of *Kansas City Illustrated,* a weekly magazine-style show, decided to accept Berdella's offer, and James McKinley, an author and professor at the University of Missouri-Kansas City, was assigned the task of interviewing Berdella. No money was paid to Berdella, and no ground rules were set.

But Berdella imposed his own ground rules once the cameras started rolling on January 2, 1989. McKinley brought a large pile of newspaper clippings with him, and conversed with Berdella for nearly three hours before the taping began. McKinley jotted down notes on some of Berdella's more pointed comments, and then asked about them on camera. But when Berdella didn't like a question, he would rock back in his chair and become unresponsive, "something that looks like shock," McKinley said later. The result was no insightful answers into how someone becomes a brutal serial killer, and extended rambling about how the police and media let such things happen all the time.

Completely distorting the facts, Berdella attacked the police investigation of James Ferris's disappearance. "Until I told those detectives that I had been questioned on Howell," Berdella said, "they were not aware that I had been investigated in any other missing person. Even when I did tell them, they did nothing to follow it up." With no reason to believe otherwise, McKinley didn't challenge Berdella's claim. McKinley asked, "If the police did their jobs, they would have caught you?"

"Maybe not caught me," Berdella replied. "Scared me off, maybe. Prevented things from happening after Howell, definitely."

"In a way, do you wish they had?" McKinley inquired.

"Yes," Berdella said unhesitatingly.

Turning his attack to the newspapers, Berdella gave his only clue as to how he perceived his own actions: "The paper was portraying me as nonhuman. Their motivation is not separate from the way I treated my victims. I treated them as something less than human, nothing more than a play toy or a play object. This is what the media's done to me, it's dehumanized me. So that it can believe, along with the public, that things like human sacrifices, Satanism, demonic practices, are more believable than me being the neighbor next door, who reached a point in his life where he could do monstrous acts. That's

351

not the same thing as being a monster."

Berdella was allowed to prattle on for about two hours, which was then edited to thirty minutes for broadcast. Following Berdella's segment, Riederer was interviewed for a response. When dealing with the media, Riederer typically is both guarded and verbose with his comments. But this time, he couldn't resist taking a few shots at Berdella and his bizarre logic that the police were somehow to blame. Riederer pointed out that the police simply didn't have enough evidence to storm Berdella's house before they did. After a full investigation uncovered the evidence, Riederer noted that Berdella felt compelled to plead guilty to six murders. "It (the investigation) was as thorough as it could possibly have been," the prosecutor commented.

Riederer was asked the question that still jump-starts conversations in Kansas City: why didn't Berdella get the death penalty? "Well, I would have liked to seen a death sentence carried out myself," Riederer said. "And I would have gladly done it after talking to him for three days and hearing the details of the most incredible crimes you can imagine." But he explained that, in the two cases where murder charges were brought, the circumstantial evidence probably was not strong enough to convince a jury to assess a death penalty as well as a guilty verdict. "I would love to see him executed," Riederer said, leaning forward in his chair, his voice rising animatedly. "You can't minimize the *inhumanity* that this guy committed on other people. But in order to get to the death penalty, we would have had to have more evidence, in my judgment. So in that sense I'm no different from anybody else, because I would love to see the plug pulled on him."

Two days after the taping, Berdella was packed into a van at 5 A.M. and driven to the state prison testing center in Fulton, Missouri, for medical checkups and mental evaluations. Dr. O'Connor, Berdella's psychologist at the Jackson County jail, had finished his assessment several days earlier, and recommended that Berdella be placed in a mental health facility, given "ongoing treatment" and not placed in a place where his "physical health problems, self-directed or internalized hostility, and tendency toward clinical depression are likely to be exacerbated." Authorities placed Berdella in the maximum security penitentiary in Jefferson City on January 10, the same day his interview aired on Channel 19. While housed in the protective custody unit, he filed various lawsuits and reportedly bragged of his crimes. On October 8, 1992, Berdella complained of chest pains. He was rushed to a hospital, but within two hours he was dead of a heart attack. Robert A. Berdella Jr. was 43 years old. His father also had died of a heart attack, at age 39.

How did an art student from Ohio become a sadistic murderer? Berdella declined to be interviewed for this book, but in other interviews he has mentioned the possibility of mental illness, and refused to blame developments in his past, or in his family, for any occurrences in his later life. "I don't think it's relevant," he said of his past, in an interview with Lisa Austin of the *Wichita Eagle*. "I did my crimes as an adult and I will take full responsibility for them." But he said he didn't know why he turned to serial homicide. "I'm the one that's asking that question more than anybody else," Berdella told Austin. "I don't know. Why the hell do people think I know? Do they really want to accept and believe that I planned all this, that I thought it out? Interesting concept."

353

Still, Berdella searched for some sort of answer. "The same people which I helped or tried to help and I had love for, turned me to rage and destruction," Berdella said in the *Eagle* interview. "There's no separating the two. There's a complete yin and yang . . . They weren't all good people. If I prevented them from doing more wrong, I'm not trying to justify anything I did. But it's an inner spiritual conflict I think you go through. . . . It helps me understand what happened inside of me. I think I saw some of my actions completely subjectively as preventing them from continuing the lifestyle they were in. Did it equal the wrongs I prevented them from doing?

"We're talking mental illness here," Berdella figured. "I did not sit down and decide. You're trying to get me to understand now what happened and why," he told Austin. "And I'm trying to find a way to, I hate to use the word rationalize, but to explain and find a reason that's communicable."

At the time, perhaps the closest comparable killer to Bob Berdella in American crime history was Chicago's John Wayne Gacy, who killed thirty-three young men between 1974 and 1978, when twenty-nine of the bodies were discovered buried in the crawl space of his home. The similarities between Gacy and Berdella are numerous and amazing. Both were born into blue-collar, traditional Midwestern, Catholic families with a dominant father and submissive mother. Both Gacy and Berdella were far closer to their mothers than their fathers, in part because both of their fathers were violent men given to beating their sons in fits of rage or abusing them verbally. Still, both sons sought the approval of their fathers, but neither received it. Both John Gacy Sr. and Robert Berdella Sr. died close to Christmas Day, and neither of their namesakes was present when the fathers died. John Gacy Jr.

was in an Iowa prison for sexually assaulting a high school boy when his father died in a Chicago hospital. Berdella's father suffered a heart attack on Christmas Day, and Berdella Jr. was at home in Cuyahoga Falls when his father died two days later in Canton.

Neither Gacy nor Berdella completed college, but both were intent on succeeding as independent, self-employed businessmen. Gacy ran his own contracting firm, hiring young boys to work on construction sites. Berdella had his own shop, and hired young men to work either in Bob's Bazaar Bizarre or around his home. Outside of work, both Gacy and Berdella established reputations for themselves as civic-minded citizens. Gacy worked for the lighting district in his township, was a member of the Chicago Democratic political organization, and did volunteer work as a clown in parades and at hospitals. Berdella headed up his neighborhood crime watch program, donated time to raise funds for Channel 19, and tried to help wayward youths by acting as an informal "big brother."

The two men both liked to project images of authority, of being well-connected to the halls of power. Gacy customized his car with police accessories to give it the impression of being an undercover vehicle, and sometimes captured his victims from the street by telling them he was a policeman. Gacy also reminded people of his ties to the political machine, and the privileges that entailed. Berdella often implied to people that he knew powerful figures or could get certain things done. He gave the impression that he was well-versed in the law, and was capable of accomplishing his desires through the courts if necessary.

Both Gacy and Berdella captured their victims after luring them back to their houses, though Gacy sometimes knocked out his victims while they rode in his car. Both men cruised the male prostitute strips in their respective cities, plucking some of their eventual victims from there. Gacy knew some of his victims, either from the strip or work, but he also killed people he met for the first time. Chris Bryson was the first person Berdella captured whom he had not known previously. Once the unconscious victims were tied up and immobilized inside Gacy's or Berdella's house, both men sodomized their young [18-25 mainly], white [all] captives repeatedly. Gacy performed some torture and did some beating, but not to the extremes that Berdella visited upon his hostages.

In the book *Buried Dreams,* Gacy indicated to Chicago reporter Russ Ewing that he was, in effect, playing God with the lives of his incapacitated guests, plunging them toward death, then reviving them briefly. Gacy wanted his victims to appreciate that he controlled their fates utterly, a self-satisfaction that Berdella also sought. In recreating a murder, Gacy told Ewing that one of his victims pleaded, "Oh God, help me." Gacy responded: "Yes my son, God will help you. God is here."

Neither Gacy nor Berdella slept much during these all-night horror sessions, and neither seemed to need much sleep in general. But Gacy did not keep his victims alive for very long, unlike Berdella. He normally finished with them after one night, then strangled or suffocated them, sometimes with their own underwear. Berdella's victims were kept for days or weeks, and most died simply from the accumulation of atrocities. Both Gacy and Berdella kept small mementos of their victims, such as wallets or identification, but Gacy did not take photos or keep notes. Gacy did not dismember his victims' bodies; he simply dropped them into a crawl space beneath his first floor and buried them neatly, sometimes spreading lime over the graveyard to hasten its collective disintegration. He also dropped several bodies into the Des Plaines River.

As with Chris Bryson, one of Gacy's victims lived, though Gacy actually allowed him to leave. Gacy expected that the police would not believe the man's story, and he was right. Gacy wasn't prosecuted for abducting and sodomizing the man, but instead continued on his killing spree. Gacy was captured after he kidnapped a drug store employee while the youth's mother waited outside. The parents of the victim quickly convinced the Des Plaines Police Department to investigate Gacy, and when police entered Gacy's house, they recognized the rancid smell of death and uncovered the hidden burial ground. Gacy was arrested on December 21, 1978, and confessed to the murders, though he didn't know the names of some of his victims and couldn't remember the exact details of each killing. Gacy went to trial in 1980 hoping for an acquittal on the grounds that a separate personality, a "Bad Jack," had overtaken him during the brief murder periods. A Cook County jury was not convinced, and convicted him of thirty-three murders. Gacy was sentenced to death, and now awaits execution at the Menard Correctional Center in Chester, Illinois. It is not known what, if anything, Bob Berdella knew about John Wayne Gacy.

One of the more frightening aspects about Bob Berdella is that he isn't that unusual. "He's very common among a unique group of people," said Ronald Holmes, author of the book *Serial Murder*. "That's what makes it so scary. We want these people to walk around with serial murderer, 'SM,' on their foreheads. They don't." Even scarier, the number of unlabeled killers currently roaming the country is estimated variously at 150 to more than 500 by assorted experts. Berdella's defining traits—torture, photographs, notes, sexual assault, dismemberment—are shared by dozens of previous killers, and doubtless dozens more still to be discovered. Berdella's distinctive feature may have been that he held his captives for days and weeks, where most killers terminate their hostages after no more than a day.

In July 1991, a killer with amazing similarities to Berdella was discovered in Milwaukee. Jeffrey Dahmer, a factory worker, grew up in Bath, Ohio, an Akron suburb about fifteen miles from Berdella's hometown of Cuyahoga Falls. Dahmer confessed to Milwaukee police that he lured his victims back to his apartment, as Berdella did, drugged his victims, had sex with them, and then killed them. When a dazed man escaped from Dahmer's apartment, still wearing handcuffs, police entered and found dozens of Polaroid photographs in the bedroom. The pictures depicted various homosexual sex acts and apparent dead bodies. One of the officers examining the photos then went to the kitchen, where he found a human head in the refrigerator.

Though both Dahmer and Berdella cut up the dead bodies in their residences, Berdella disposed of the parts, while Dahmer kept and had eaten some of them. The remains of eleven men were found in Dahmer's apartment, and police say he has confessed to seventeen killings. As with Berdella, almost all of the victims were gay, injected with drugs, tortured and photographed. Unlike Berdella, Dahmer cooperated with police almost immediately, providing an early confession with names and details of the repulsive crimes he had committed. Because Dahmer didn't remove the evidence of his crimes, as Berdella did, and because he confessed right away, his case drew far more national attention than Berdella's. At the height of publicity on the Dahmer case, Berdella telephoned the *Kansas City Star* to declare that Dahmer must be lying, that he couldn't really have killed that many people.

Berdella, of course, did not want to discuss how he or Dahmer reached the level of serial killer. Others, however, have numerous theories on what might have contributed to Berdella's psychological makeup. One idea cited by several people was a possible lack of development in Berdella's early life. Helen Morrison, a Chicago psychologist who has done extensive interviews with serial killers such as Gacy and Atlanta's Wayne Williams, perceived that with Berdella, "There's no sense of early childhood. There's some definite difficulty in how he did develop in the first year of life. . . . In early development, sex and aggression are mixed up together. This fusion is something that most people theoretically are born with close together. Only with time do they develop into separate elements. But they never got separated with these people [sexual killers], just as they never progress to the stage of sexual identity."

Reid Meloy, a San Diego Psychiatrist and author of *The Psychopathic Mind,* made a similar observation in analyzing Berdella's crimes. "The early psychosexual stages become horribly obvious," Meloy said. "I think that during and just prior to the act, you're going to see behaviors that are acted out that are very regressive. Whether they are fixated, who knows?" Morrison noted that as such killers grow into childhood, their fathers seem to be the main disciplinary or limiting influence. "The fathers have a function of enclosing them in a box so they know how far they can go," Morrison said. "They provide a sense of limits. . . . while the mothers are passive or noninvolved." When the fathers leave the home or die while

359

the child is still living there, Morrison said, "there's no control, no external structure."

Berdella posed no known disciplinary problems outside the home, and was an excellent student throughout his years in Cuyahoga Falls. Inside the home, though, Berdella's scholastic and artistic achievements apparently weren't enough for his father, who Berdella claims abused him physically and verbally. Some experts theorized that this could have created a deep-seated resentment that Berdella sought to purge by taking out his frustrations on his victims. "You have Berdella recreating his relationship with his dad in a more bizarre way," Meloy said. "Initially, he sees himself as the father figure," attempting to nurture and assist the young men who live with him. "Then, he shifts and becomes the predator. The victim shifts and becomes the child he can dominate. . . . My hunch is, in the throes of hurting somebody badly, this person is carrying a lot of Berdella's projections about himself. All the hateful things about yourself, childhood things, that devalues the victim even more. It stimulates your hatred so you desire to destroy this object." Holmes said much the same thing when he commented: "You lash out at those people that remind you too much of yourself."

At some stage in his adolescent development, some believe, Berdella may have begun having sexual fantasies that, over the years, gradually escalated both in intensity and violence. Many studies have found fantasies to be a common trait in serial killers. "It's an escalating masturbatory fantasy," said Joel Norris, psychologist and author of *Serial Killers: The Growing Menace*. "They have hallucinations of fantasies that are intense, that they can't get rid of. . . . After you start the killings, you can't stop."

As with many of his killing cohorts, Berdella maintained an external cloak of normalcy. In part, Norris has

360

written, this is because serial killers have practiced and perfected their crimes, and masking them is part of the procedure. They've been doing it for years, and fantasizing about it for far longer. In Berdella's case, part of the fantasy obviously was the abduction and extended captivity of his victims. Most observers feel the complete subjugation served to dehumanize the victim, and inflate Berdella's own sense of worth. Meloy said: "One of the dynamics of a psychopath is, to shore up their own self-esteem, they have to devalue other people. They tend to be arrogant, condescending, with an intellectual narcissism. When they're around other people, they devalue them. It gives their own grandiosity a pump."

Along the same lines, the pleasure of domination for Berdella was not so much in the sexual activity as in the torture and full control. "It's a total body experience," said Morrison. "Sometimes they don't have sex. They're into the torturing relationship, which is always so one-sided. There's no sense of relationship. They're not capable of it." Cole, after sitting through Berdella's confession for three days, likened the situation to a sadistic doctor-patient relationship, with Berdella drawing enjoyment not only from the domination but the carefully notated experiments with the drugs and the electric shocks.

How does a person's personality evolve to a point where inflicting pain is a positive thing? Norris believes that "by the time he was seeing these young men, he [Berdella] had mislearned about people. His idea about having an intimate companion had evolved to where he saw he needed complete control." Unable to initiate or maintain a normal relationship, the extended captures became necessary, then, "to keep them close," Norris theorized. "He had a companion." Morrison added: "It's similar to a young infant manipulating his environment. He plays and

361

plays and doesn't stop. . . . This person belongs to them. Whatever is theirs is theirs, and they'll keep it as long as they can."

Norris discussed another component of Berdella's modus operandi. "Sick as it is, you're looking at a real serious pathology. I think that's why they keep the trophies, the skulls or the photos. It's like a memento." Keeping items from the crimes is not unusual among killers, and a commonly held belief among experts is that victims' body parts or personal belongings are kept as reminders of the triumph of the crime, or committing murder and getting away with it. That self-satisfaction in turn becomes a source of sexual excitement. Berdella admitted as much in his confession.

Berdella also said in his confession that after killing Jerry Howell, he initially was repulsed by the crime, and blocked it out of his mind completely. But eventually it became an acceptable and then desirable act, and the urge to do it again arose. Holmes and others said it was "normal" among serial killers for the longest interval between murders to occur between the first and the second killings. But after the second death, the interval between number two and number three invariably is shorter, as it was with Berdella. The three killings in 1985, after Howell's in 1984, made several experts wonder if Berdella was hiding murders he may have committed in 1986 and 1987, where he claims to have killed only one.

However, one aspect that defined Berdella's murderous pattern was the increasing length of the captivities. Starting with the third man, each subsequent victim was kept in Berdella's house for a longer period than the previous victim, and it appears Chris Bryson was meant to be held for a long time as well. Holmes explained that Berdella was more of a "thrill killer" than a "lust killer." Holmes categorizes killers by whether they murder quickly or over an elongated period of time. Holmes said, "Dahmer was a lust killer, who was also into necrophilia. With Berdella, once the person's dead, the whole thrill is gone. You feed off the fear and frenzy and the horror that this person is going through. Once that's gone, you drop him and go on to the next one."

Toward the end, whether it's just laziness or an unconscious desire to get caught, the killers tend to become more careless. Gacy abducted his final victim while the victim's mother waited nearby, practically ensuring that Gacy would become a prime suspect. Both Dahmer and Berdella were discovered after their last victims escaped, escapes the killers had never allowed to happen before. Once the killer is captured, he sometimes confesses immediately, as Gacy and Dahmer did, or waits until denial is no longer plausible, as did Ted Bundy and Bob Berdella. Almost all serial killers confess completely at some stage, gaining a final measure of enjoyment. "It is among the controls they still have," Morrison said. "I think the excitement is in controlling the interview." Holmes confirmed Cole's observation that Berdella seemed to enjoy his confession. "When you talk about it, you relive it," Holmes said. "I imagine a lot of the time he [Berdella] was talking about it, he had an erection."

Still, the question: why Berdella? As with many serial killers, he had a slightly traumatic background, but hardly as bad as those who grow up in ghettos or broken homes. He may have been delusional or mentally ill, but so are hundreds of thousands of other Americans who do not became serial killers. Both Norris and Morrison are developing theories that examine the effect of physical trauma to the brain, organic malfunction or brain defect. Norris suggested in a recent book on Texas serial killer

363

Henry Lee Lucas that brain damage caused by repeated beatings, drugs and toxic substances may have led to his "behavioral impairment." At one time, Lucas took credit for more than 360 murders, though he now claims far fewer.

Lucas may or may not be the worst serial killer of all time. But contrary to popular belief, serial killers are hardly a new phenomenon. There have been serial killers in America at least dating back to the beginning of this century, and their numbers were just as grisly as today's murderers. Holmes has compiled a list of more than 135 killers, beginning in 1900 with a California man who killed twelve of his employees, to 1991's Donald Leroy Evans, a Mississippi man who claims to have killed more than sixty people throughout the country. It seems possible that the genre simply wasn't recognized as such until recent years, that multiple killings were viewed more as an aberration than a trend, and only in the last decade have professionals begun to closely examine the similarities between killers.

In the past, law enforcement may have been slow to diagnose the trend as well. Agencies separated by state lines, or even city borders, often were reluctant to share information, and patterns of similar killings could have gone unnoticed. The gathering and dissemination of such data wasn't computerized, either, making the recognition of patterns that much more difficult. Such a difficulty led the FBI to begin the National Center for the Analysis of Violent Crime, which collects unsolved murder data from around the country and tries to assist agencies who might otherwise be unaware of the links between crimes in two different areas. Now that law enforcement, and the news media, have a heightened awareness of the continuing presence of serial killers, the problem has received greater public attention in recent years, and perhaps spawned the misperception that serial murder is a new, emerging development.

The FBI's program also has undertaken studies of known serial killers, searching for strands of consistency that might provide insights in tracking or stopping future murder sprees. In a way, the increased attention that these grisly crimes have received serves some positive purpose. Academics, social workers and even policy makers are more likely to study the problem closely, seek out indicators or warning signs, maybe even apply them in clinical or judicial settings. Though Bob Berdella wasn't one of them, many serial killers have contact with the justice system before they begin their bloody rampages. Recognizing the circumstances that create such personalities, or the late-stage alarms that flash in the moments before the fatal darkness, could one day prevent some of these killers from living out their devastating fantasies.

Acknowledgments

This was an easy book to write, because of the assistance of so many helpful people. Besides the Kansas City Police Department, we must thank the dozens of people who knew or worked with Bob Berdella at some point in his life, many of whom agreed to be interviewed or contributed valuable information. All the dialogue in this book was recalled by at least one if not both parties to the conversation, either to the authors directly or to detectives in police reports. Similarly, the thoughts or reactions attributed to many of those in this book were described directly to the authors, or in some instances may have been described to a police investigator. The names of some of Berdella's former acquaintances have been changed to protect their identities, but all other names, events and places are as accurate as possible.

Berdella refused to be interviewed for this book. He was never offered any money to participate, and he will not receive any proceeds from its sales. In a series of letters to the authors, Berdella initially declined even to meet with the authors. Then he wrote that "I do not wish to be an uncooperative party by any means." Later, he declared that he would be filing suit to keep the police department from cooperating with the book. He never filed such a suit before his death.

Information on Berdella's state of mind after his arrest was obtained partially through statements he made in the

366

three-day confession session, and also through comments he made to friends and visitors while he was in jail. Berdella's lawyers refused to discuss the case, citing attorney-client privilege guidelines.

At the time this book was being prepared, Berdella was engaged in a series of legal battles with Chris Bryson and four of the families of men he killed, and spent much of his time doing legal research. In January 1992, the family of Todd Stoops won a wrongful death suit against Berdella, and a Jackson County jury awarded them five billion dollars the largest jury award ever in the United States in a personal injury or wrongful death suit. The award was later reduced to eighteen million dollars in a special settlement.

A writer who signed a contract with Chris Bryson in 1988 declined to allow Bryson to be interviewed. The authors were unable to locate Bryson for comment.

We must thank the Kansas City Police Department for allowing us to consult their files on the Berdella case. Thanks in particular go to the Board of Police Commissioners, led by William Ray Price, and also former police Chief Larry J. Joiner, his successor Chief Steven Bishop, the police legal advisers David Swartzbaugh and Dale Close, Gary Howell of the crime lab, and the numerous detectives and officers who gave their time and consideration to be interviewed for this book. We are also grateful to past and present members of the Jackson County prosecutor's office, especially Albert Riederer and Pat Hall, for their cooperation.

[In a tragic postscript, Hall died in his home of a sudden heart attack on February 14, 1992. He was 41 years old.]

We also appreciate the help of the *Kansas City Star* reporters David Goldstein and Melissa Berg for providing information from their files, photographers Alison K.

Barnes, Steve Gonzales and Tammy Ljungblad for their assistance, and the editors who supported this project, notably Bob Lynn, Darryl Levings and David Hayes. Thanks also to Lisa Austin, formerly of the *Wichita Eagle,* and Luci Williams of the *Cleveland Plain-Dealer* for their assistance, and to Cindy Eberting for her thorough Nexis research. The comments and guidance provided by Scott and Jill Canon and Bill Luening were greatly appreciated. The support of people such as John, Karen, Robert and Angela Martellaro, and Jeff and Ann Spivak, were invaluable throughout the preparation of the book.

Finally, we are most thankful to Rick Balkin, the agent who worked exceedingly hard to get this book into print, and to Paul Dinas, who actually agreed to publish it. On the home front, we will always be grateful to Jan Cole, who continues to tolerate Troy for reasons unknown, and to Sigrid and Bill Jackman, who supported Tom both morally and financially, simply because they are terrific parents. This book exists because of Jan, Sigrid and Bill, and we gladly dedicate it to them. Thanks for everything.

Tom Jackman
Troy Cole
June 1992